Gabriele Stein

English Word-Formation over two Centuries

In Honour of Hans Marchand
on the Occasion of his Sixty-Fifth-Birthday

Tübinger Beiträge zur Linguistik

herausgegeben von Gunter Narr

34

Gabriele Stein

English Word-Formation
over two Centuries

In Honour of Hans Marchand
on the Occasion of his Sixty-Fifth Birthday, 1 October 1972

Tübingen 1973

Druck: Becht Druck + Co. · Ammerbuch Pfäffingen
ISBN 3-87808-034-4

For Professor Hans Marchand
on the occasion of his 65th birthday

During the past two years, my colleagues and I have been exercised to
find appropriate ways both of recognising this sixty-fifth birthday
and also of conveying some token of our gratitude and esteem. It will
be generally recognised that there is need for a full theoretical and
historical study of the way word-formation research has developed over
the past two hundred years, crowned in 1960 with what will long remain
the standard work on English word-formation. I have tried to begin laying
the foundation for such a study by compiling the bibliographical data
which I have pleasure now in presenting. In addition, I hope this contribution will serve the dedicatee and other scholars in providing them
with some of the modest but essential tools for their current researches.

Tübingen,
1 October 1972

Gabriele Stein

ACKNOWLEDGMENTS

I am indebted to Professor Randolph Quirk, University College London, who gave me welcome advice and generous practical assistance in arranging access to library facilities in London.

I am also grateful to Mr. Iain Clarkson, Lecturer at the English Seminar of Tübingen University, for reading the manuscript of the introduction and making helpful suggestions to improve its English style.

G. S.

CONTENTS

III. GENERAL STUDIES ON DERIVATION IN ENGLISH

II.

Particular Aspects That Have Been Studied In English Word-Formation

IX. WORD - FORMATION AND GRAPHEMICS

X, WORD - FORMATION AND PHONEMICS

(Stress, phonemic reduction of vowel quantity...)

XI, CONTRASTIVE STUDIES

XII, WORD - FORMATION IN SPECIFIC AUTHORS, IN SPECIFIC WORKS

ABBREVIATIONS

(Most of the abbreviations of Russian publications are those used by B. Butte-
K. Hansen in their extensive bibliography on Russian publications in ZAA)

AGI	: Archivio Glottologico Italiano, Firenze.
Allg. Litblatt	: Allgemeines Literaturblatt.
AmA	: American Anthropologist, Menasha, Wisc..
Anon.	: Anonymous.
ANUkr - L	: Akademija Nauk Ukrainskoj SSR, otdelenie literatury, jazyka i iskusstvovedenija.
app.	: appendix.
Bašk U	: Baškirskij gosudarstvennyj universitet, Ufa.
BNF	: Beiträge zur Namensforschung. Neue Folge. Heidelberg.
BSL	: Bulletin de la Société de Linguistique de Paris, Paris.
č.	: cast' (part)
Chab Ped I	: Chabarovskij gosudarstvennyj pedagogičeskij institut, Chabarovsk.
Charkov U	: Char'kovskij gosudarstvennyj universitet, Char'kov.
ČMF	: Časopis pro moderní filologii, Praha.
DAb	: Dissertation Abstracts. Abstracts of dissertations available on microfilm, Ann Arbor, Mich..
Dagest U	: Dagestanskij gosudarstvennyj universitet, Machačkala.
Dal U	: Dal'nevostočnogo universiteta, serija filologičeskaja, Vladivostok.
Diss.	: dissertation
DLit	: Doslidžennja z literaturoznavstva ta movoznavstva (Kyjiv U), Kyjiv.
DLZ	: Deutsche Literaturzeitung für Kritik der internationalen Wissenschaft, Berlin.
DSi.Ja	: Doklady i Soobščenija Instituta Jazykoznanija Akademij Nauk SSSR, Moskva.
dt.	: deutsch (German)
DVost U	: Dal'nevostočnyj gosudarstvennyj universitet, Vladivostok.

EA	: Etudes Anglaises, Paris.
ed.	: edition, edited
engl.	: englisch (English)
Erasmus	: Erasmus. Speculum Scientiarum. International Bulletin of Contemporary Scholarship, Wiesbaden.
Erev U	: Erevkanskogo gosudarstvennogo universiteta. Serija filologičeskich nauk, Erevan.
esp.	: especially
ETC	: ETC. A Review of General Semantics, Chicago.
FAJa	: fakul'tet anglijskogo jazyka
fasc.	: fascicule
FIJa	: fakul'tet inostrannych jazykov
FilN	: filologičeskie nauki
FilS	: filologičeskaja serija
frz.	: französisch (French)
FS	: French Studies, Oxford.
FUF	: Finnisch-ugrische Forschungen. Zeitschrift für finnisch-ugrische Sprach- und Volkskunde, Helsinki.
GFFNS	: Godisnjak Filozofskog Fakulteta u Novom Sadu, Novi Sad.
germ.	: germanisch (Germanic)
Germanistik	: Germanistik. Internationales Referatenorgan mit bibliographischen Hinweisen, Tübingen.
GL	: General Linguistics, University Park, Pa..
Gork Ped I	: Gor'kovskij gosudarstvennyj pedagogičeskij institut inostrannych jazykov, Gor'kij.
GSUF	: Godisnik na Sofijskija Universitet, Filologičeski fakultet, Sofija.
Hand NPh C	: Handelingen van het Nederlands Philologen - Congres, Groningen.
HFYW	: Hsi-fang Yü-wen (Western Languages and Literatures), Peking.
HNR	: Hikone Ronso (Hikone Journal, Cultural Science Edition Hikone, Japan.

IJa	: inostrannye jazyki
IJaš	: Inostrannye jazyki v škole, Moskva.
Issl AFil	: Issledovanija po anglijskoj filologii, Leningrad.
It Stud Konf	: Itogovaja studenčeskaja naučnaja konferencija posvjaš-čennaja 91-j godovščine so dnja roždenija V. I. Lenina (Charkov U). Tezisy dokladov, Char'kov, 1961.
Ivan Ped I	: Ivanovskij gosudarstvennyj pedagogičeskij institut, Ivanovo.
Izv AN	: Izvestija Akademii Nauk SSR, otdelenie literatury i jazyka, Moskva - Leningrad.
JAfrL	: Journal of African Languages, London.
JbAm	: Jahrbuch für Amerikastudien, Heidelberg.
Kanaz Jk	: Kanazawa Daigaku Kyoyobu Ronshu Jinbunkagakuhen (Studies in Humanities, College of Liberal Arts), Kanazawa (University), Kanazawa, Japan.
Kiev IFK	: Kievskij gosudarstvennyj institut fizičeskoj kul'tury Kiev.
Kiev Ped I	: Kievskij gosudarstvennyj pedagogiceskij institut inostrannych jazykov, Kiev.
Kiev U	: Kievskij gosudarstvennyj universitet im. T. G. Ševčenko, Kiev.
KIJa	: kafedra inostrannych jazykov
Kišin Ped I	: Kišinevskij gosudarstvennyj pedagogičeskij institut, Kišinev.
KLFA Ja	: kafedra leksiki i fonetiki anglijskogo jazyka
KNf	: Kwartalnik Neofilologiczny, Warszawa.
Kyjiv U	: Kyjivs'kyj deržavnyj universytet im. T. G. Ševčenka, Kyjiv.
KZJa	: kafedra zapadnych inostrannych jazykov
LaS	: Language and Style, Carbondale, Ill..
Latomus	: Latomus. Revue d'études latines, Bruxelles.
Latv U	: Latvijskij gosudarstvennyj universitet, Riga.
LB Bijbl	: Leuvense Bijdragen. Tijdschrift voor Germaanse filologie, Leuven.
Le St	: Lingua e Stile. Quaderni dell'Istituto di Glottologia dell' Università degli Studi di Bologna, Bologna.

LIAvP	: Leningradskij institut aviacionnogo priborostroenija, Leningrad.
Litbl.	: Literaturblatt
Litcbl.	: Literarisches Centralblatt
Litteris	: Litteris. An International Critical Review of the Humanities, Lund.
L Ped I	: Leningradskij gosudarstvennyj pedagogičeskij institut im. A. I. Gercena, Leningrad.
1 - L Ped I	: I - j Leningradskij pedagogičeskij institut inostrannych jazykov, Leningrad.
LPosn	: Lingua Posnaniensis. Czasoposmo poświę cone językoznawstwu porównawczemu i ogólnemu, Poznań.
LSb	: Leksikograficeskij sbornik Moskva
LT	: Levende Talen, Groningen.
LU	: Leningradskij gosudarstvennyj universitet im. A. A. Ždanova, Leningrad.
lvs.	: leaves
lvs.n.	: leaves numbered (refers to numbered pages of unpublished manuscripts)
MAev	: Medium Aevum, Oxford.
Magnit Ped I	: Magnitogorskij gosudarstvennyj pedagogičeskij institut, Magnitogorsk.
Masch. verv.	: Maschinenschrift vervielfältigt (typewritten manuscript polycopied)
Mat TD	: Materialy i tezisy dokladov XIV itogovoj naučnoj konferencii (Orenb Ped I), 1965.
M Gor Ped I	: Moskovskij gorodskoj pedagogičeskij institut im. V. P. Potemkina, Moskva.
MObl Ped I	: Moskovskij oblastnoj pedagogičeskij institut im. N. K. Krupskoj, Moskva.
Mor U	: Mordovskogo universiteta. Serija filologičeskich nauk. Saransk.
M Ped I	: Moskovskij gosudarstvennyj pedagogičeskij institut im. V. I. Lenina, Moskva.
1 - MPed I	: I - j Moskovskij gosudarstvennyj pedagogičeskij institut inostrannych jazykov im. M. Toreza, Moskva.

MPh	: Modern Philology, Chicago.
Mu	: Muttersprache. Zeitschrift zur Pflege und Erforschung der deutschen Sprache, Mannheim.
Museum	: Maandblad voor philologie en geschiedenis, Leiden.
Names	: Names. Journal of the American Name Society, Potsdam, N. Y..
NDVŠ - F	: Naučnye doklady Vysšej školy filologičeskie nauki, Moskva.
N. F.	: Neue Folge (new series)
NMet Konf	: Naučno-metodičeskaja konferencija prepodavatelej inostrannych jazykov Kazachskoj SSR. Programma i tezisy dokladov, Alma-Ata, 1961.
NoB	: Namn och Bygd. Tidskrift för nordisk ortnamnforskning, Uppsala.
N & Q	: Notes and Queries for Readers and Writers, Collectors, and Librarians, London.
n.s.	: new series
NTS	: Norsk Tidsskrift for Sprogvidenskap, Oslo.
NZ	: Naučnye zapiski
NZ Kiev P II n	: Naučnye zapiski Kievskogo pedagogičeskogo instituta inostrannych jazykov, Kiev.
Orenb Ped I	: Orenburgskij gosudarstvennyj pedagogičeskij institut, Orenburg.
PADS	: Publications of the American Dialect Society, Gainesville, Fla.
Paideia	: Paideia. Rivista letteraria di informazione bibliografica, Brescia.
PAPhilosS	: Proceedings of the American Philosophical Society, Philadelphia.
Pjat Ped I	: Pjatigorskij gosudarstvennyj pedagogičeskij institut inostrannych jazykov, Pjatigorsk.
PMLA	: Publications of the Modern Language Association of America, New York.

Praxis	: Praxis des neusprachlichen Unterrichts, Dortmund.
Probl Morf	: Problemy morfologičeskogo stroja germanskich jazykov, Moskva, 1963.
Probl sravnit filol	: Problemy sravnitel'noj filologii. Sbornik statej 70 - letiju člena-korrespondenta AN SSSR V. M. Žirmunskogo (Red. kollegija : M. P. Alekseev (otv. red.) i dr.), Moscow - Leningrad : Izd. " Nauka" (AN SSSR otd. lit. i jazyka), 1964, 496 p., front. (portr.), tab..
Proc.	: Proceedings
Proc Razv	: Processy razvitija v jazyke, Moskva, 1959.
QJSp	: The Quarterly Journal of Speech, Columbia, Missouri.
RBPh	: Revue Belge de Philologie et d'Histoire, Bruxelles.
repr.	: reprint, reprinted
RESl	: Revue des Etudes Slaves, Paris.
Resp Konf	: Respublikanskaja konferencija po voprosam jazykoznanij i metodiki prepodavanija inostrannych jazykov. Tezisy kladov 2., Alma-Ata, 1964.
rev.	: revised
RF	: Romanische Forschungen. Vierteljahresschrift für romanische Sprachen und Literaturen, Frankfurt a. M..
RFRG	: Revista de Filologie Romanică si Germanică, Bucaresti.
RGFil	: Romano-germanskaja filologija, Moskva.
Rjazan Ped I (Rjaz P I)	: Rjazanskij gosudarstvennyj pedagogičeskij institut, Rjazan.
RLaV	: Revue des Langues Vivantes, Bruxelles.
RLB	: Recueil Linguistique de Bratislava, Bratislava.
rom.	: romanisch (Romance)
RPF	: Revista Portuguesa de Filologia, Coimbra.
RRLing	: Revue Roumaine de Linguistique, Bucarest.
Sat. Rev.Lit.	: The Saturday Review of Literature, New York.
Scriptorium	: Scriptorium. Revue internationale des études relatives aux manuscrits, Anvers & Bruxelles.
SFFUK	: Sbornik Filozofickej Fakulty Univerzity Komenského, Philologica, Bratislava.

SFilN	: Serija filologičeskich nauk
SIL	: Studies in Linguistics, Dallas, Texas.
SPFUK - Ph	: Sbornik Pedagogické Fakulty University Karlovy. Philologica, Praha.
Symposium	: Symposium. A Journal Devoted to Modern Foreign Languages and Literatures, Syracuse, N. Y..
t.	: tom (volume)
TAPA	: Transactions and Proceedings of the American Philological Association, Ithaca, N. Y..
TAPS	: Transactions of the American Philosophical Society, Philadelphia.
Tartu U	: Tartuskij gosudarstvennyj universitet, Tartu.
Tašk Ped I	: Taškentskij gosudarstvennyj pedagogičeskij institut inostrannych jazykov, Taškent.
(UZ) Taš P IIn	: (UZ) Taškentskogo pedagogičeskogo instituta inostrannych jazykov, Taškent.
Tbil U	: Tbilisskij gosudarstvennyj universitet, Tbilisi.
TD Met Konf	: Tezisy dokladov k naučno-metodičeskoj konferencii (Leningradskij politechničeskij institut, kafedra russkogo jazyka, kafedra inostrannych jazykov), Leningrad, 1965.
T Konf	: Tezisy naučnoj konferencii fakul'teta inostrannych jazykov Odesskogo universiteta, Odessa, 1965.
TLS	: The Times Literary Supplement
TPS	: Transactions of the Philological Society, Oxford.
Tul Ped I	: Tul'skij gosudarstvennyj pedagogičeskij institut, Tula.
Univ.	: University , Universität
UZ	: Učenye zapiski
UZ IMO	: Učenye zapiski, institut mezdunarodnych otnošenij, Moskva.
Viln Ped I	: Vil'njusskij gosudarstvennyj pedagogičeskij institut, Vil'njus.
VJa	: Voprosy jazykoznanija, Moskva.
VJa Met	: Voprosy jazykoznanija i metodiki prepodavanija inostrannych jazykov, Alma-Ata, 1965.

VKyjiv U	: Visnyk Kyjivskoho universytetu, serija filologij ta žurnalistyky, Kyjiv.
VMU	: Vestnik Moskovskogo universiteta, filologija, žurnalistika, Moskva.
VObsc	: Voprosy obščego i romano-germanskogo jazykoznanija. Tezisy dokladov IV naučnoj konferencii jazykovedov (Bask U), Ufa, 1965.
Voen I	: Voennyj institut inostrannych jazykov, Moskva.
Volog Ped I	: Vologodskij gosudarstvennyj pedagogičeskij institut, Vologda.
Voron U	: Voronežskij gosudarstvennyj universiteta, Voronež.
VPIMD	: Vilniaus Pedagoginio Instituto Mokslo darbai, Vilnius.
vyp.	: vypusk
WZPhP	: Wissenschaftliche Zeitschrift der Pädagogischen Hochschule Potsdam. Historisch-Philosophische Reihe. Potsdam.
WZTUD	: Wissenschaftliche Zeitschrift der Technischen Universität Dresden, Dresden.
WZUB	: Wissenschaftliche Zeitschrift der Humboldt-Universität Berlin. Gesellschafts- und Sprachwissenschaftliche Reihe.
WZUL	: Wissenschaftliche Zeitschrift der Karl-Marx-Universität Leipzig. Gesellschafts- und Sprachwissenschaftliche Reihe.
ZbR	: Zbirnyk robit aspirantiv romano-germans'koji klasycnoji filolohiji, L'viv.
ZFSL	: Zeitschrift für französische Sprache und Literatur, Wiesbaden.
ZMaF	: Zeitschrift für Mundartforschung, Wiesbaden.

INTRODUCTION

Nobody, we think, will deny that linguistics has become one of the most im-
portant and interesting fields of research in our century. Never, it seems,
has theoretical linguistic discussion been more animated and varied than
during the last two decades. And the scope of linguistics itself is becoming
wider and wider as more and more disciplines develop within the field of
linguistics. The time is long past when illustrious scholars could encom-
pass the whole of linguistics, or of Romance or Germanic linguistics. The
twentieth century is the century of specialists and in linguistics, too,
one has to specialize if one wants to keep up with the most recent theoretical developments. But even then, it is difficult to keep up with all
the published work: the linguistic market is and is being flooded with
new publications from all over the world.

One of the immediate consequences of this situation is that more
and more linguists, above all of the younger generation, have read the
latest contributions to their specific field of research and joined the
theoretical discussions on it, without knowing the works that have been
written on the same topic in the not too distant past. How many books
and articles could have remained unwritten if their authors had realized
that they were just repeating what others had written before.

A time characterized by what could almost be called an overpro-
duction in scientific publication has to face this phenomenon which is
already a serious problem. But facing a problem implies also attempting
to overcome it.

Different steps could be taken to remedy the situation. Research
centres, for instance, could collect and publish the bibliographical data

on the most recent publications in their specific fields. Periodicals, mush-
rooming as never before, could join in a kind of international bibliographical cooperation; each one would include a section on recent publications.
But instead of listing new publications in general, it would be much better
if certain periodicals were to specialize in specific subjects so that the
linguist interested in a particular field of research would know that a specific periodical will supply him with the latest contributions on his subject. We do not deny that there are various book series collecting and listing the year's published work, but they very often appear as much as two or
three years late; or not infrequently they are too general, as they have not
been compiled by specialists.

Bibliographies on specific subjects would then give the most extensive and comprehensive information - provided they are properly compiled
and arranged. There is an increasing need for bibliographies and there have
already been numerous attempts to meet this need. There are, however, bibliographies and bibliographies. Writing a bibliography is not an easy task, but
if it is done at all, it should be done properly. If not, it serves no pur-
pose at all. Writing a bibliography does not, in any case, consist in a mere
collecting and arranging of bibliographical material. This, however, is the
impression one gets when one looks through recent bibliographies: for instance Krenn - Müllner's bibliography on transformational grammar to name
just one.

A good bibliography, we think, should satisfy at least the following three
demands:

1) <u>The subject matter has to be defined</u>

The field covered in a bibliography should be defined as clearly as possible.
If this is not done the bibliography will become unreliable, leaving out
data that should have been included, and including material that does not be-

long in it.

This presupposes that the persons writing the bibliography have a good know-ledge of the subject matter, are specialists. Specialists, however, will hard-ly ever undertake such a time-consuming task as compiling a bibliography. Here too, international cooperation between specialists in the same field seems to be the best solution.

2) The data given in a bibliography should be reliable

The first condition is a well-defined subject matter. There are two others:

a) The data given in a bibliography should be checked by the author. If the data have not been checked, errors and misprints are taken over from one bibliography into another. Occasionally the titles of publications are misleading. There was, for instance, a reference to an article *Word Build-ing for Infant Schools*, London: T.Nelson and Sons (1898), 12 p.. Yet on checking the reference we found that the book did not deal with word-for-mation at all; what had been called ' word building' was nothing more than a search for minimal pairs: cf. word building with *-at: bat, cat, fat, hat* ....

On the other hand, everybody will admit that it is quite impossible to check all the references collected. It would take the author years and years and even then his task might not be finished, since checking a re-ference almost inevitably means finding others to be checked. It would therefore be unwise to expect a bibliography to have been checked in de-tail and completely. If this were to be accepted the writers of biblio-graphies would no longer need to suggest or maintain that they had check-ed all the material. They could openly admit that some of the material had been checked, while other parts had not. Only in this way will the user know how reliable the bibliography in question really is.

b) Reliability depends on yet another factor. Once it has been admitted that no bibliography can and will be exhaustive, one should think of how close one can practically come to this goal. Bibliographies should be supplementable. They can, however, only be supplemented, if one knows what has been checked and what has not. Therefore, in order to facilitate international cooperation in supplementing already existing bibliographies, authors should quote the sources checked. If a bibliography lists all the bibliographies, periodicals, dissertations etc. that have been consulted, a scholar working in another country might want to prepare a supplement dealing with publications not included which have , however, appeared in his country. In this manner bibliographical work could be reasonably divided up on an international level; and many hands make light work.

3) <u>Arrangement of the material collected</u>

The most common arrangement of all the references collected is by alphabetical listing. This is the easiest way of writing a bibliography but it is not the most informative one. A bibliography which attempts to point out the development of the research field under discussion and the apparent direction of the development so that the reader becomes familiar with specific aspects that have been studied or neglected would be of much greater use and effect. Since all the data contained in a bibliography cannot - as we have tried to show above - be checked, an arrangement with regard to the subject matter instead of an alphabetical listing by authors - though apparently the best - meets with almost insurmountable difficulties. The question to be decided is whether or not an alphabetical listing of authors is to be preferred to an arrangement according to the subject matter (as it will include a certain percentage

of errors due to references which were inaccessible to the bibliographer).
Critical reviews of the present bibliography will answer this question.

This book is a bibliography of English word-formation. We have not included works on word-formation in the Germanic languages; the reader is therefore
referred to Marchand and Seymour. It is a well-known fact that word-formation
has not yet received as much attention as phonology, syntax or semantics. It
is significant that we accept that this is so without surprise : if nowadays,
due to the rise of generative-transformational grammar, the creative aspect in
language is again stressed, one is astonished to see that the interest in linguistic creativity seems to be confined to syntax, whereas it could be most
easily observed in word-formation. The question of how a child acquires its
word building faculty is at least as interesting as that of how a child acquires its capacity to generate sentences. And where could the operations of semantic features, selection restrictions etc. be better observed and described
than in word-formation?

We do not yet have at our disposal a 'research report' on English word-formation for which our bibliography is intended to pave the way. There are, however, several short accounts of the state of research in English word-formation.
These are :

HOOPS, J.   : *Englische Sprachkunde*, Stuttgart - Gotha : Verlag Friedrich An-
                dreas Perthes A.-G., 1923, x, 127 p. (= Wissenschaftliche For-
                schungsberichte ed. by Prof.Dr.Karl Hönn, Geisteswissenschaft-
                liche Reihe 1914-1920, Englische Sprachkunde),pp. 98 - 105.

HORN, W.   : *Die englische Sprachwissenschaft*, in Stand und Aufgaben der
                Sprachwissenschaft, Festschrift für Wilhelm Streitberg, Heidel-
                berg : Carl Winters Universitätsbuchhandlung, 1924, xix, (1),
                683 p.; pp. 512 - 584)
                (esp. pp. 558 - 561)

         - : *Englische Sprachforschung*, in Germanische Philologie, Ergeb-
                nisse und Aufgaben, Festschrift für Otto Behagel, edited by

Alfred Goetze, Wilhelm Horn, Friedrich Maurer, Heidelberg :
Carl Winters Universitätsbuchhandlung, 1934 (= Germanische
Bibliothek, 1. Abteilung: Sammlung germanischer Elementar-
und Handbücher. 1. Reihe: Grammatiken, 19. Bd.: Germanische
Philologie) viii, 573 p.,(1), table of contents; pp. 259-290.
(esp. pp. 280 - 281)

FUNKE, O. : *Englische Sprachkunde. Ein Überblick ab 1935*, Bern: A. Francke
AG, 1950 (= Wissenschaftliche Forschungsberichte. Geisteswissenschaftliche Reihe, edited by Prof. Dr. Karl Hönn, Bd. 10)
163 p..
(esp. pp. 123 - 129)

The most recent has been written by Esko Pennanen:

PENNANEN, E. :*Current Views of Word-Formation,*NphM 73, 1972, pp. 292 - 308.

The present-day standard work on English word-formation is the impressive
book written by Hans Marchand, *The Categories and Types of Present-Day English Word-Formation. A Synchronic-Diachronic Approach,* second, completely
revised and enlarged edition, München: C.H. Beck'sche Verlagsbuchhandlung
1969, xxvi, 545 p.. One of the improvements over the first edition (Wiesbaden: Otto Harrassowitz, 1960, xx, 379 p.) is the inclusion of an extensive bibliography on English and general word-formation.

Richard K. Seymour's book, *A Bibliography of Word-Formation in the Germanic Languages,*Duke University Press, Durham N.C., 1968, xi, 158 p., repre-
sents a first attempt at writing a bibliography of word-formation and should
be welcomed as such, though its short-comings are quite obvious, cf. the
reviews by Klaus R.Grinda (Anglia 89, 1971, pp. 241 - 243) and Klaus Hansen (ZAA 17, 1969, pp. 310 - 312). But if the inadequacies of Seymour's
bibliography had been less conspicuous - such as the omission of many standard publications, immediately obvious to the specialist - the present bibliography might never have been written.

The main objections we have to raise against Seymour's bibliography may be summarized as follows:

1) Seymour does not indicate which sources and reference books he has consulted and checked. If he had done so one would perhaps know why so many references have been omitted which should have been included. Since there is no trace whatsoever of a systematic checking of a number of sources we would prefer to call his book a good and useful collection of publications on word-formation in the Germanic languages, but not a bibliography. As such it would not then lay claim to a reliability to which it cannot pretend.

2) Seymour rightly encloses in brackets those monographs and articles which have not been available for inspection. But the unbracketed articles which have been consulted should be given with the full number of pages relevant to the subject. Cf. for instance the following numbers:

No.					
185	, 117 ff	instead of	117 - 136		
463	, 27 ff	instead of	27 - 42		
	127 ff	instead of	127 - 141		
577	, 260 ff	instead of	260 - 273		
691	, 342 ff	instead of	342 - 358		
884	, 24 ff	instead of	25 - 66		
	279 ff	instead of	279 - 286		
896	, 181 ff	instead of	181 - 188		
926	, 50 ff	instead of	50 - 72	etc...

Nor does he indicate the numbers of pages for unbracketed books. The titles of checked references are often incomplete (cf. for instance No. 66, 150, 452, 466, 471, 775, 835, 932 etc.).

3)We are fully aware of the difficulties of defining the field of word-formation. But we do not think that a bibliography of word-formation in the Germanic languages should include works dealing with Latin, Greek, French etc. if they discuss or treat a suffix borrowed into Germanic or one of the Germanic languages and the subsequent development of that suffix. If one adheres to this principle, then its application in a bibliography should be consistent. How far would one have to go back to the origins of derivational morphemes?

The material of the present bibliography listing items from 1803 to 1972 has been compiled by a systematic checking of

a) catalogues of dissertations

b) periodicals

c) bibliographies and reference books

d) bibliographies in books checked

As to the choice of our periodicals we have endeavoured to include those periodicals which are the most widely read in English and modern linguistics.

The catalogues, periodicals and bibliographies checked are:

1) Bibliographies:

SEYMOUR, R.K.   : *A Bibliography of Word-Formation in the Germanic Languages,* Duke University Press, Durham N.C. 1968, xi, 158 p

KENNEDY, A.G.   : *A Bibliography of Writings on the English Language from the Beginning of Printing to the End of 1922,* Cambridge & New Haven : Harvard University Press - Yale University Press, 1927, xvii,(1), 517 p.

SCHEURWEGHS, G. : *Analytical Bibliography of Writings on Modern English Morphology and Syntax. 1877 - 1960.*
Vol. I with an Appendix on Japanese Publications by Prof. Hideo Yamaguchi (Fukui, Japan), Louvain (Belgium) : Nauwelaerts, 1963, xviii, 293 p..

Vol. II with Appendixes on Japanese Publications by Prof. Hideo Yamaguchi (Fukui, Japan) and on Czechoslovak Publications by Dr. Ján Simko (Bratislava) , Louvain (Belgium) : Nauwelaerts, 1965, xviii, 232 p., 2 p. corrigenda.

Vol. III - I. Docent G.G. Pocheptsov : Soviet Research on English Morphology and Syntax, II. M. Mincoff, A. Resz-kiewicz, L. Levitchi, R. Filipovič : English Studies in Bulgaria, Poland, Rumania and Yugoslavia, Louvain (Belgium) : Nauwelaerts, 1968, xvii, (1), 267 p..

Vol. IV Addenda and General Indexes, continued by E.Vorlat with a Few Addenda by Dr. Ján Simko (Bratislava), Louvain (Belgium) : Nauwelaerts, 1968, x, 123 p..

BIBLIOGRAPHIE LINGUISTIQUE DE L'ANNEE - LINGUISTIC BIBLIOGRAPHY FOR THE YEAR   published by the permanent international committee of linguists under the auspices of the international council for philosophy and humanistic studies, Spectrum, Utrecht - Antwerp

1939/1947 - 1969

2) Dissertations:

McNAMEE, L.F. : *Dissertations in English and American Literature. Theses Accepted by American, British and German Universities, 1865 - 1964,*New York - London : R.R. Bowker Company , 1968, xi, 1124 p..

- : *Dissertations in English and American Literature. Supplement One. Theses Accepted by American, British and German Universities 1964 - 1968,* New York - London : R.R. Bowker Company, 1969, x, 450 p..

RUTHERFORD, Ph.R.:*A Bibliography of American Dissertations in Linguistics 1900 - 1964,*Center for Applied Linguistics, Washington 1968, iv, 139 p..

a)America: *Dissertation Abstracts A, The Humanities and Social Sciences, Abstracts of Dissertations Available on Microfilm or as Xerographic Reproductions,* Ann Arbor, Michigan, University Microfilms, A Xerox Company

Vol. I,1 (1938) - Vol. 32,12 (1972)

b) Austria : *Verzeichnis über die seit dem Jahre 1872 an der philosophischen Fakultät der Universität in Wien eingereichten und approbierten Dissertationen*

Vol. I (1935)
II (1936)
III (1936)
IV (1937) - *Verzeichnis der 1934 - 1937 an der philosophischen Fakultät in Wien und der 1872 bis 1937 an der philosophischen Fakultät der Universität in Innsbruck eingereichten und approbierten Dissertationen*

(Abbr. as Vienna 1, 2, 3, 4)

- :*Verzeichnis der an der Universität Wien approbierten Dissertationen,* edited by Dr. Lisl Alker

1937 - 1944
1945 - 1949
1950 - 1957
1958 - 1963
1964 - 1965

(Abbr. as Vienna 1937 - 1944, 1945 - 1949 etc.)

- : *Dissertationen-Verzeichnis der Universität Graz 1872 - 1963,* edited by Franz Kroller

1964
1964 - 1965 (with addenda)

(Abbr. as Graz 1, 2, 3)

- : *Gesamtverzeichnis österreichischer Dissertationen,* Verlag Notring der wissenschaftlichen Verbände Österreichs, Wien 1967 ff

Vol. I   (1966)

    II   (1967)

    III   (1968)

(Abbr. as Austria I, II, III)

c)England :*Index to Theses Accepted For Higher Degrees in the Universities of Great Britain and Ireland,* edited by P.D. Record, London :Aslib, 1954 ff

Vol. I   (1950/51)   -   Vol. XIX   (1968/69)

(Abbr. as England I,II, III etc.)

- :*Subjects of Dissertations and Theses and Published Work. Presented by Successful Candidates at Examinations for Higher Degrees,* University of London

    1929 - 1936

    1937 - 1944

    1945 - 1960

    1960 - 1965

    1965 - 1970

d)Germany :*Jahresverzeichnis der an den Deutschen Universitäten erschienenen Schriften*

Vol. I   (1885/86) - Vol. 82,7   (1966)

(Abbr. as Germany 1, 2, 3, 4, etc.)

- :*Deutsche Nationalbibliographie und Bibliographie des im Ausland erschienenen deutschsprachigen Schrifttums*

    Reihe B   1966

              1967

    Reihe C   1968

              1969

              1970

              1971

              1972   (without No 12)

- :*English and German Studies in German. Summaries of Theses and Monographs. Supplements to Anglia,* edited by Werner Habicht,

Tübingen: Max Niemeyer Verlag

1968
1969
1970
1971

e)Switzerland :*Jahresverzeichnis der Schweizer Universitätsschriften*, Basel:
Schweighauserische Buchdruckerei, 1898 ff

Vol. 1897/98 - 1968

3)Periodicals:

The abbreviations are those of the Bibliographie linguistique de l'année
(Utrecht: Spectrum). The following periodicals are not mentioned in it:
Anglia Beiblatt , Englische Studien, Linguistic Inquiry and Linguistik und
Didaktik. In these cases the abbreviations are either the customary ones
or our own :

AL : *Acta Linguistica Hafniensia. International Journal of
Structural Linguistics.* Copenhagen .
Vol. 1 (1939) - 13 (1970)

ALH : *Acta Linguistica Academiae Scientiarum Hungaricae.* Budapest .
Vol. 1 (1951) - 21 (1971)

Anglia : *Anglia. Zeitschrift für Englische Philologie.* Tübingen .
Vol. 1 (1878) - 89 (1971)

Anglia B : *Beiblatt zur Anglia.* Halle .
Vol. 1 (1890) - 54 (1943/44)

ArchL : *Archivum Linguisticum. A Review of Comparative Philology and
General Linguistics.* Glasgow .
Vol. 1 (1949) - 17 (1965)
n.s. 1 (1970) - 3 (1972)

AS : *American Speech.* New York .
Vol. 1 (1925/26)- 40/41 (1965/66)

ASNS   : *Archiv für das Studium der neueren Sprachen.* Braunschweig.

            Vol. 1 (1846) - 208 (1971/72)

AUMLA   :*AUMLA. Journal of the Australasian Universities Language and Literature Association.* Christchurch, N.Z.

            Vol. 1 (1953) - 36 (1971)

BLI   :*Beiträge zur Linguistik und Informationsverarbeitung.* München & Wien.

            Vol. 1 (1963) - 21 (1971)

BSE   :*Brno Studies in English.* Brno.

            Vol. 1 (1959) - 5 (1964)

CFS   :*Cahiers Ferdinand de Saussure.* Genève.

            Vol. 1 (1941) - 26 (1969)

CJL   :*Canadian Journal of Linguistics / Revue Canadienne de linguistique.* Toronto.

            Vol. 7 (1961) - 17,1 (1971)

CLex   :*Cahiers de lexicologie.* Besançon.

            Vol. 1 (1959) - 19 (1971)

ELT   :*English Language Teaching.* London.

            Vol. 1 (1946) - 24 (1969/70)

ES   :*English Studies. A Journal of English Letters and Philology.* Amsterdam.

            Vol. 1 (1919) - 53,2 (1972)

ESt   :*Englische Studien.* Leipzig.

            Vol. 1 (1877) - 76 (1944)

FL   :*Foundations of Language. International Journal of Language and Philosophy.* Dordrecht. The Netherlands.

            Vol. 1 (1965) - 8,2 (1972)

FMLS :*Forum for Modern Language Studies.*St. Andrews.

        Vol. 1 (1965) - 6 (1970)

FoL :*Folia linguistica.Acta Societatis Linguisticae Europaeae.*The Hague

        Vol. 1 (1967) - 5,2 (1971)

Glossa :*Glossa. A Journal of Linguistics.* Burnaby,B.C.

        Vol. 1 (1967) - 5 (1971)

GRM :*Germanisch-Romanische Monatsschrift.*Heidelberg.

        Vol. 1 (1909) - 31 (1943)
        n.s. 1 (1950/51)- 53,2 (1972)

Idioma :*Idioma. International Modern Language Review.*München.

        Vol. 1 (1964) - 6 (1969)

IF :*Indogermanische Forschungen. Zeitschrift für Indogermanistik und Allgemeine Sprachwissenschaft.*Berlin.

        Vol. 1 (1892) - 75 (1970)

IJAL : *International Journal of American Linguistics.*Baltimore.

        Vol. 1 (1917/20)- 37 (1971)

IRAL : *IRAL.International Review of Applied Linguistics in Language Teaching.Internationale Zeitschrift für angewandte Linguistik in der Spracherziehung.*Heidelberg.

        Vol. 1 (1963) - 10,1 (1972)

JEGP :*The Journal of English and Germanic Philology.*Urbana,Ill.

        Vol. 1 (1897) - 70,1 (1972)

JEL :*Journal of English Linguistics.*Bellingham,Wash.

        Vol. 1 (1967) - 6 (1972)

JL :*Journal of Linguistics.*London.

        Vol. 1 (1965) - 8,1 (1972)

Kratylos : *Kratylos. Kritisches Berichts- und Rezensionsorgan für indo-germanische und allgemeine Sprachwissenschaft.* Wiesbaden .

Vol. 1 (1956) - 15,1 (1970) 1972

Langages : *Langages.* Paris .

Vol. 1 (1966) - 24 (1971)

LBer : *Linguistische Berichte.* Braunschweig .

Vol. 1 (1969) - 18 (1972)

Lexis : *Lexis. Studien zur Sprachphilosophie, Sprachgeschichte und Begriffsforschung.* Lahr (Baden) .

Vol. 1 (1948) - 4,1 (1954)

Lg : *Language. Journal of the Linguistic Society of America.* Baltimore .

Vol. 1 (1925) - 47,2 (1972)

Ling I : *Linguistic Inquiry.* Cambridge, Mass. & London ..

Vol. 1 (1970) - 3,3 (1972)

Lingua : *Lingua. International Review of General Linguistics / Revue internationale de linguistique générale.* Amsterdam .

Vol. 1 (1947/48)- 29,2 (1972)

Linguistics : *Linguistics. An International Review.* The Hague .

Vol. 1 (1963) - 81 (1972)

Linguistique: *La Linguistique. Revue internationale de linguistique géné-rale.* Paris .

Vol. 1,1(1965) - 7,2 (1971)

LuD : *Linguistik und Didaktik.* München .

Vol. 1 (1970) - 11 (1972)

L & S : *Language and Speech.* Teddington, Middlesex, England .

Vol. 1 (1958) - 15,1 (1972)

LL : *Language Learning.*Ann Arbor .

      Vol. 1 (1948) - 21,2 (1971)

MLN : *Modern Language Notes.*Baltimore .

      Vol. 1 (1886) - 87,3 (1972)

MLQ : *Modern Language Quarterly.*Seattle .

      Vol. 1 (1940) - 32 (1971)

MLR : *The Modern Language Review.*Cambridge .

      Vol. 1 (1905/6) - 67,3 (1972)

Nph : *Neophilologus.*Groningen .

      Vol. 1 (1916) - 55 (1971)

NphM : *Neuphilologische Mitteilungen./Bulletin de la Société néophi-*
*lologique de Helsinki.*Helsinki .

      Vol. 1 (1899) - 73,2 (1972)

NphZ : *Neuphilologische Zeitschrift.* Berlin & Hannover .

      Vol. 1 (1949) - 4 (1952)

NS : *Die Neueren Sprachen.* Frankfurt (Main) .

      Vol. 1 (1894) - 50 (1942)
      N.F. 1 (1952) - 21,8 (1972)

Orbis : *Orbis. Bulletin international de documentation linguistique.*
Louvain .

      Vol. 1 (1952) - 20,2 (1971)

Phonetica : *Phonetica. Internationale Zeitschrift für Phonetik./Inter-*
*national Journal of Phonetics.*Basel & New York .
      Vol. 1 (1957) - 25,1 (1972)

PhP : *Philologica Pragensia.* Praha .

      Vol. 1 (1958) - 11 (1968)

PhQ : *Philological Quarterly.*Iowa City .

      Vol. 1 (1922) - 50 (1971)

RES : *The Review of English Studies.* London .

Vol. 1 (1925) - 25 (1949)
n.s. 1 (1950) - 22 (1971)

SL : *Studia Linguistica. Revue de linguistique générale et comparée.* Lund .

Vol. 1 (1947) - 26,1 (1972)

SMSpr : *Studier i Modern Sprakvetenskap./ Stockholm Studies in Modern Philology.* Stockholm .

Vol. 1 (1898) - 19 (1956)
n.s. 1 (1960) - 3 (1968)

SNPh : *Studia Neophilologica. A Journal of Germanic and Romanic Philology.* Uppsala

Vol. 1 (1928) - 43 (1971)

SPh : *Studies in Philology.* Chapel Hill, N.C.

Vol. 1 (1906) - 68 (1971)

Sprache : *Die Sprache. Zeitschrift für Sprachwissenschaft.* Wien .

Vol. 1 (1949) - 18,1 (1972)

SRAZ : *Studia Romanica et Anglica Zagrabiensia.* Zagreb .

Vol. 1 (1956) - 32 (1971)

TSLL : *Texas Studies in Literature and Language.* Austin .

Vol. 1 (1959) - 12 (1970/71)

Word : *Word. Journal of the Linguistic Circle of New York.* New York .

Vol. 1 (1945) - 25,3 (1969)

ZAA : *Zeitschrift für Anglistik und Amerikanistik.* Leipzig .

Vol. 1 (1953) - 22,2 (1972)

In order to avoid our bibliography extending into too many subfields of linguistics we have limited the scope of word-formation as follows : in general, we have not included studies on place-names and personal names for which there are already good reference books. If, however, a suffix enjoys wide currency in the formation of other types of words, as for instance -*ing*, we have also included it in its place-name forming function. Books on loan words and borrowings and monographs on the influence of other languages, such as for instance French, German etc.,upon English have only been included in so far as they were found in the course of compilation. They usually contain some pages on those word-forming patterns that have been taken over into English. Since books and articles on the influence of French, German etc. on English are so numerous that they would in themselves fill another bibliography, we have tried not to extend our coverage beyond those works listed.

Studies on the language or vocabulary of specific authors also have only been included if they turned up while checking the works quoted above.

If a book or an article the title of which promised something about word-formation turned out not to deal with word-formation at all, - cf. the example quoted *Word Building For Infant Schools* - we did not include it.

The bibliography thus lists first all the references found for those ways of forming new words in English that are based on a syntagmatic relationship of its constituents such as compounding, prefixation, suffixation, and conversion. It then includes studies on backformation, blends, clippings, portmanteau-words, reduplicative combinations and words based on phonetic symbolism which cannot be analysed on a determinant-determinatum basis, but are linguistically motivated. We have introduced a third section 'neologisms' which will show which word-forming procedures are employed for new coinages.

Since there are no clear-cut delimitations in language we had to account for various border-line cases which we had decided to include. These are: 1) substantivation of adjectives, adjectivization of nouns which do not usually figure in word-formation (vs. derivation by means of a zero-morpheme); 2) syntactic groups of the type *stone wall, gold watch* (vs. full compounds); 3) phrasal verbs which on the one hand can be analysed and thus reveal new formations, but which on the other hand are on their way to lexicalization or are already completely lexicalized.

As to the presentation of the data compiled there are different possible approaches:

a) alphabetical listing of the authors

b) chronological arrangement according to the date of publication

c) chronological arrangement according to the historical periods of the English language, OE, ME, EMOE, MoE

d) arrangement according to the methods employed

e) arrangement according to the fields of the subject matter in question

None of these approaches could, however, be applied in its pure form. Each approach will have to contain aspects of the others. a) would give the least information about those sections that have already been investigated and those that have not yet been investigated. This task would be left to the user of the bibliography. b) has to be combined with a). Since publications may, however, be delayed, we do not consider b) a much better or more informative arrangement than a). c) combined with a) and b) would give the most valuable information as to the amount of studies on word-formation in Old English, Middle English etc.. d) would be an interesting undertaking but it presupposes a detailed knowledge of all the items. The optimal solution would be to combine e) with a), b) and c), and arrange the material according to the subject matter (for instance : compounding, prefixation etc.)-

and within these sections in turn into OE, ME, EMoE and MoE - and then alphabetically and in the case of specific authors, chronologically. Since
our interest is less in the historical side and since an attempt at an arrangement, though superior to that in previous works, yet does not result
in the optimal presentation, we have decided on arrangement e) without, however, taking into account the historical periods of English.

Although there are often discrepancies between what a title of a book
or article promises and the type of word-formation which is really dealt
with therein and although we know that the presentation of the material collected is extremely difficult and therefore most open to criticisms, we have
endeavoured as far as possible to classify the material compiled.

The material has been arranged according to the following principles:
on the one hand, we have tried to make the presentation as hierarchic as
possible, thus dividing it up into the main sections recognised within word-
formation : compounding, derivation etc.. In general, all items covering compounding and derivation are included in the section ' General Studies on English Word-Formation', as well as studies on the vocabulary in specific
authors and studies on the influence of other languages upon English unless
they were found, on checking, to deal only with derivation. In order to avoid
too many cross-references, contributions made to derivation covering several
affixes, as for instance, *pre-*, *re-*, *-ist*, *-ness* etc. figure only under 'General Studies on Derivation' and not under the affixes *pre-*, *re-*, *-ist*,
-ness respectively.

If the main sections distinguished are not based on a hierarchic order, -
for instance, derivation and derivation by means of a zero-morpheme, cross-
references are given.

The second principle underlying our arrangement has been that of trying to

focus the reader's attention on certain subjects which have attracted particular interest in research work. We have, therefore, collected the contributions made to these subjects and presented them as such : viz. obscured compounds, compounds with locative particles, diminutives, agent noun
formations etc..

The main sections have then been subdivided according to the word class
criterion and classified according to the word class membership of the de-
terminatum, such as for example : compounds functioning as substantives, as
adjectives etc., derivatives functioning as substantives, as adjectives, as
verbs etc.. Within these subsections items are arranged by alphabetical listing of authors. If an author has written several items on the same topic
these will be listed chronologically.

   Two remarks should be made concerning our alphabetical listing of affixes:

1) In order not to complicate the arrangement too much we have not distinguished between derivational morphemes inherited or borrowed and those
   which originated through the process of irradiation. *-burger*, *-scape* ,
   etc. will thus figure as suffixes.

2) Our decision not to take into account the historical stages in the development of the English language accounts for the fact that we have not
   distinguished in our alphabetical listing of affixes between those affixes which only occurred in Old English or Middle English or Modern English.

Since we decided to include border-line cases we had to find a section under which to classify formations of the type *stone wall*, *gold watch*. Faute
de mieux we have classed them together with those formations which were
evolved by the process of premodification. This classification, however, is
not very satisfactory.

Part II lists the material collected in Part I according to the aspects studied within English word-formation. It thus shows, for instance, how the emphasis in research interests has been changing. Although this bibliography
only paves the way for a future research report, the mere arrangement of
Part II already provides an interesting documentation in itself : studies in
English word-formation using the contrastive approach have been increasing fo
the last ten, twenty years, and cover all the different methods of coining
new words. The great majority of these studies have been written by German
speaking authors comparing English and German. Studies written before or
even during the nineteenth century are almost all rooted in the tradition of
historical-comparative linguistics. They therefore only deal with a specific
word-formation pattern in languages belonging to the same language family;
the favourite topics are comparative studies of English and Germanic, the
differences in stress and prefixation. Recent studies, however, deal with
languages from different language families.

Studies on word-formation in specific authors or in specific works show a
pre-occupation with Shakespeare, Carlyle, Chaucer, and the Beowulf epic. In
this case also, the items we have compiled indicate that most of the studies
have been written in the German-speaking countries Austria and Germany. The
topic seems to have been the subject for dissertations in linguistics and
its motivation is easily accounted for. Contributions in Germany go back
to the nineteenth century, the richest periods are the years 1900 - 1910
and 1950 - 1960, the last decade shows a decline in interest. Austria has
contributed works since 1900, the most productive period being that between
1940 and 1960. Whereas America manifested little interest in the early twentieth century interest has been noticeably increasing there within the last
ten years.

Although the chapters XIII to XVIII contain very few items and could have been treated in a chapter ' Varia' we have dealt with them in a special chapter. We think that there are quite a number of aspects which have not yet been studied, but which could be investigated in word-formation. Our opinion as to how research work in word-formation could be further developed and what aspects could or should be taken into account, is reflected in the headings of chapter XIII ' Word-Formation and Aphasia', XIV ' Word-Formation and Child Language', XV ' Word-Formation and the Teaching of English', XVI ' Word-Formation and Computer Studies', XVII 'Word-Formation and Sociolinguistics' and XVIII ' Word-Formation and Statistics', which we have deliberately chosen in order to attract the reader's attention to them.

Some technical details should be mentioned :

1) Works marked by ' before the number have not been checked.

2) Anonymous works are generally listed before those of known authors.

3) Titles in Russian, Polish etc., that is languages unfortunately unfamiliar to a wide readership, are also given in English. The English version has either been taken over from the source or is a rendering, not a literal translation, of what the article is about.

4) In order to avoid unnecessary repetition the full bibliographical data are only given at the first mention of an item. The reader is therefore referred to this first mention.

5) Reviews are only listed for monographs and articles dealing exclusively with word-formation. They are not relisted after the first entry.

6) All -ing-forms are only listed once, in the chapter on derivation of substantives; as to the adjectival function of -ing the reader is therefore referred to this chapter.

7) The figures in the index of authors at the end of the bibliography refer to page numbers.

8) Unfortunately some cross-references were unwillingly omitted in the course
   of compilation. It was decided in these cases to introduce numbers combined
   with lower case letters (...a, ...b). By doing so we salvaged our number-
   ing system : the first entry numbers remain successive; cross-reference number
   are always lower than the immediately preceding first entry number.

It finally remains to be said that I am aware of certain short-comings in my
approach to this undertaking. I would sincerely welcome suggestions for im-
provement, and general ideas as to the effectiveness of my approach. If some
investigator should feel induced to improve this or that point by presenting
material from sources I had no access to then the time for the preparation of
this bibliography will have been well spent.

I.

I. GENERAL STUDIES ON ENGLISH WORD - FORMATION
(General studies, compounding and derivation ...)

' 1 Anon.   : *Words and Meanings*, New Britannica Book of the Year 1952,
                    pp. 741 - 742.
                    (Coinages of 1951, or earlier, which became prominent in
                    1951, prepared by New Words Research Committee of American
                    Dialect Society, I. Willis Russell, chairman)

  2 Anon.   : *Word-Work for Word-Building, Spelling, Sentence-Building
                    and Transcription, Standards I and II*, Birmingham : Davis
                    & Moughton 1896 - 1900, iv, 48 p..
                    (pp. 34 - 36)

  3 ABBOTT, E.A.:*A Shakespearean Grammar. (An Attempt to Illustrate Some
                    of the Differences Between Elizabethan and Modern English)*,
                    London : MacMillan and Co., 1869, viii, 136 p..
                    (3rd ed. 1870, xxiv, 511 p.; 1878 : xix, 511 p.; 1886,1909)

' 4 ADAMS,V.   : *Introduction to Modern English Word-Formation*, London :
                    Longman, 1973.

' 5 AJZENŠTADT,E.I.: *Nekotorye sredstva leksičeskogo vyraženija emfazy v
                    sovremennom anglijskom jazyke* , (Lexical devices for ex-
                    pressing emphasis in modern English), IJaŠ 1964, No. 5,
                    pp. 29 - 34.

  6 ALLEN,A. - CORNWELL,J.: *A New English Grammar With Very Copious Exer-
                    cises and a Systematic View of the Formation and Deriva-
                    tion of Words*, London : Simpkin, Marshall & Co., 1841,
                    xv, 168 p..
                    (esp. pp. 70 - 97)
                    Review:
                    ' -   : Eclectic Review, n.s. 9, pp. 693 - 702

' 7 ANDREWS,E.   : *A History of Scientific English. The Story of its Evolu-*
                     tion Based on a Study of Biomedical Terminology. With a
                     Foreword by A.B. Luckhardt, 1947.

8 ANIKA,H.   : *Wortbildende Kräfte in der englischen Pressesprache des*
                     letzten Jahrzehnts, Diss. Hamburg 8.8.1951,(2),115 lvs.,
                     Appendix 14 lvs.,(2),(1).

' 9 ARNOL'D, I.V.: *Leksikologija sovremennogo anglijskogo jazyka*, Moskva,
                     1959.

10 ARONSTEIN, Ph.:*Englische Wortkunde*, Leipzig : Verlag und Druck von B.
                     G.Teubner, Berlin, 1925, viii, 130 p..
                     Reviews:

Aronstein,Ph.	:	GRM 14, 1926, 464
C.,W.E.	:	MLR 24, 1929, 107 - 108
Franz,W.	:	ESt 62, 1927/28, 419 - 422
Humpf,G.	:	Zeitschrift für franz. u. engl. Unter-richt mit Berücksichtigung der übrigen neueren Fremdsprachen 25, 1926, 570
Karpf,F.	:	NS 35, 1927, 549 - 554
Lindelöf,U.	:	NphM 27, 1926, 240 - 241
Malone,K.	:	MLN 41, 1926, 471 - 473
Northup,C.S.	:	JEGP 27, 1928, 393 - 396
Redin,M.	:	MSpråk 20,1926 , 154 - 156

'11 ARUTJUNOVA,N.D.: *Stat'i G.Marčanda po teorii sinchronnogo slovoobrazo-*
                     vanija (H.Marchand's articles on the theory of synchron-
                     ic word-formation), VJa 1959, 2, pp. 127 - 131.

'12 BADENHAUSEN,I.: *Die Sprache Virginia Woolfs. Ein Beitrag zur Stilistik*
                     des modernen englischen Romans, Diss. Marburg 7.3.1932;
                     Marburg, 63 p.,vita.
                     (Germany 48, p. 543)

'13 BANKEVITCH,L. : *English Word-Building*, Leningrad, 1961.

'14 BARAK,S.M.   : *K voprosu o sposobach obrazovanija naučno-techničeskich*
                     terminov. (Na materiale anglijskogo jazyka) (On the

methods of forming scientific and technical terms. (Using English material)), *Voprosy leksiki i fraseologii anglijskogo i nemeckogo jazykov* (Ministerstvo vysšego i srednogo special'nogo obrazovanija USSR, Char'kov 1964, vyp. 1, pp. 3 - 11.

15 BARBER,Ch. : *Linguistic Change in Present-Day English*, Edinburgh & London : Oliver & Boyd, 1964, ix, 154 p.; reprint 1966. (esp. pp. 77 - 107)

16 BAREŠ,K. : *Morfologiké rysy odborné angličtiny*, (The morphological features of technical English), ČMF 51, 1969, pp. 209 - 218; p. 218 English summary.

17 BAUER,R. : *Erhaltung und Förderung ursprünglich britischen Wortgutes im modernen Amerikanischen*, Diss. Erlangen 20.8. 1955; (1955), 43 p. (Masch. verv.). (Germany 71, p. 167)

18 BAUGH,A.C. : *A History of the English Language*, London : Routledge & Kegan Paul Ltd., second ed. (revised) 1959, xiii, (3), 506 p.. (esp. pp. 73 - 77, 104, 365 - 370)

19 BAYLEY,H. : *The Shakespeare Symphony. An Introduction to the Ethics of the Elizabethan Drama*, London : Chapman and Hall Ltd., 1906, ix, 393 p.. (esp. Chapter X : The Word Makers, pp. 202 - 229)

20 BELENKAYA,V.D.: *Modern English Morphology* , Moscow State University, Philological Faculty, English Department, 1966.

21 BEYER,E. : *Studien zur amerikanischen Sportsprache unter Berücksichtigung des Baseballspieles und seines Wortschatzes*, Diss. Marburg 2.11.1948; Marburg , 1948, 315 lvs.n.. (Germany 65, p. 360)

22 BINDMANN,W. : *Wortschatz und Syntax bei Benjamin Disraeli (Lord Beaconsfield). Unter besonderer Berücksichtigung der Neologis-*

men und moderner syntaktischer Erscheinungen, Diss. Jena
22.7.1957; (1957),xxxv, 203 lvs.n..
(Germany 73, p. 440)

23 BLOOMFIELD,L.: *Language*, London: George Allan & Unwin Ltd., 1969, ix,
566 p. (1rst ed. 1933).

24 BLOOMFIELD,M.W. - NEWMARK,L.: *A Linguistic Introduction to the History
of English*, New York : A.A.Knopf, 1963, xvi, (2), 375 p.
xx.
(Esp. pp. 326 - 366 : The English Vocabulary and English
Word-Formation)

'25 BONELIS,M.D. : *Ob osnovnych sposobach obrazovanija gornych terminov
v sovremennoj anglijskoj gornorudnoj terminologii*,
(On the main means of forming mineral terms in modern
English mining terminology), UZ 1-MPed I 1961, t. 26,
pp. 204 - 242.

'26   - : *Obščaja charakteristika leksičeskogo sostava sovremennoj
anglijskoj gornorudnoj terminologii i osnovnye sposoby
obrazovanija gornych terminov*, (On mining terminology),
Diss. Moskva (1-MPed I), 1962.

27 BRADLEY,H.   : *The Making of English*, London : The MacMillan Company,
1906, viii, 245 p. (1rst ed. March 1904).
(esp. pp. 111 - 154)

'28 BRAŽNIKOVA,G.F.: *Grammatika sovremennogo anglijskogo jazyka (Teoreti-
českij kurs). Morfologija*, (A Modern English Grammar.
(A Theoretical Course). Morphology), Kiev (Radjanska sko-
la), 1960, 184 p. (in Ukrainian).

'29 BRETZFELDER-THALMESINGER,L.: *Lydgate's Sprache im 'Siege of Thebes'*,
Diss. München 18.6.1920; München, xviii, 96 lvs..
(Germany 30, p. 698)

'30 BULAVIN,N.M. : *Sootnositel'naja charakteristika novoobrazovanij v britanskom anglijskom jazyke i ego amerikanskom variante (leksika i slovoobrazovanie) v svjazi s teoriej " amerikanskogo jazyka"* , (Comparing characteristics of new formations in British and American English (Lexicon and word-formation)), Diss. Moskva 1956 (MU).

'31   - : *Suščestvujut li različija v sposobach slovoobrazovanija meždu anglijskim jazykom Velikobritanii i ego amerikanskim variantom?* (Is there a distinction between Britain and American word-formation?), UZ IMO 1958, KIJa zapadnogo fakul'teta, vyp. 1, pp. 59 - 82.

'32   - : *O tendencijach dopolnenija slovarnogo sostava britanskogo i amerikanskogo variantov anglijskogo jazyka* , (On the tendencies of expanding the British and Amerian lexicon), UZ IMO 1960, KZJa, vyp. 3, pp. 104 - 141.

33 CALVET,L.-J. : *Sur une conception fantaisiste de la langue: la "newspeak" de George Orwell,* Linguistique 1, 1969, pp.101-104.

34 CAMPBELL,H.F. : *English Word Study. A Series of Exercises in English Etymology. To Which are Appended Exercises in Analysis and Composition,* London : Longmans, Green & Co., 1883, 110 p..

35 CARSTENSEN,B. : *Zur Systematik und Terminologie deutsch-englischer Lehnbeziehungen,* in Wortbildung, Syntax und Morphologie, Festschrift zum 60. Geburtstag von Hans Marchand am 1.Oktober 1967, edited by Herbert E.Brekle and Leonhard Lipka, Paris - The Hague : Mouton, 1968, 250 p.; pp. 32 - 45.

36 CHAPIN,P. : *On the Syntax of Word-Formation in English,* Ph. D. M.I.T. ,Eric Document Reproduction Service (ED 019648), Bethesda, 1967, 197 p., vita.

37 CHARLESTON,B.M.: *Studies on the Emotional and Affective Means of Expression in Modern English,* Bern :Francke Verlag, 1960,

(= Schweizer anglistische Arbeiten - Swiss Studies in English, Vol. 46), 357 p..
(A shortened form of a Habilitationsschrift, Bern 1957).

'38 CHOMJAKOV,V.A.: *O douch sposobach obrazovanija slov slenga v amerikanskom variante anglijskogo jazyka* (On two types of word-formation in American slang), UZ Volog Ped I 1964, t. 28 pp. 257 - 275.

39 COATES,W.A. : *Meaning in Morphemes and Compound Lexical Units,* in Proceedings of the Ninth International Congress of Linguists Cambridge, Mass., August 27 - 31, 1962, ed. by H.G.Lunt, Mouton & Co., 1964, xxii,1174 p.; pp. 1046 - 1051 (discussion pp. 1051 - 1052).

'40 COWDREY,M.B. : *The Linguistic Experiments of James Joyce,* Horn Book Magazine 6, Boston, 1933, pp. 16 - 19.

'41 CRABB,G. : *Neue practische Englische Grammatik,* 4th rev. ed. Frankfurt 1825 (first ed. 1803).

42 CRAIGIE,W.A. : *The Growth of American English. I,* S.P.E. Tract No. 56, Oxford : Clarendon Press, 1940, pp. 197 - 222.

43 - : *The Growth of American English. II,* S.P.E. Tract No. 57, Oxford : Clarendon Press, 1940, pp. 223 - 264.

'44 DALY,B.A. : *The Sources of New Words and New Meanings in English Since 1800,* CJ 34, 1939, pp. 488.

'45 DANKOVA,M. : *Mnogočlennye obrazovanija v različných sintaksičeskich funkcijach i nekotorye slučai ich stilističeskogo ispol'zavanija v publicistike* (Multicomponent formations in various syntactic functions and some examples in modern journalism), Resp Konf , pp. 24 -25.

'46 DAVENPORT,B. : *The Joycean Language,* Blue Pencil 1.2.,New York, 1934, pp. 4 - 5.

'47 DETLEFSEN,H. : *Die Namengebung in den Dramen der Vorgänger Shake-*
speares, Diss. Kiel 12.2.1914; Schleswig: Bergas,1914,
ix, 60 p..
(Germany 30, p. 672)

48 DEUTSCHBEIN,K. : *Shakespeare-Grammatik für Deutsche oder Übersicht über*
die grammatischen Abweichungen vom heutigen Sprachge-
brauch bei Shakespeare, second rev. ed. Cöthen : Verlag
Otto v. Schulze, 1897,viii, 84 p.
(esp. pp 36 - 37)
(The first ed. 1882 was a Separatabdruck of two Pro-
grammabhandlungen published with Programm der Zwickauer
Realschule, Ostern 1881 and 1882).

49 DEWITT,N.W. : *On Making New Words,* The Classical Weekly Vol.XV, 12,
1922, pp. 89 - 91.

'50 DIETRICH,H. : *Sprache und Stil James T. Farrells. Möglichkeiten und*
Grenzen des psychologischen Naturalismus , Diss. Leip-
zig 5.7.1966; Leipzig, 1966, xiv, 285 lvs.n.,Masch. verv..
(DNB B 1967,11; p. 1157)

51 DYBOSKI,R. : *Über Wortbildung und Wortgebrauch bei Tennyson,* Bausteine I, 3, 1905, pp. 165 - 223.

52 - : *Zur Wortbildung in Tennysons Jugendgedichten,* Bausteine
I, 3, 1905, pp. 239 - 241.

53 - : *Tennysons Sprache und Stil,* Diss. Wien, 1905, Wien -
Leipzig : W. Braumüller, 1907, xxxvii, 544 p..
(= Wiener Beiträge zur englischen Philologie, Vol.25).

54 ECKHARDT,E. : *Die neuenglische Verkürzung langer Tonsilbenvokale in*
abgeleiteten und zusammengesetzten Wörtern, ESt 50,
1916/1917, pp. 199 - 299.

55 - : *Nochmals zur neuenglischen Vokalverkürzung in Ablei-*
tungen und Zusammensetzungen, ESt 55, 1921, pp. 226 -
230.
(refers to Luick)

56 ECKHARDT,E.   : *Reim und Stabreim im Dienste der englischen Wortbil-*
                      dung, ESt 72, 1937/1938, pp. 161 - 191.

57 ELLEGÅRD,A.   : *English, Latin, and Morphemic Analysis,* Gothenburg
                      Studies in English 15, Acta Universitatis Gothoburgen-
                      sis 1963, 20 p..
                      Reviews:
                      Marchand,H.   : ES 47 , 1966, 466 - 467
                      Pilch, H.   : ASNS 202, 1966,464 - 465

'58 ELMAYER von VESTENBRUGG,R. : *Studien zum Darstellungsbereich und Wort-*
                      schatz des Beowulf-Epos, Diss. Graz, 1958, 275 lvs..
                      (Graz 1, p. 160, 2693)

'59 ERLEBACH,P.   : *Bildungstypen englischer Zunamen französischer Her-*
                      kunft, Diss. Mainz 12.7.1968; Mainz, 1968, 123 p..
                      (DNB C 1970,4; p. 20)

'60 ERLER,E.   : *Die Namengebung bei Shakespeare,* Diss. Jena 30.6.1913;
                      Heidelberg: Winter, 1913, viii, 24 p..
                      (complete ed. as Anglistische Arbeiten 2)
                      (Germany 29, p. 635)

'61 ERNST, M.S.   : *Words: English Roots and How They Grow,* 2nd ed. rev.
                      New York : Knopf, 1950, x, 116 p..

'62   - : *More About Words,* New York : Knopf, 1951, vi, 233 p.,
                      xi.

'63 ESCENKO,Ju.F. : *K voprosu o putjach sozdanija tehničeskoj terminologii*
                      v anglijskom jazyke (On the ways of forming technical
                      terms in English) , It Stud Konf, pp. 364 - 366.

'64 ESTRICH,R.M. - SPERBER,H. : *Three Keys to Language ,* New York, 1952,
                      358 p..
                      (esp. pp. 276 - 309 : On humour in language and word-
                      formation)

65 F.,F.A.   : *Die englische Lexikographie in Deutschland seit Adelung*
                      (1783), ASNS 8, 1851, pp. 249 - 290.

66 FICHTNER,E.G.   : *The Trager - Smith Levels of English. A Reinterpreta-*
                       tion, IRAL 10,1, 1972, pp. 21 - 33.

67 FIEDLER,E.   : *Wissenschaftliche Grammatik der englischen Sprache,*
                       Vol. I : *Geschichte der englischen Sprache, Lautlehre,*
                       Wortbildung und Formenlehre, Leipzig : W.Violet,1861,
                       xix, 313 p..
                       (esp. pp. 158 - 218)

'68 FILIPOVIĆ,R.   : *Descriptivna gramatika engleskog jezika* (Descriptive
                       grammar of the English language); Vol. II, fasc. 4:
                       Tvorba riječi (Word-formation), Zagreb, 1960, 97 p..
                       (2nd ed. 1963: 98 p.)

69 FISIAK,J.   : *A Short Grammar of Middle English,* Part One: *Graphe-*
                       mics, Phonemics, and Morphemics, Warszawa : PWN -
                       Polish Scientific Publishers - London : Oxford Univer-
                       sity Press, 1968, 139 p..
                       (esp. pp. 111 - 120)

70 FRANCIS,N.W.   : *The Structure of American English with a Chapter on*
                       American English Dialects by Raven I. McDavid Jr. ,
                       New York : The Ronald Press Company, 1958, vii, 614 p..
                       (1rst ed. 1954)
                       (esp. pp. 196 - 208)

71   - : *The English Language. An Introduction,* London : The
                       English Universities Press Ltd., rev. English ed.,
                       1967, x, 273 p..
                       (esp. pp 33 - 37, 152 - 164)

'72 FRANK,E.O.   : *Modern American Language in the Service of Present-*
                       Day Advertisement (a Survey of the Linguistic Means
                       Available for the Psychology of Selling), Diss. Vienna
                       1947, 138 lvs..
                       (Vienna 1945 - 1949, p. 54, 1145)

73 FRANKE,W.   : *Über Wortbildung und Wortgebrauch im Englischen und*
                       Amerikanischen der Gegenwart, NphZ 2, 1950, pp. 12-21.
                       (Prefixation, Suffixation, Conversion, Blends...)

74 FRANZ,W.   : *Zu Schmeding, Über Wortbildung bei Carlyle*, ASNS 109, 1902, pp. 129 - 130.

75   - : *Die Wortbildung bei Shakespeare*, ESt 35, 1905, pp.34 - 85.

76   - : *Orthographie, Lautgebung und Wortbildung in den Werken Shakespeares mit Ausspracheproben*, Heidelberg : Carl Winters Universitätsbuchhandlung, 1905, vi, 125 p..
Reviews:

Bastide,Ch.   : Revue Critique d'histoire et de litté-
                    rature n.s. 61, 1906, 465 - 466
Brotanek,R.   : Shakespeare - Jahrbuch 42, 1906, 248
                    - 254
Dyboski,R.   : Allgemeines Literaturblatt 17, 1908,
                    col. 81
Ekwall,E.   : DLZ 28, 1907, col. 103 - 104
Mawer,A.   : MLR 1 , 1905/o6, 342
Pr.,Ldw.   : Literarisches Centralblatt 57, 1906,
                    col. 578 - 579
Splettstösser,W.:ASNS 118, 1907, 211
Western,A.   : ESt 37, 1907, 212 - 217

77   - : *Shakespeare-Grammatik* , 2nd ed., largely augmented and rev., Heidelberg : Carl Winters Universitätsbuchhandlung, 1909, xxviii, 602 p..
(word-formation pp. 95 - 149)

78   - : *Shakespeare-Grammatik*, 3rd ed. rev.,Heidelberg :Carl Winters Universitätsbuchhandlung, 1924, xxxiv, 640 p..
(= Germanistische Bibliothek, ed. by W. Streitberg I. Reihe,II)

79   - : *Die Sprache Shakespeares in Vers und Prosa unter Berücksichtigung des Amerikanischen entwicklungsgeschichtlich dargestellt*, 4th ed. rev. and largely augmented, Halle: Max Niemeyer, 1939, xxxx, 730 p..

80 FRANZ,W.   : *Shakespeares Blankvers mit Nachträgen zu des Verfassers*
                        Shakespeare-Grammatik (3rd ed.), 2nd ed., Tübingen:
                        Komm.-Verlag der Osianderschen Buchhandlung, 1935, 104 p..

'81 FROMM,Ch.   : *Über den verbalen Wortschatz in Sir Thomas Malorys Ro-*
                        man ' Le Morte Darthur, Diss. Marburg 21.2.1915, Mar-
                        burg 1914, Borna-Leipzig : Noske, x, 103 p..
                        (Germany 31, p. 364)

82 FUNKE,O.   : *Zum Problem 'Sprachkörper und Sprachfunktion'*, in Neu-
                        sprachliche Studien, Festgabe Karl Luick zu seinem
                        sechzigsten Geburtstage dargebracht von Freunden und
                        Schülern, Marburg : N.G. Elwert'sche Verlagsbuchhand-
                        lung, G. Braun, 1925 (= Die Neueren Sprachen, 6. Bei-
                        heft), pp. 102 - 121.
                        (esp. pp. 108 - 110)

83   - : *Englische Sprachkunde. Ein Überblick ab 1935*, Bern :
                        A.Francke AG., 1950 (= Wissenschaftliche Forschungs-
                        berichte. Geisteswissenschaftliche Reihe, ed. by Prof.
                        Dr. Karl Hönn, Vol. 10), 163 p..
                        (esp. pp. 123 - 129)

84   - : *Neue Sprachforschung unter besonderer Berücksichti-*
                        gung des modernen Englisch, in Sprache und Literatur
                        Englands und Amerikas, Forschungsberichte und Einfüh-
                        rung in die Gegenwartsströmungen. Lehrgangs-Vorträge
                        der Akademie Comburg. In Gemeinschaft mit A.Heidelber-
                        ger,H.Metzger und G.Müller-Schwefe, ed. by C.A.Weber,
                        Tübingen : Max Niemeyer, 1952, pp. 1 - 27.
                        (esp. pp. 14 -15, 22 - 23)

85 GALINSKY,H.   : *Die Sprache des Amerikaners. Eine Einführung in die*
                        Hauptunterschiede zwischen amerikanischem und briti-
                        schem Englisch der Gegenwart, Vol. II : *Wortschatz*
                        und Wortbildung.Syntax und Flexion, Heidelberg :F.H.
                        Kerle Verlag, 1952, x, 521 p., (1).
                        (esp. pp. 61 - 119)

86   - : *Unterschiede und Gemeinsamkeiten des amerikanischen*
                        und britischen Englisch : Ein Forschungsbericht, in

Sprache und Literatur Englands und Amerikas: Forschungsberichte und Einführung in die Gegenwartsströmungen, ed.
by C.A.Weber, Tübingen : Max Niemeyer, 1952, pp. 29 - 59.
(esp. pp. 53 - 54)

87   - : *Amerikanisches und Britisches Englisch. Zwei Studien zum
Problem der Einheit und Verschiedenheit einer Weltsprache,*
München : Max Hueber, 1rst ed. 1957, 2nd ed. 1967, (=
Studien und Texte zur englischen Philologie, ed. by J.
Raith, Vol. 4) , (6), 100 p..
(esp. pp. 55 - 63, 71 - 73 : -rama, -matic, -ennial,
blending ...)

88   - : *Gedanken zu einer neuen Darstellung der englischen Wortbildung,* NS, N.F., 11, 1962, pp. 97 - 121.

89   - : *Stylistic Aspects of Linguistic Borrowing: A Stylistic
and Comparative View of American Elements in Modern German, and British English,* JbAm 8, 1963, pp. 98 - 135.

90 GIBBS,J.W.   : *Teutonic Etymology. The Formation of Teutonic Words in
the English Language,* New Haven : Peck, White & Peck,N.Y.
1860, vii, 139 p..
Reviews:
Anon.   : The New Englander 18, 1860, 1097 - 1099

'91 GIELEN,R.   : *Untersuchungen zur Namengebung bei Beaumont, Fletcher
und Massinger,* Diss. Münster 29.7.1929; Quakenbrück :
Kleinert, 1929, x, 82 p..
(Germany 45, p. 455)

'92 GINZBURG,R.S. - CHIDEKEL,S.S. - KNYAZEVA,G.Y. - SANKIN,A.A. :
A Course in Modern English Lexicology, Moskva, 1966.

93 GNEUSS,H.   : *Lehnbildungen und Lehnbedeutungen im Altenglischen,*
Diss. Berlin 31.7.1953; Berlin - Bielefeld - München:
Erich Schmidt Verlag, 1955, viii, 184 p..

Reviews:

Brunner,K.	:	Anglia	75	, 1957,	347	- 348
Dobbie,E.V.K.	:	Word	13	, 1957,	172	- 175
Einarsson,S.	:	MLN	71	, 1956,	207	- 208
Funke,O.	:	ES	39	, 1958,	130	- 131
Girvan,R.	:	RES n.s.8		, 1957,	45	- 51
Graband,G.	:	ZAA	3	, 1955,	369	- 371
Haugen,E.	:	Lg	32	, 1956,	761	- 766
Kuhn,S.M.	:	JEGP	57	, 1958,	329	- 331
Polomé,E.	:	Latomus	14,	1955,	583	- 584
Quirk,R.	:	PBB (T)78		, 1956,	315	- 317
Reed,C.E.	:	MLQ	17	, 1956,		371
Rynell,A.	:	SNPh	30	, 1958,	111	- 112
Schneider,K.	:	ASNS	192	, 1956,		201
Stanley,E.G.	:	MLR	50	, 1955,		565

94 GOEDERS,Ch.   : *Zur Analogiebildung im Mittel- und Neuenglischen, ein*
Beitrag zur Kenntnis der Sprachgeschichte, Diss. Kiel;
Kiel : Verlag von Lipsius & Tischer, 1884, 39 p..

'95 GOLLE,G.   : *Sprache und Stil bei Erskine Caldwell,* Diss. Jena 20.12.
1961; Jena, 1961, xl, 282 lvs.n.,Masch. verv..
(Germany 78, p. 462)

'96 GONDA,J.   : *Some Remarks on Onomatopoeia, Sound Symbolism and Word-*
Formation à propos of the Theories of C.N. Maxwell,
Tijdschrift voor Indische taal-, land- en volkenkunde
80, 1940, pp. 133 - 211.

'97 GOTTLIEB,A.   : *Zur Sprache John Taylors,* Diss. Vienna; Vienna 1906,
170 lvs..
(Vienna 2, 1965)

98 GOVE,Ph.B.   : *Self-Explanatory Words,* AS 41, 1966, pp. 182 - 198.

99 GRADUATE and HEAD-TEACHER : *Handbook of English, Consisting of Grammar,*
Analysis, and Word-Building, with Special Application
to Correct Writing and Speaking, Blackburn : R.Denham
& Co.; London : Simpkin, Marshall Hamilton, Kent & Co.,
1893, 56 p..

100 GREENOUGH, J. B. - KITTREDGE, G. L. : *Words and Their Ways in English Speech*, New York : The Macmillan Company; London : Macmillan & Co., Ltd.; 1901, x, 431 p..
(esp. : pp. 185 - 192 : Chapter XIV : The Development of Words. II. Derivation and Composition)

101 GREEVER, G. and BACHELOR, J. M. : *The Century Vocabulary Builder*, Century Hand-Book Series, New York Century Co.; 1922, xi, 320 p..

'102 GRINBERG, L. E. - KUZNETS, M. D. - KUMACEVA, A. V. - MELTSER, E. M. : *Exercises in Modern English Lexicology*, Moscow, second ed. 1966.

'103 GRZEBIENIOWSKI, T. : *Gramatyka oposiwa języka angielskiego* (A descriptive grammar of the English language) , Warszawa (PWN), 1954, 276 p..

104 - : *Słownictwo i sł owotwórstwo angielskie* (English vocabulary and word-formation), Warszawa (PWN), 1962, 281, (1) p..

'105 - : *Morfologie i składnia języka angielskiego* (Morphology and syntax of the English language), Warszawa (PWN), 1964, 314 p..
(This is the second edition, completely revised and enlarged of the original *Gramatyka*)

'106 HAASE, A. : *Englisches Arbeitswörterbuch. Der aktive englische Wortschatz nach Wertigkeitsstufen und Sachgruppen, sowie mit Berücksichtigung des amerikanischen Sprachgebrauchs, der Phonetik und der Wortbildungslehre*, Frankfurt : M. Diesterweg, 1959, 273 p.
Reviews:
Rück, H. : NS, N.F., 9, 1960, 51 - 53

107 HALDEMAN, S. S.: *Word-Building : for the Use of Classes in Etymology*, Philadelphia: J. B. Lippincott & Co., 1881, 55 p..

108 HALL, R.   : *John Locke's Unnoticed Vocabulary I*, N & Q 206, 1961, pp. 186 - 191, 207 - 210.

109   - : *John Locke's Unnoticed Vocabulary II*, N & Q 206, 1961, pp. 247 - 250, 330 - 335, 432 - 433.

110   - : *More Words From John Locke*, N & Q 211, January 1966, pp. 29 - 31.

111 HAMEL, G.   : *Zur Sprache der englischen Reklame*, NS, N.F., 18, 1969, pp. 223 - 234.

112 HANSEN, K.   : *Englisch. Abriss der modernen Wortbildung.* (Lehrbriefe für das Fernstudium der Lehrer),Berlin, 1964, 134 p.. (2nd ed. rev., Berlin, 1968,ix, 136 p.; 3rd rev. ed., Berlin, 1971, ix, 137 p.)

113   - : *Die Bedeutung der Worttypenlehre für das Wörterbuch*, ZAA 14, 1966, pp. 160 - 178.

'114   - : *Zur Wortbildungsanalyse im modernen Englisch*, Fremdsprachenunterricht 13, 1969, pp. 380 - 395.

115   - : *Bemerkungen zur Lehrbuchreihe ' English for you' (Teile 1-4) und zu den Unterrichtshilfen*, Fremdsprachenunterricht 14, 1970, pp. 592 - 600, 605. (esp. pp. : 598 - 600 : 3. Wortbildung)

116   - : *Ein bedeutender Beitrag zur Theorie der Wortbildung*, ZAA 19, 1971, pp. 59 - 67. (refers to Marchand, H. : *The Categories and Types of Present-Day English Word-Formation*, 2nd ed.)

117 HARWOOD, F.W. - WRIGHT, A. M.: *Statistical Study of English Word-Formation*, Lg 32, 1956, pp. 260 - 273.

118 HASCHKA, G.   : *Studien zur Wortbildung und zu den Wortformen in Dramen von Philip Massinger und ein Vergleich mit der Sprache Th. Middletons*, Diss. Graz, 1950, iv, 165 lvs.. (Graz 1, 2702)

'119 HASCHKA, H.   : *Bedeutungswandel und Wortbildung in Adam Smiths "An*
                       Inquiry into the Nature and Causes of the Wealth of
                       Nations, Diss. Graz, 1952, 188 lvs..
                       (Graz 1, 2720)

120 HAUGEN, E.   : *The Analysis of Linguistic Borrowing*, Lg 26, 1950, pp.
                       210 - 231.
                       (esp. pp. 218 - 219, 221)

121 HAYDEN, M. G.   : *Terms of Disparagement in American Dialect Speech*,
                       Dialect Notes 4,3, 1915, pp. 194 - 223.

'122 HIGGINSON, F. H. : *James Joyce, Linguist*, Word Study 31, 1956, pp. 1 - 3.

'123 HINZE, O.   : *Studien zu Ben Jonsons Namengebung in seinen Dramen*,
                       Diss. Leipzig 8.7.1918 (1919), Weida i. Th. : Thomas
                       & Hubert, 1919, 84 p..
                       (Germany 35, p. 426)

124 HITTMAIR, R.   : *Wortbildende Kräfte im heutigen Englisch*, in Aus
                       Schrifttum der Angelsachsen, ed. by R. Hittmair and
                       R. Spindler, Vol. 7, Leipzig :R. Noske, 1937, 40 p..
                       Reviews:
                       L., G.   : ASNS 171, 1937, 257

'125 HIXSON, J. C.   : *English Word-Building*, Words 4, 1938, pp. 41 - 43.

'126 HÖLLER, H.   : *Wortbildung und Wortformen in den Dramen Thomas Middle-*
                       tons. Ein Vergleich mit der Sprache Shakespeares, Diss
                       Graz, 1950, iv, 155 lvs..
                       (Graz 1, 2704)

'127 HOFFMANN, A.   : *Nominale Ausdrucksweise im modernen Englisch*, Diss.
                       P.H. Potsdam 12.11.1970, Potsdam 1970, vi, 273 lvs.
                       n..
                       (DNB C 1971, 10; p. 15 (153))

128 HOOPS, J.   : *Englische Sprachkunde*, Stuttgart - Gotha : Verlag F.
                       A. Perthes A.-G., 1923, x,127 p. (= Wissenschaftliche
                       Forschungsberichte ed. by Prof. K. Hönn, Geisteswis-
                       senschaftliche Reihe 1914-1920, Englische Sprachkunde)
                       (esp. pp. 98 - 105)

129 HORN, W.
: *Sprachkörper und Sprachfunktion*, Palaestra 135, Berlin : Mayer & Müller, 1921, iv, (4), 144 p.. (2nd ed. 1923) (esp. pp. 3 - 8, 74)

130
- : *Die englische Sprachwissenschaft*, in Stand und Aufgaben der Sprachwissenschaft, Festschrift für Wilhelm Streitberg, Heidelberg : Carl Winters Universitätsbuchhandlung, 1924, xix, (1), 683 p.; pp. 512 - 584. (esp. pp. 558 - 561)

131
- : *Englische Sprachforschung*, in Germanische Philologie, Ergebnisse und Aufgaben, Festschrift für Otto Behagel, edited by Alfred Goetze, Wilhelm Horn, Friedrich Maurer, Heidelberg : Carl Winters Universitätsbuchhandlung, 1934 (= Germanische Bibliothek, 1. Abteilung : Sammlung germanischer Elementar- und Handbücher. 1. Reihe: Grammatiken, 19. Bd. : Germanische Philologie) viii, 573 p., (1), table of contents; pp. 259 - 290. (esp. pp. 280 - 281)

'132 HORTEN, F.
: *Studien über die Sprache Defoes*, Bonn, 1914.

'133 HÜCKEL, W.
: *Einige Fragen des Wortverbandes im Englischen, sein Verhältnis zum Einzelwort und seine Stellung zum Satz*, Diss. Leipzig 16.7.1971, Leipzig 1971, 292 lvs.n.,ann., (Masch. verv.). (DNB C 1972,4; p. 13 (132)

'134 HUFNAGEL, J.
: *Wortschatz von Thomas Nash*, Diss. Freiburg 8.1.1926, Freiburg, xxxii,180 lvs.. (Germany 42, p. 168)

'135 HUMBACH, Ä.
: *Aspekte der Wortbildung bei Herman Melville*,Diss. Freiburg 28.7.1959, Mecklinghausen (Westf.), (1959), 181 lvs.n.. (Germany 76, p. 254)

'136 IL'IŠ, B. A.   : *Stroi anglijskogo jazyka* (The structure of English), Leningrad, 1935, 32 p. (Research Institute of Linguistics of the Leningrad Institue of History, Philosophy, Linguistics and Literature (LIFLI), Series " Structure of Languages", Gen. ed. by A. P. Riflin, Fasc. 1).

'137 ISHIBASHI, K.   : *A New Advanced English Grammar*, Osaka : The Osaka Kyōiku Tosho Company, 1951; 4th rev. ed. , 1953-1954, 2, 6, 143 p..

138 JÄP, G.   : *Warum wendet sich die englische Sprache beim Entlehnen und Zusammensetzen neuer Worte vorzüglich an die klassischen Sprachen des Alterthums, statt den Wortschatz und die Plasticität des deutschen Sprachelements in Anspruch zu nehmen?* ASNS 9, 1851, pp. 1 - 21.

'139 JAESCHKE, K.   : *Beiträge zur Frage des Wortschwundes im Englischen*, Breslau, 1931.

'140 JENISCH, O.   : *Der Wortschatz des Chronisten Wace. Nach seiner Chronik*, Diss. Prag, Prag, 1939, 197 lvs.n.. (Germany 60, p. 735)

141 JENSEN, J.   : *Die I. und II. Ablautsreihe in der ae. Wortbildung*, Diss. Kiel 23.6.1913, Kiel : H. Fiencke, 1913, 150, (1) p., vita. (Germany 29, p. 655)

142 JESPERSEN, O.   : *Growth and Structure of the English Language*, Leipzig : B.G. Teubner, 1905, iv, 260 p..

143   - : *Nature and Art in Language*, AS 5, 1929/1930, pp. 89 - 103.

144   - : *A Modern English Grammar on Historical Principles*, Part VI : *Morphology, written with the assistance of Paul Christophersen, Niels Haislund and Knud*

Schibsbye, London : George Allen & Unwin Ltd., 1946
(first published in G.B.;)x, 570 p.
(first ed. 1942)
Reviews :

Bodelsen, C.A.	:	AL	2,	1940/41,	259 - 261
Koziol, H.	:	ESt	76,	1944	, 121 - 124
Potter, S.	:	MLR	42,	1947	, 368 - 370
Preusler, W.	:	Anglia	B 54,	1943/44,	13 - 15
Zandvoort, R. W.	:	ES	26,	1944/45	, 145 - 151

'145 JOHNSON, M. J. : *The Modern Vocabulary and Technical Jargon of Adver-*
tising, M.A. Wales, Bangor.
(England 19, p. 14; 343)

146 KÄSMANN, H. : *Studien zum kirchlichen Wortschatz des Mittelengli-*
schen 1100 - 1350. Ein Beitrag zum Problem der Sprach-
mischung, Habilitationsschrift Berlin F.U. 24.2.1960,
Tübingen : M. Niemeyer Verlag, 1961 (= Buchreihe der
Anglia, Zeitschrift für englische Philologie, Vol. 9)
viii, 380 p..

'147 KALAČEVSKAJA, N. : *Očerk morfologii anglijskogo jazyka. Časti reči i ich*
funkcii v sovremennom anglijskom jazyke (An outline
of English morphology. Parts of speech and their functions in modern English),Kiev U 1946, 444 p. (in
English).

148 KASTOVSKY, D. : *Wortbildung und Nullmorphem*, LBer 2, 1969, pp. 1 - 13.

'149 KELLOGG, B. and REED, A. : *The English Language. A Brief History of its*
Grammatical Changes and its Vocabulary. With Exercises
on Synonyms, Prefixes and Suffixes, Word-Analysis and
Word-Building, New York : Maynard & Co., 1891, v, (1),
170 p..
(new ed. 1893, 1894)

'150 KELLOGG, B. - REED, A. : *Word-Building with Roots, or Stems, and Prefixes*
and Suffixes, New York : E. Maynard & Co., 1892, 63 p..

'151 KENNEDY, A. G.   : *Current English; a Study of Present-Day Usages and Tendencies, Including Pronunciation, Spelling, Grammatical Practice, Word-Coining, and the Shifting of Meanings*, Boston, New York : Ginn and Company (1935) xiii, 737 p..

'152 KIENDLER, H.   : *Wortformen und Wortbildung in den Dramen F. Beaumonts und J. Fletchers. Ein Vergleich mit der Sprache Shakespeares sowie Middletons und Massingers,* Diss. Graz 1952, vi, 177 lvs..
(Graz 1, 2706)

153 KIRCHNER, G.   : *"Neue Synthese" im Gegenwartsenglisch,* in Festschrift für Walter Fischer, Heidelberg : Carl Winter - Universitätsverlag, 1959, viii, 332 p.; pp. 302 - 322.

154   - : *Amerikanisches in Wortschatz, Wortbildung und Syntax von Herman Melvilles "Moby Dick",* in Mélanges de linguistique et de philologie, Ferdinand Mossé in memoriam, Paris : Didier, 1959, 534 p.; pp. 208 - 217.

'155 KITTNER, H.   : *Studien zum Wortschatz William Langlands,* Diss. Hal 27.5.1937, Würzburg : Triltsch, 1937, xiii, 131 p..
(Germany 53, p. 304)

156 KOCH, C. F.   : *Historische Grammatik der englischen Sprache,*Vol. III : *Die Wortbildung der englischen Sprache,* Cassel & Göttingen : G. H. Wigand, 1868
Part I : *Angelsächsisch nebst den anderen germanischen Elementen,* xvi, 184 p..
Part II : *Fremde Elemente,* Cassel & Göttingen : G. H. Wigand, 1869, x, 231 p..
(2nd ed. edited by R. Wülker, 1891)

157 KOEPPEL, E.   : *Zur englischen Wortbildungslehre,* ASNS 104, 1900, pp. 25 - 66, 279 - 286.

158 KOHL, N.   : *Das Wortspiel in der Shakespeareschen Komödie. Stu-*

dien zur Interdependenz von verbalem und aktionalem
Spiel in den frühen Komödien und den späten Stücken,
Diss. Frankfurt 23.2.1966, Frankfurt, 273 p.,(1), vita.

'159 KONOVALOVA, E. D. : *Puti obrazovanija substantivnych odnoslovnych metal-*
lurgičeskich terminov v anglijskom jazyke (Means of
forming metallurgical single word substantival terms
in English), TIMet Konf , pp. 34 - 35.

160 KOZIOL, H. : *Handbuch der englischen Wortbildungslehre,* Heidelberg:
Carl Winters Universitätsbuchhandlung, 1937 (= Germanische Bibliothek begründet v. W. Streitberg, 1.Ab-
teilung : Sammlung germanischer Lehr- und Handbücher,
1.Reihe: Grammatiken, Vol. 21), xv, (1), 260 p..
Reviews:

Heraucourt, W.	: NS 46, 1938, 332 - 333
Holthausen, F.	: ESt 73, 1938/39, 70 - 71
Horn, W.	: ASNS 173, 1938, 235 - 239
'Lehnert, M.	: Geistige Arbeit 5, 1938, No. 17, 10 a - 10 b
Liljegren, S. B.	: Anglia B 49, 1938, 37 - 47
Potter, S.	: MLR 33, 1938, 621
Zandvoort, R. W.	: ES 26, 1944/45, 151 - 153

(2nd rev. ed. forthcoming)

161 - : *Zur Wortbildung im Englischen,* Anglia 65, 1941, pp.
51 - 63.

162 - : *Förderung und Hemmung analoger Wortbildungen im En-*
glischen, in Anglo-Americana, Festschrift zum 70. Geburtstag von Prof.Dr. Leo Hibler-Lebmannsport, ed.
by Dr. Karl Brunner, Wien IX - Stuttgart : W. Braumüller (= Wiener Beiträge zur englischen Philologie,
Vol. 63), 1955, pp. 101 - 110.
(esp. -ese, -en, -ster, -trix, -ess)

163 - : *Zur Aufnahme von Wortneubildungen im Englischen,*
Orbis 4, 1955, pp. 452 - 458.

164   - : *Zur Wortbildung im amerikanischen Englisch,* in
Anglistische Studien : Festschrift zum 70. Geburts-
tag von Professor Friedrich Wild, ed. by Dr. Karl
Brunner, Dr. Herbert Koziol, Dr. Siegfried Korninger, Wien IX - Stuttgart : W. Braumüller, 1958 ,
(= Wiener Beiträge zur englischen Philologie, Vol.
66), pp. 127 - 138.

165   - : *Untersuchungen zur englischen Wortbildung,* Forschungen und Fortschritte 33, 1959, pp. 378 - 380.

166   - : *Zu Neubildungen und Lehnwörtern im amerikanischen
Englisch,* Orbis 10, 1961, pp. 169 - 174.

167 KRAEMER, H.   : *Der deutsche Einfluss auf den englischen Wortschatz
(Ein Beitrag zur Geschichte der deutsch-englischen
Sprach- und Kulturbeziehungen),* Diss. Tübingen
3.3.1952, (1952), 137 lvs.n., vita.

168 KREUTZER, E.   : *Sprache und Spiel im 'Ulysses' von James Joyce,*
Diss. Bonn 14.2.1968, Bonn : H. Bouvier und Co.
Verlag, 1969 (= Studien zur englischen Literatur,
ed.by Johannes Kleinstück, Vol. 2), ix,(1), 307 p.

169 KROESCH, S.   : *Semantic Borrowing in Old English,* in Studies in
English Philology: A Miscellany in Honor of Fre-
derick Klaeber, ed. by K. Malone and M.B. Ruud,
Minneapolis, 1929, pp. 50 - 72.

170 KRÜGER, G.   : *Zu Henry Bradleys 'Making of English',* ASNS 117,
1906, pp. 58 - 67.

171   - : *Schwierigkeiten des Englischen.*Part III : *Syntax
der englischen Sprache, vom englischen und deut-
schen Standpunkte,nebst Beiträgen zur Stilistik,
Wortkunde und Wortbildung,*Dresden and Leipzig :
C. A. Kochs Verlagsbuchhandlung (H.Ehlers), 1904,
xxiv, 778 p..
(esp. pp. 640 - 649)

172   - : *Schwierigkeiten des Englischen. Umfassende Darstellung des lebenden Englisch.* Part II : *Syntax.* 1.Abteilung : *Hauptwort,* Dresden and Leipzig : C. A. Kochs Verlagsbuchhandlung (H. Ehlers), 2nd, rev. and enlarged ed., 1914, x, 217 p..
(esp. pp. 188 - 192, 193 - 196)

173   - : Part II : *Syntax.* 2.Abteilung : *Eigenschaftswort, Umstandswort,* 2nd, rev. and enlarged ed., Dresden and Leipzig : C. A. Kochs Verlagsbuchhandlung (H. Ehlers), 1914, xii, pp. 219 - 712.
(esp. pp. 219 - 234, 262 - 318, 378 - 380, 381 - 412)

174   - : Part II :*Syntax.* 4.Abteilung : *Zeitwort,* 2nd, rev. and enlarged ed., Dresden and Leipzig : C. A. Kochs Verlagsbuchhandlung (H.Ehlers), 1914, xviii, (2), pp. 1027 - 1523.
(esp. pp. 1040 - 1046)

175   - : Part II : *Syntax.* 6.Abteilung : *Verhältniswort, Gefühlswörter, Ausrufe, Schreibung,* 2nd, rev. and enlarged ed., Dresden and Leipzig : C. A. Kochs Verlagsbuchhandlung (H. Ehlers), 1916, xi, (1), pp. 1727 - 2136.
(esp. pp. 2123 - 2127)

'176 KRUEGER, H.   : *Wirkungselemente im englischen Zeitungsstil. Der Versuch einer sprachlich-stilistischen Deutung bei volkstümlichen Massenblättern in England* , Diss. München 19.8.1949;1949, 130, vi lvs n., sev. tabl..
(Germany 65, p. 418)

177 KRUISINGA, E.   : *A Handbook of Present-Day English.* Part II : *English Accidence and Syntax 3,* 4th ed., Utrecht : Kemink en Zoon, 1925, xii, 360 p..
(1rst ed. 1911)
(esp. pp. 3 - 131)

178 KRUMMACHER, M.   : *Notizen über den Sprachgebrauch Carlyle's* , ESt 6,
                        1883, pp. 352 - 397.

179   - : *Sprache und Stil in Carlyle's "Friedrich"*, ESt 11,
                        1888, pp. 67 - 91.

180   - : *Sprache und Stil in Carlyle's " Friedrich II"* (Forts.)
                        ESt 11, 1888, pp. 433 - 457.

181   - : *Sprache und Stil in Carlyle's " Friedrich II"*,
                        ESt 12, 1889, pp. 38 - 59.

182 KRUSIUS, P.   : *Eine Untersuchung der Sprache John Webster's*, Diss.
                        Halle 3.9.1908, Halle : Wischau & Burkhardt, 1908,
                        217,(1) p.,vita.
                        (Germany 24, p. 278)

183 KULLNICK, M.   : *Studien über den Wortschatz in Sir Gawayne and the
                        Grene Knyʒt*, Diss. Berlin 7.6.1902, Berlin : Mayer
                        & Müller, 1902, 54 p.,(1), vita.
                        (Germany 17, p. 145)

'184 LAAFTMAN, E.   : *Studier i ordbildning i en keps : hur vi benämna
                        engelska ting* , Boraas, 1940 (= Redogörelse f. högre
                        allmänna laroverket i Boraas 1939-1940, Bilaga).

'185 LAIG, F.   : *Englische und französische Elemente in Sir William
                        Davenants dramatischer Kunst* , Diss. Münster 16.5.
                        1934, Emsdetten :Lechte, 1934, vi, 133p..
                        (Germany 50, p. 529)

'186 LANDAU, E.   : *Wortspiele bei Beaumont und Fletcher*, Diss. Vienna,
                        1960, 181 lvs..
                        (Vienna 1958 - 1963, p. 48; 866)

187 LANG, W.   : *Sprache und Stil in Katherine Mansfields Kurzge-
                        schichten*, Diss. Tübingen 26.8.1936, Tübingen :
                        Becht, 1936, 58 p. (also as Aus Schrifttum und
                        Sprache der Angelsachsen, Vol. 5, Leipzig : Noske).
                        (Germany 52, p. 671)

188 LATHAM, R. G.　　: *The English Language* , London : Walton and Maberly,
　　　　　　　　　　　　Longman, Green, Longman, and Roberts, 5th ed., rev.
　　　　　　　　　　　　and enlarged, 1862, xxx, 720 p..
　　　　　　　　　　　　(1rst ed. 1841)
　　　　　　　　　　　　(esp. pp. 464 - 507)

189 LEEB-LUNDBERG, W.　: *Word-Formation in Kipling. A Stylistic-Philological*
　　　　　　　　　　　　Study, Lund : Lindstedts Univ.-Bokhandel (A. & O.
　　　　　　　　　　　　Schedin), Cambridge : W. Heffer & Sons, 1909, 116 p..
　　　　　　　　　　　　Reviews :
　　　　　　　　　　　　Ericson, E. E.　: Anglia B 43, 1932, 227 (refers to Fehr)
　　　　　　　　　　　　Fehr, B.　　　　: Anglia B 24,1913, 178 - 182
　　　　　　　　　　　　Paues, A. C.　　: MLR 9, 1914 , 410 - 412

190 LEECH, G. N.　　　 : *Language of Commercial Television Advertisements*,
　　　　　　　　　　　　M.A. London, 1962/1963 .
　　　　　　　　　　　　(England 13, 147)

191　　　　　　　　 - : *English in Advertising. A Linguistic Study of Adver-*
　　　　　　　　　　　　tising in Great Britain, English Language Series,
　　　　　　　　　　　　London : Longmans, 1966, xiv, 210 p..
　　　　　　　　　　　　(esp. pp. 135 - 141)

192 LEHNERT, M.　　　　: *Morphem, Wort und Satz : eine kritische Betrachtung*
　　　　　　　　　　　　zur neueren Linguistik, ZAA 17, 1969, pp. 5 - 40,
　　　　　　　　　　　　117 - 158.
　　　　　　　　　　　　(also in Sitzungsberichte der Deutschen Akademie
　　　　　　　　　　　　der Wissenschaften zu Berlin, Klasse für Sprachen,
　　　　　　　　　　　　Literatur und Kunst, Jahrgang 1969, No. 1)

193 LEIDIG, P.　　　　 : *Französische Lehnwörter und Lehnbedeutungen im*
　　　　　　　　　　　　Englischen des 18. Jahrhunderts. Ein Spiegelbild
　　　　　　　　　　　　französischer Kultureinwirkung, Habilitationsschrift
　　　　　　　　　　　　Kiel 17.6.1938, Kiel : Schmidt & Klaunig, 1938,18 p..
　　　　　　　　　　　　(Germany 54, p. 394)
　　　　　　　　　　　　(complete ed. Bochum-Langendreer : H. Pöppinghaus
　　　　　　　　　　　　o. H.-G., 1941, xxxii, 408 p. (= Beiträge zur
　　　　　　　　　　　　englischen Philologie, Vol. 37)

194 LEISI, E.   : *Das heutige Englisch. Wesenszüge und Probleme,* 2nd ed., Heidelberg : Carl Winters Universitätsverlag, 1960, 224 p.. (1rst ed., 1955) (esp. pp. 88 - 118)

195   - : *Der Wortinhalt. Seine Struktur im Deutschen und Englischen,* 3rd, rev. and enlarged ed., Heidelberg : Quelle & Meyer, 1967, 135 p. (Habilitationsschrift Zürich 1950; first ed. 1952) (only very occasionally)

196 LENZ, K.   : *Zur Lautlehre der französischen Elemente in den schot tischen Dichtungen von 1500 - 1550 (G. Douglas; W. Dunbar; D. Lyndesay; Clariodus). Mit Bemerkungen zur Wortbildung und Wortbedeutung,* Diss. Marburg, 1911, Marburg : R. Friedrich's Universitäts-Buchdruckerei, 1913, x, 346 p., vita.

197 LEVIN, S. R.   : *Homonyms and English Form-Class Analysis,* AS 35, 1960, pp. 243 - 251.

'198 LINDHEIM, B. v.   : *Die Sprache des Ywain und Gawein und des Pricke of Conscience by Richard Rolle de Hampole,* Diss. Vienna, 1935. (Vienna 4, p. 67; 834)

199 LIPKA, L.   : *Grammatical Categories, Lexical Items and Word-Formation,* FL 7, 1971, pp. 211 - 238.

200 LOTH, J.   : *Etymologische angelsaechsisch-englische Grammatik,* Eberfeld :R. L. Friderichs, 1870, xii, 481 p.. (esp. pp. 223 - 481)

201 LÜTJEN, H. P.   : *Kontrastive Grammatik des Deutschen und Englischen: Wortbildung,* LBer 9, 1970, pp. 29 - 34.

202 LUICK, K.   : *Über Vokalverkürzung in abgeleiteten und zusammengesetzten Wörtern,* ESt 54, 1920, pp. 177 - 186.

203 McATEE, W. L. : *Bird Names With Animal or Plant Components*, AS 30, 1955, pp. 176 - 185.

204 MACDERMOTT, D. : *Vegetable Power*, Idioma 6, 1969, pp. 163 - 166.

205 MCELROY, J. G. R. : *Essential Lessons in English Etymology, Comprising the History, Derivation, Composition and Relationship of English Words; with Lists of Prefixes, Suffixes, Stems, Doublets, Homonyms, etc..For the Use of Schools*, Philadelphia : J. E. Potter and Company, (C1886), viii, 11 - 322 p..

206 MACGILLIVRAY, H. S.: *Der Einfluss des Christentums auf den Wortschatz des Altenglischen.* Part I, 1st half, Diss. Göttingen 26.5.1898, Halle a. S. : E. Karras, 1898, 50 p.. (Germany 13, p. 104; 72) (complete ed. Halle : Max Niemeyer, 1902, xxviii, 171 p. (= Studien zur englischen Philologie, Vol. VIII))

'207 McKNIGHT, G. H. : *English Words and Their Background*, New York, 1923, x, (2), 449 p..

208 MÄTZNER, E. : *Englische Grammatik.* Part I : *Die Lehre vom Worte*, 3rd ed., Berlin : Weidmannsche Buchhandlung, 1880, viii, 583 p.. (esp. pp. 479 - 564)

'209 MAGOUN, F. P. Jr. : *Word Formation in N. H. Turk : " An Anglo-Saxon Reader*, New York, rev.ed. 1930, 48 a - 48 m.

'210 MAHOOD, M. M. : *Shakespeare's Wordplay*, London, 1957.

'211 MAL'KOVSKIJ, G. E. : *Variantnost' ustojčivych slovosočetanij v sovremennom anglijskom jazyke* (" Receiver end = receiving end; tractive wheel = traction wheel etc. " in modern English), NDVS - F 7, 1964, No. 2, pp. 88 - 97.

212 MARCHAND, H. : *Phonology, Morphophonology, and Word-Formation*, NphM 52, 1951, pp. 87 - 95.

213   — : *Synchronic Analysis and Word-Formation*, CFS 13, 1955, pp. 7 - 18.

214   — : *Phonetic Symbolism in English Word-Formation*, IF 64, 1958, pp. 146 - 168, 256 - 277.

215   — : *Das amerikanische Element in der englischen Wortbildung*, in Sprache und Literatur Englands und Amerikas III, Die wissenschaftliche Erschliessung der Prosa. Lehrgangsvorträge der Akademie Comburg. In Gemeinschaft mit Hermann Metzger ed. by Gerhard Müller-Schwefe, Tübingen : Max Niemeyer Verlag, 1959, pp. 155 - 166.

216   — : *The Categories and Types of Present-Day English Word-Formation. A Synchronic-Diachronic Approach*, Wiesbaden : O. Harrassowitz, 1960, xx, 379 p..
Reviews :
Anon.   : Lebende Sprachen 8, 1963, 27 - 28
Berndt, R. : ZAA 11, 1963 , 304 - 308
Galinsky, H.:NS, N.F.,11, 1962, 97 - 121
Gaweľko, M. :KNf 15 , 1968, 105 - 111
Hartmann, P.:Kratylos 8, 1963, 81 - 85
'Kubrjakova, E. S. - Anackij, J. N. : VJa 1963, No.1, 135 - 142
Pilch, H.   : JbAm 6, 1961, 343 - 345
'Schmidt-Hidding, W. : Mitteilungsblatt des Allg. Deutschen Neuphilologenverbandes 15, 1962, 1 - 7
Standop, E. : Anglia 79, 1961, 64 - 69
'Tellier, R. : EA 14, 1961, 357 - 359
Zandvoort, R.W. : ES 42, 1961, 120 - 125

2nd, completely revised and enlarged edition, München : C. H. Beck'sche Verlagsbuchhandlung, 1969, xxvi, 545 p..
Reviews :

Adams, V   : JL 7, 1971 , 125 - 131
Bauer, G.   : Sprache 16, 1970, 189 - 190
Moessner, L. : Kratylos 14, 1969 (1972), 199 - 205
Pederson, L. : GL 2, 1970, 132 - 138
Standop, E.   : Anglia 88, 1970, 347 - 349
'Tevernier-Vereecken, C.: De Vlaamse Gids ,1971,
                  vol.1, 32 - 34
Thompson, S. A.: Lingua 27, 1971, 82 - 92
Viereck, W.   : NS, N.F., 21, 1972, 493 - 494

217   - : *Expansion, Transposition, and Derivation*, Lingui-
                     stique 1, 1967, pp. 13 - 26.

218 MARCUS, H.   : *Sprachliche Neubildungen in der englischen Gegen-
                        wartsliteratur (3. Folge)*,Neuphilologische Monats-
                        schrift 11, 1940, pp. 29 - 37.

219 MATTHEWS, B.   : *The Advertiser's Artful Aid*, The Bookman (New York:
                        George H. Doran Company), vol. 48, Sept. 1918 -
                        Feb. 1919, pp. 659 - 664.

220 MAYER, E.   : *Sekundäre Motivation. Untersuchungen zur Volksetymo-
                        logie und verwandter Erscheinungen im Englischen*,
                        Diss. Köln 1.10.1962, Köln, 1962, vii,(1), 369 p.,
                        vita.
                        (Germany 78, p. 519)

221 MEAD, L.   : *Word-Coinage by Living American Authors*, The Chau-
                        tauquan 30, 1899 - 1900, pp. 131 - 135.

222   - : *Word-Coinage; Being an Inquiry into Recent Neolo-
                     gisms, also a Brief Study of Literary Style, Slang,
                     and Provincialisms*, New York : T. Y. Crowell & Co.,
                     (1902), xi, 281 p..
                     (Published in 1907 under the title ' How Words
                     Grow')

223 MEDNIKOVA, E. M.   : *Modern English Lexicology*, Moscow, 1964.

'224 MEDNIKOVA, E. M. - KARAVKINA, T. Ju. : *Socio-lingvističeskij aspekt pro-*
duktivnogo slovoobrazovanija (na materiale anglijs-
kogo jazyka) (The socio-linguistic aspect of productive word-formation in English), VMU 19, 1964,
No. 5, pp. 80 - 88, tab..

'225 MEL'CER, E. M.   : *K voprosu o processach slovoobrazovanija sovremen-*
nogo anglijskogo jazyka (On the processes of word-
formation in present-day English), IJaŠ 1957, 4, pp.
17 - 27.

226 MENCKEN, H. L.   : *The American Language. An Inquiry into the Develop-*
ment of English in the United States, 3rd rev. and
enlarged ed., New York : A. A. Knopf, 1923, ix, 489 p
(first ed. 1919)
(esp. pp 189 - 204 : Processes of Word-Formation)

'227   - : *Postscripts to the American Language, Scented Words,*
New Yorker, April 2, 1949, pp. 70 - 74.
(Lists some of the euphemisms coined in order to
dignify common occupations : mortician, realtor,
custodian, engireer, nutritionist, shoe rebuilder)

'228 MERITT, H.   : *Some Minor Ways of Word-Formation in Old English*,
Stanford Studies in Language and Literature, 1941,
pp. 74 - 80.

'229 MIKLAŠEVSKAJA, G. A.:*Naibolee produktivnye sposoby obrazovanija neolo-*
gizmov za period s 1946 po 1957 god (The most pro-
ductive means of forming neologisms during the period of 1946 - 1957), NZ Kiev PIIn 5, 1963, pp. 61
- 77.

230 MINTON, A.   : *Names of Self-Service Laundries,* AS 33,2, 1958, pp.
5 - 16.

231   - : *Some Popular Components of Trade Names*, AS 33, 2,
1958, pp. 17 - 28.
(esp. -master, -mat(ic), -rama, -ramia)

232 MONSON, S. C.   : *Word Building* , New York : The MacMillan Company, 1958, 153 p..

233 MORRIS, R.   : *Historical Outlines of English Accidence, Comprising Chapters on the History and Development of the Language, and on Word-Formation,* London : MacMillan and Co., 1872, xii, 378 p..

(esp. pp. 211 - 248)

Reviews :

Anon.   : The Nation, (N.Y.), 15, 1872, pp. 154 - 155

234   - : *Elementary Lessons in Historical English Grammar, Containing Accidence and Word-Formation,* London : MacMillan and Co., 1874, xii, 254 p..

(More elementary work than 'Historical Outlines')

235   - : *Historical Outlines of English Accidence, Comprising Chapters on the History and Development of the Language, and on Word-Formation,* 2nd ed., rev. by L. Kellner with the assistance of Henry Bradley, London : MacMillan and Co., and New York, 1895,xiii, 463 p..

(The chapter on word-formation has been completely rewritten)

Reviews :

'Binz, G.   : Litbl. 18, 13 - 15

Bülbring, K. D. : Anglia B 7, 1896/97, 226 - 233

'Holthausen, F.: Lit.Cbl. 1896, 1577

Swaen, A. E. M. : ESt 23, 1897, 299 - 304

Tanger, G.   : ASNS 99, 1897, 152 - 157

236 MOSER, O.   : *Untersuchungen über die Sprache John Bale's,* Diss. Berlin 14.5.1902, Berlin : Mayer & Müller , 1902, 31 p., (1), vita.

(Scarcely any word-formation)

(Germany 17, p. 17; 158)

237 MOSSE, F. : *Esquisse d'une histoire de la langue anglaise,* Collection " Les langues du monde", publiée sous la direction de Henri Hierche, Série Grammaire, Philologie, Littérature, Vol. II, Lyon : IAC, 1947, xvi, 268 p..
(esp. pp. 34 - 36, 93, 195 - 201)

238 - : *Manuel de l'Anglais du Moyen Age des origines au XIVe siècle. I. Vieil-Anglais,* Tome Premier :*Grammaire et Textes,* Paris : Aubier, 1950, 345 p., planches. (= Bibliothèque de philologie germanique, Vol. VIII).
(esp. pp. 123 - 136)

239 MÜLLER-SCHOTTE, H. : *Zur typisch-englischen Kürze und Bündigkeit des Ausdrucks. (Beispiele zur Erläuterung der zur Anwendung kommenden sprachlichen Mittel,* NS, N.J. 6, 1957, pp. 219 - 228.

240 NECK, M. G. van : *On Derivation and Composition,* Taalstudie 9, 1888, pp. 282 - 292 (to be continued).
(Only suffixation)
'(cf. Germ. Jahresbericht 10, p. 265)

241 NELLE, P. : *Das Wortspiel im englischen Drama des 16. Jahrhunderts vor Shakspere,* Diss. Halle 4.8.1900, Halle : Heinrich John, 1900, 53 p., (1), (1), vita.

242 NEUMANN, J. H. : *Poe's Contributions to English,* AS 18, 1943, pp. 73 - 74.

'243 NOSEK, J. : *Základy mlnvnice moderní angličtiny* (Essentials of a grammar of modern English), Praha, 1960, 164 p..
(2nd ed. 1962, 157 p.)

244 OBERDÖRFFER, W. : *Das Aussterben altenglischer Adjektive und ihr Ersatz im Verlaufe der englischen Sprachgeschich-*

81

te, Diss. Kiel 13.7.1908, Kiel : H. Fiencke, 1908,
(2), 55 p., vita.
(Germany 23, p. 352; 74)

'245 OCHOTSKAJA, G. P.   : *Slovoslozenie i slovoproizvodstvo fiziceskich terminov i ich perevod na russkij jazyke* (Compounding
and derivation of physical terms and their translation into Russian), N Met Konf 1961, 40.

'246 OFFE, J.   : *Das Aussterben alter Verba und ihr Ersatz im Verlaufe der englischen Sprachgeschichte*, Diss. Kiel,
12.1.1908, Kiel : Schmidt & Klaunig, 1908, 79 p..
(Germany 23, p. 353; 76)

'247 OLEKSENKO, N. G.   : *O nekotorych sredstvach i sposobach obogascenija
slovarnogo sostava sovremennogo anglijskogo jazyka*
(On some means and methods of enriching the modern English vocabulary), UZ 1-MPed I, 1961, t.
25, pp. 271 - 294.

248 PALMER, H. E.   : *A Grammar of Spoken English. On a Strictly Phonetic Basis*, Cambridge : W. Heffer & Sons Ltd.,
1924, xxxvi, 293 p..

'249 PEDČENKO, E. D.   : *Slovoobrazovatel'naja rol' skandinavskich suscestvitel'nych v dal'nejsem obogascenii slovar-
nogo sostava anglijskogo jazyka* (The role of
Scandinavian substantives in word-formation as
to the further enrichment of the English vocabulary), UZ Kišin Ped I, 1958, t. 8.

250 PENNANEN, E. V.   : *Chapters on the Language in Ben Jonson's Dramatic
Works*, Annales Universitatis Turkuensis, Series B,
39, Turku, 1951, xvi, 334 p., 1 table.
(A diss. of Turun Yliogisto, the Finnish University of Turku, 1951)
(esp. pp. 47 - 76, 77 - 87, 88 - 110, 154 - 179,
180 - 203)

251 — : *Current Views of Word-Formation,* NphM 73, 1972, pp. 292 - 308.

'252 PETITJEAN, A. : *El tratamiento del lenguaje en Joyce*, SUR 78, 1971 pp. 42 - 59.

253 PILCH, H. : *Modelle der englischen Wortbildung*, in Wortbildung, Syntax und Morphologie, Festschrift zum 60. Geburtstag von Hans Marchand am 1. Oktober 1967, ed. by Herbert E. Brekle and Leonhard Lipka, The Hague - Paris : Mouton, 1968, 250 p.; pp. 160 - 178.

254 — : *Altenglische Grammatik, Dialektologie, Phonologie, Morphologie, Syntax,* München : Max Hueber Verlag, 1970, 267 p.. (= Commentationes Societatis Linguisticae Europaeae I,1). (esp. pp. 109 - 113, 117 - 119, 129 - 135)

255 PINSKER, H. E. : *Historische englische Grammatik. Elemente der Laut-, Formen- und Wortbildungslehre*, München : M. Hueber, 3rd ed. 1969, xvi, 282 p.. (1rst ed., 1959; 2nd ed., 1963) (esp. pp. 207 - 258)

'256 POELL, M. : *Wortformen und Syntax in Thomas Nashs " Unfortunate Traveller" : ein Vergleich mit der Sprache Shakespeares*, Diss. Graz 1950, ix, 163 lvs.. (Graz 1, p. 161; 2711)

'257 PONOMARENKO, L. : *Kal'kirovanie kak vid vlijanija odnogo jazyka na drugoj . (Na materiale anglijskich kalek s russkogo jazyka)* (Loan formation as a kind of influence of one language on another. Using material of English loans from Russian) , ANUkr-L Diss. Kiev, 1965.

'258 POSSANER - EHRENTHAL, H. : *Die Namengebung bei John Galsworthy* , Diss. Vienna, 1939, x, 100 lvs.. (Vienna 1937 - 1944, p. 103; 2227)

259 POTTER, S.   : *Our Language*, London : Pelican Books A 227, 1950,
                          202 p..
                          (esp. pp. 78 - 89)

260   - : *Trends in Current English*, MSpråk 50, 1956, pp.
                          255 - 267.

261   - : *Modern Linguistics* , New York, Language Library,
                          1964, 192 p..
                          (esp. pp. 78 - 103)

262   - : *Changes in Present-Day English*, ELT 21, 1966/67,
                          pp. 6 - 11.

263   - : *Changing English*, London : Andre Deutsch, 1969,
                          192 p. (= The Language Library).
                          (esp. pp. 61 - 176)

264 POUND, L.   : *Word-Coinage and Modern Trade-Names*, Dialect Notes
                          4,1, 1913, pp. 29 - 41.

'265   - : *On Indefinite Composites and Word-Coinage*, The Uni-
                          versity Studies of the University of Nebraska 13, 19
                          1913, pp. 407 ff.

266 POUTSMA, H.   : *A Grammar of Late Modern English for the Use of*
                          Continental, Especially Dutch, Students, Part II:
                          The Parts of Speech.
                          Section I, A : *Nouns, Adjectives, and Particles*,
                          Groningen : P. Noordhoff, 1914, xii, 703 p..
                          (esp. pp. 1- 22, 365 - 426)
                          Section I, B : *Verbs and Particles*,Groningen : P.
                          Noordhoff,
                          (esp. pp. 619 - 661)

'267 PRANINSKAS, J.   : *The Processes and Patterns of Trade Name Creation*,
                          Ph.D. University of Illinois, 1963, 208 p..
                          (DAb 24, 10, 1964, 4186)

268 PRESCOTT, J. : *James Joyce : A Study in Words*, PMLA 54, 1939,
pp. 304 - 315.

269 PYLES, Th. : *Words and Ways of American English. An Authoritative
Account of the Origins, Growth and Present State of
the English Language in America*, London : A. Melrose
1954, 240 p..
(esp. pp. 11 - 28, 118 - 143)

270 - : *The Origins and Development of the English Language*,
2nd ed., New York, Chicago, San Francisco : Atlanta,
1971, x, 413 p..
(1rst ed. 1964)
(esp. pp. 275 - 312)

271 QUIRK, R. - WRENN, C. L. : *An Old English Grammar*, London : Methuen & Co.,
(= Methuen's Old English Library) 1955, x, 166 p..
(esp. pp. 104 - 119)

272 QUIRK, R. - GREENBAUM, S. - LEECH, G. - SVARTVIK, J. : *A Grammar of Contemporary English*, London : Longman Group Ltd. ,
1972, xii, 1120 p..
(esp. pp. 973 - 1032, 1034 - 1040)

'273 RAYEVSKAYA, N. : *English Lexicology*, Kiev, 1957.

274 REISMÜLLER, G. : *Romanische Lehnwörter bei Lydgate*, Diss. München
23.7.1909, Naumburg : Lippert, 1909, (4), 53 p.,
vita.
(Appears in a complete ed. in Münchener Beiträge
zur rom. und engl. Philologie, Vol. 48)
(Germany 25, p. 613)

'275 REISS, S. : *The Rise of Words and Their Meaning*, New York :
Philosophical Library, 1950, 301 p..

276 REMUS, H. : *Die kirchlichen und speciell wissenschaftlichen
romanischen Lehnworte Chaucers*, Halle : Max Niemeyer, 1906, xii, 154 p..
(= Studien zur engl. Philologie, Vol. 14)

'277 RIESS, A.   : *Verbaltechnik bei Rudyard Kipling*, Diss. Vienna, 1938, v, 111 lvs..
(Vienna 1937 - 1944, p. 104; 2235)

278 RITCHIE, F.   : *Exercises in English Word-Formation and Derivation*, London : Swan Sonnenschein, Lowrey & Co., 1887, 55 p..
(Derivation only)

279 RÖSENER, F.   : *Die französischen Lehnwörter im Frühneuenglischen*, Diss. Marburg 23.7.1907, Marburg : R. Friedrich, 1907, 59 p., vita.
(esp. pp. 40 - 46)
(Germany 22, p. 484; 96)

280 RÜHMEKORB, W.   : *Wortbildende Kräfte in der heutigen anglo-amerikanischen Presse- und Umgangssprache und im Slang*, Diss. Kiel 8.11.1954, (1954), ix, 226 lvs.n..
(Germany 70, p. 428)

'281 ŠACHRAJ, O. B.   : *Grečeskij element v leksike anglijskogo jazyka. Očerk istorii slov grečeskogo proischoždenija i ich oformlenija v anglijskom jazyke* (The Greek element in English vocabulary. Historical outline of the words of Greek origin and of their formation in English), Diss. Leningrad, 1963 (LU).

282 SALOMON, H. I.   : *Wörter mit Doppelakzent im Neuenglischen*, Diss. Königsberg 15.3.1933, Breslau : Priebatsch, 1933, (6), 131 p..
(= Sprache und Kultur der germanischen und rom. Völker. A. Anglistische Reihe, 11)
(Germany 49, p. 139)

'283 SANKIN, A. A.   : *Ob osnovnych sposobach obrazovanija naučno- techničeskich terminov* (On the main methods of forming scientific-technical terms), UZ 1-MPed I, 1956, t. 10, pp. 81 - 96.

'284 SANNIKOV, N. G. : *K voprosu o složnoproizvodnych slovach v anglijs-kom jazyke* (On the question of derived compounds in English), UZ 1-MPed-I, 1961, pp. 285 - 300.

· 285 SCHAU, K. : *Sprache und Grammatik der Dramen Marlowes*, Diss. Leipzig 30.4.1902, Halle : H. John, 1901, 102 p., vita.
(esp. pp. 24 -25, 27)
(Germany 17, p. 245; 406)

'286 SCHINDL, E. : *Studien zum Wortschatz Sir Philip Sidneys : Neu-bildungen und Entlehnungen*, Diss. Vienna, 1955, 141 lvs..

'287 SCHLAUCH, M. : *The Language of James Joyce*, Science & Society 3, 1939, pp. 482 - 497.

288 SCHMEDING, O. : *Über Wortbildung bei Carlyle*, Diss. Göttingen 21.8.1899, Halle : E. Karras, 1899, 74 p..
(complete ed. : *Über Wortbildung bei Carlyle*, Halle : M. Niemeyer, 1900, xiii, 352 p. (= Stu-dien zur engl. Philologie, Vol. 5).
Reviews :
Franz, W.   :   ASNS 108, 1902, 208 - 212
              ASNS 109, 1902, 129 - 130

'289 SCHMETZ, L. : *Sprache und Charakter im Drama Shakespeare's*, Diss. München 19.7.1950; 1949, 190 lvs.n..
(Germany 66, p. 459)

290 SCHMIDT, I. : *Grammatik der englischen Sprache für obere Klas-sen höherer Lehranstalten*, 3rd rev. and enlarged ed. (Lehrbuch der englischen Sprache. Part II), Berlin : Hande- und Spener'sche Buchhandlung, 1883 xii, 585 p..
(esp. pp. 195 - 239)

291 SCHNEIDER, D. B. : *Wordsworth's " Prelude" and the O.E.D. : Word-Combinations*, N & Q 209, March 1964, pp. 100 - 102.

292 SCHÖNFELDER, K.-H. : *Ausdrücke aus dem deutschen Bildungswesen im amerikanischen Englisch*, ZAA 3, 1955, pp. 419 - 431.

293 - : *Deutsches Lehngut im amerikanischen Englisch. Ein Beitrag zum Problem der Völker- und Sprachmischung*, Halle : VEB Max Niemeyer Verlag, 1957, ix, 288 p.. (esp. pp. 229 - 259)

294 SCHOPPER, G. : *Aufbau und Sprache von Congreves Incognita*, Diss. Mainz, Mainz, 1967, (6), iv, 125 p., (1), vita. (esp. pp. 62 - 70) (DNB C, 1969, 2; p. 19, 212)

295 SCHRÖER, M. M. A. : *Supplement zur englischen Schulgrammatik. Einleitung und Paradigmen zur Lehre von der Aussprache und Wortbildung. Mit einem Anhange, enthaltend Transkriptionsproben zu R. Sonnenburgs Grammatik (- H. Bergers Lehrbuch -) der englischen Sprache*, Wien, 1885, vi, 34 p..

296 - : *Erklärung zu meinem " Supplement zur englischen Schulgrammatik"*, ESt 10, 1887, pp. 529 - 531.

297 - : *Neuenglische Elementargrammatik. Lautlehre, Formenlehre, Beispielsätze, Wortbildungslehre, mit phonetischer Aussprachebezeichnung, etc.*, Heidelberg : Winter, 1909, viii, 216 p..

298 SEALE, L.L. : *A Note on Coinages*, AS 30, 1955, pp. 69 - 70.

'299 SEVERN, W. : *People Words*, New York : Washburn, 1966, 184 p.. (A popular treatment of words derived from proper names)

300 SHEARD, J. A. : *The Words We Use*, London : Andre Deutsch, 2nd ed., 1954, 344 p.. (esp. pp. 35 - 93 : Word-formation and extension of vocabulary) (first ed. 1954)

88

'301 SIL'ČENKO, E. K.   : *Obosoblenie formy množestvennogo čisla suščestvi-*
tel'nych v anglijskom jazyke kak sposob sloovobra-
zovanija (The isolation of the substantive plural
form in English as a means in word-formation), UZ
Dagest U , Saratov, 1962, t. 8, Fil. S., pp. 99 -
114.

'302 SIMONINI, R. C. jr. : *Word-Making in Present-Day English*, English Journal
55, 6, 1966, pp. 752 - 757.

303 SIMONS, R.   : *Worte und Wortverbindungen der echten Schriften*
Cynewulfs, Diss. Bonn 6.8.1898, Bonn : Universitäts-
buchdruckerei von Carl Georgi, 1898, 32 p..
(Complete ed. under the title *Cynewulfs Wortschatz*,
Bonner Beiträge zur Anglistik, Vol. 3)
(Germany 14, p. 29; 60)

'304 SKOROCHOD'KO, E. F. : *Strukturno-semantičeskij analiz anglijskich naučno-*
techničeskich terminov (Structural and semantic ana-
lysis of English scientific-technical terms), DLit,
1961, c. 2, pp. 124 - 131.

'305   - : *Struktura i semantika anglijskich naučno-techničes-*
kich terminov (Structure and semantics of English
scientific-technical terms), Prikladnaja lingvistika
i mašinnyj perevod, Kiev 1962, pp. 30 - 65.

'306   - : *Voprosy teorii anglijskogo slovoobrazovanija i ee*
primenenie k mašinnomu perevodu (Theoretical que-
stions of English word-formation and their treatment in machine-translation), Kiev, 1964.

'307 SMEATON, W.   : *An Etymological Manual of the English Language;*
Comprising the Prefixes, Affixes and Principal La-
tin, Greek and Saxon Roots of the English Language,
New Haven : J. P. Hart, 1843, iv, (5), 96 p..

'308 SMIRNICKIJ, A. I.   : *Morfologia anglijskogo jazyka*, red. V.V. Passek
(English Morphology, ed. by V. V. Passek), Moscow
(ILIY), 1954, 440 p. (Library of a Philologist).

'309   : *Leksikologija anglijskogo jazyka*, Moskva, 1956.

310 SMITH, L. P.   : *Needed Words* , Oxford : Clarendon Press, 1928,
S.P.E. Tract No 31, pp. 311 - 329.
(Only very occasionally)

'311 SOBOLEVA, P. A.   : *Komponentnyj analiz značenij glagola na osnove slovoobrazovatel'nogo priznaka* (Componental analysis
of verbal meanings on the basis of word-building
properties), in Problemy strukturnoj lingvistiki.
Sbornik statej, Moscow, 1962, pp. 175 - 189.
(Engl. summary)

'312 SOBOTKA, R.   : *Die englische Sprache in den Schlagzeilen der anglo-amerikanischen periodischen Presse*, Diss. Vien-
na, 1951, xii, 168 lvs..
(Vienna 1950 - 1957, p. 72; 1449)

313 SOHRAUER, M.   : *Kleine Beiträge zur altenglischen Grammatik*, Diss.
Berlin, 1886, Berlin : G. Bernstein, 1886, 53 p.,
vita, (1).

'314 SOKOLOVA, M. A.   : *Obrazovanie special'noj terminologii na osnove by-
tovoj leksiki* (The formation of technical termi-
nology on the basis of the common vocabulary),
Trudy Voron U 1958, t. 51, Sb. rabot istoriko -
filologičeskogo fakul'teta, vyp. 2, pp. 131 - 136.

'315   - : *O smyslorazličitel'noj funkcii vtorogo sil'nogo
i vtorostepennogo udarenij v anglijskom jazyke*
(On the distinctive function of the second main
stress and secondary stress in English), UZ MObl
Ped I, 1959, t. 73, Trudy KIJa, vyp. 5, pp. 207 -
211.

'316 SOLOV'EVA, T. A.   : *K voprosu o slovoobrazovanii v sovremennom anglijskom jazyke putem leksikalizacii formy množestven-
nogo čisla suščestvitel'nych* (On word-formation
by lexicalization of the substantive plural form
in English), UZ Ivan Ped I, 1962, t. 30, vyp. 2,
pp. 68 - 82.

317 SONNEFELD, G. : *Stilistisches und Wortschatz im Beowulf, ein Bei-*
trag zur Kritik des Epos, Diss. Strassburg, 1892,
Würzburg : Etlingers Buchdruckerei, 1892, 98 p.,
vita, (1), (1 : contents), (1 : errata).
(Germany 9, p. 236; 80)

318 SPIES, H. : *Kultur und Sprache im Neuen England*, Leipzig - Berlin : B. G. Teubner, 1925, xiv, (2), 216 p..
(esp. pp. 125 - 130)

'319 SPITZBARDT, H. : *Die Ausdrucksverstärkung im heutigen Englisch*,
Habilitationsschrift Jena 7.11.1960, Jena, 1960,
ii, 325 lvs.n..
(Germany 77, p. 449)

320 - : *Lebendiges Englisch. Stilistisch-syntaktische Mit-*
tel der Ausdrucksverstärkung, Halle : VEB Max Niemeyer Verlag, 1962, 287 p..
(esp. pp. 100 - 103, 110, 121)

321 STAHL, H. E. : *Schöpferische Wortbildung bei Shakespeare?* Shakespeare-Jahrbuch 90, 1954, pp. 252 - 278.

322 STEIN, G. : *Einführung in die englische Wortbildungslehre*, Stu-
dieneinheit für das Deutsche Institut für Fernstu-
dien (DIFF), Tübingen, 1971, 66 p..

323 STONE, R. M. : *Studien über den deutschen Einfluss auf das ame-*
rikanische Englisch, Diss. Marburg , 1934 (1933),
Bochum-Langendreer : H. Pöppinghaus, 1934, vii,
(1), 90 p., bibliographical note.
(esp. pp. 15 - 16, 21 - 22, 27 - 28, 33, 39 - 40,
90)

324 STRANG, B. M. H. : *Modern English Structure*, London : Edward Arnold
Publishers, 2nd ed., 1968, xiii, (1), 264 p..
(first ed. , 1962)

325   - : *A History of English*, London : Methuen & Co., 1970, xxiv, 453 p..

'326 STRAUMANN, H.   : *Newspaper Headlines; a Study in Linguistic Method*, Habilitationsschrift Phil. I, Univ. Zürich, London : George Allen & Unwin Ltd., 1935, 263 p..

327 STROHEKER, F.   : *Doppelformen und Rhythmus bei Marlowe und Kyd*, Diss. Heidelberg 12.4.1913, Heidelberg : Carl Winter; Tübingen : H. Laupp, 1913, xi, (1), 105 p., (1), vita.
(esp. pp. 24 - 38)
(Germany 29, p. 624)

328 STUBELIUS, S.   : *Airship, Aeroplane, Aircraft. Studies in the History of Terms for Aircraft in English*, Göteborg (= Gothenburg Studies in English 7), Stockholm : Almqvist & Wiksell, Lund : Carl Bloms Boktryckeri A.-B., 1958, x, 342 p..

329   - : *Balloon, Flying - Machine, Helicopter. Further Studies in the History of Terms for Aircraft in English*, Götegorg, Acta Universitatis Gothoburgensis. Göteborgs Universitets Årsskrift, Vol. 66, 1960,5 (also published as : Gothenburg Studies in English 9) xi, (3), 396 p..

'330 STUMMER, P.   : *Sprachliche und stoffliche Ausdrucksformen in den Romanen von Thomas Hardy*, Diss. München 9.10.1969, München, 1969, 190 p..
(DNB C 1971, 6; p. 24; 283)

331 SUTHERLAND, R. D.   : *Language and Lewis Carroll*, The Hague - Paris : Mouton, 1970, 245 p.(Ph.D. Iowa State Univ.,1964)
(DAb 25, 4, 1964, 2522 - 2523)

332 SWEET, H.   : *A Short Historical English Grammar* , Oxford : Clarendon Press, 1892, xii, 264 p..
(esp. pp. 208 - 260)

333   - : *A New English Grammar. Logical and Historical.*
                 Part I : *Introduction, Phonology, and Accidence,*
                 Oxford : Clarendon Press, 1900, xxiv, 499 p..
                 (esp. pp. 24 - 27, 444 - 499)

334 TAUBE, E. M.   : *German Influence on the English Vocabulary in the*
                 19th Century, JEGP 39, 1940, pp. 486 - 493.

'335 TAYLOR, A. M.   : *The Language of World War II. Abbreviations, Cap-*
                 tions, Quotations, Slogans, Titles, and Other Terms
                 and Phrases, rev. and enlarged ed., New York : H.
                 W. Wilson Co., 1948, 265 p..

336 TEICHERT, F.   : *Über das Aussterben alter Wörter im Verlaufe der*
                 englischen Sprachgeschichte, Diss. Kiel, Erlangen:
                 K. B. Hof- und Universitäts-Buchdruckerei von Jun-
                 ge & Sohn, 1912, (3), 77 p., vita.

337 THEOBALD, R. M.   : *Word-Coinage in Shakespeare and Others*, Baconiana
                 4, 3rd Series, London : Gay & Bird, 1906, pp. 239
                 - 244.
                 (Criticisms of the 10th chapter "On Word-Makers"
                 in Harold Bayley's *Shakespeare Symphony* (cf. No.
                 19))
                 (cf. Bayley, H. : *To the Editor*, Baconiana 4, 3rd
                 Series, 1906, pp. 244 - 246)

'338 TRNKA, B.   : *Rozbor nynější spisovné angličtiny. II. Morfologie*
                 slovnich druhu a tooyení slov (Analysis of pre-
                 sent-day literary English. II. Morphology of the
                 word classes and word-formation), Praha Státuí pe-
                 dag. naklad., 1954, 169 p..
                 (2nd ed., 1962 : 190 p.)

339 TUCKER, G. M.   : *Grammatical Suggestions from a Workshop*, New En-
                 glander 8, (n.s.), (= Vol. 44 of the complete se-
                 ries), 1885, pp. 391 - 402.
                 (Comments on different linguistic phenomena, also
                 on word-formation)

340 VALLINS, G. H.   : *The Making and Meaning of Words. A Companion to the Dictionary*, London : Adam and Charles Black, 1949, vii, 216 p.. (esp. pp. 91 - 109)

'341 VASIL'EV, V. A.   : *Rol' fonetičeskogo stroja v slovoobrazovanii i slovoizmenenii sovremennogo anglijskogo jazyka* (The role of phenetic structure in contemporary English word-formation and word-change), Proc Razv, pp. 79 - 114.

'342 VESNIK, D. - ČIDEKEL, S. : *Exercises in Modern English Word-Building*, Moscow, 1964.

'343 VILJUMAN, V. G.   : *O sposobach obrazovanija slov slenga v sovremennom anglijskom jazyke* (On the methods of forming slang words in modern English), UZ LPed I, 1955, t. 3, pp. 137 - 139.

*344 VÖGELE, H.   : *Aufbau und Sprache in Charlotte Brontës " Jane Eyre" und Emily Brontës " Wuthering Heights"*. *Ein Vergleich*, Diss. Freiburg 9.7.1954, Freiburg , 1954, ii, 227 lvs.n.. (Germany 70, p. 227)

345 VOLKLAND, L.   : *Wörterbuch zu den englischen Dichtungen von Percy Bysshe Shelley*, Part I : A - M, Diss. Leipzig 5.3.1910, Borna - Leipzig : Noske, 1910, x, 81 p.. (Germany 25, p. 540)

346 VORONCOVA, G. N.   : *Očerki po grammatike anglijskogo jazyka* (Essays on English grammar), Moscow (ILIY), 1960, 399 p.. (Library of a Philologist)

347 W., J.   : *Etymological Guide to the English Language; Being a Collection, Alphabetically Arranged, of the Principal Roots, Affixes, and Prefixes, with Their Derivatives and Compounds*, 3rd ed., greatly enlarged, Edinburgh : Oliver & Boyd; London : Simpkin & Marshall 1837, 234 p..

'348 WÄCHTLER, K.　　　: *Studien zum informellen Wortschatz, zur Headline-Syntax und zum betont informellen Stil in amerika-nischen Tageszeitungen und Wochenschriften*, Diss. Marburg 6.3.1951, Stuttgart, 1951, vi, 142 lvs.n..
(Germany 68, p. 566)

349　　　　　　　　　- : *Studien zur amerikanischen headline Syntax*, NS, N.F., 2, 1953, pp. 201 - 210.

350 WALLAS, G.　　　　: *Notes on Jeremy Bentham's Attitude to Word-Creation and Other Notes on Needed Words*, S.P.E. 31, Oxford: Clarendon Press, 1928, pp. 333 - 334.

'351 WANETSCHEK, G.　　: *Studien zum Wortschatz von Samuel Taylor Coleridge*, Diss. Vienna, 1956, 105 lvs..
(Vienna 1950 - 1957, p. 73; 1465)

'352 WEBB, A. C.　　　　: *The Model Etymology with Sentences Showing the Cor-rect Use of Words; and a Key Giving the Analysis of English Words*, Philadelphia : Eldredge & Bro., 1867, 169 p..
(= The Model Work Book, No. 2)
(Rev. ed., 1879, 255 p.)

'353　　　　　　　　　- : *A Manual of Etymology; Containing Latin and Greek Derivatives, with a Key, Giving the Prefix, Root and Suffix*, Philadelphia : Eldredge & Bro., 1879, 317 p..
(= The Model Work Book, No. 3)

354 WEBER, G.　　　　: *Der Bau der englischen Sprache*, Palaestra 192, Leipzig : Mayer & Müller, 1934, iv, 135 p..

355 WEEKLEY, E.　　　　: *The English Language, with a Chapter on the History of American English* by Professor John W. Clark, London : A. Deutsch, 1952, 138 p..
(esp. pp. 87 - 96)

'356　　　　　　　　　- : *Words Ancient and Modern*, Forest Hills, N. Y. :

Transatlantic Press, 214 p..

'357 WIENCKE, H.   : *Die Sprache Caxtons*, Diss. Köln 10.2.1930, Leipzig: Tauchnitz, 1930, 226 p..
(= Kölner Anglistische Arbeiten 11)
(Germany 46, p. 385)

'358 WIGZELL, R. J.   : *Nominalization and Compounding in Modern English*, Ph.D. Manchester.
(England 19, p. 14; 338)

'359 WINTER, E. O. O.   : *The Language of Contemporary Newspaper Advertisements in English*, MA London, U.C..
(England 14, p. 9; 173)

360 WÖLCKEN, F.   : *Entwicklungsstufen der Wortbildung aus Initialen*, Anglia 75, 1957, pp. 317 - 333.

361 WOLFF, D.   : *Statistische Untersuchungen zum Wortschatz englischer Zeitungen*, Diss. Saarbrücken 17.1.1969, Saarbrücken, 1969, 285 p., (1).
(DNB C 1969, 10; p. 26; 296)

'362 WOLFF, E.   : *Entwicklungen und Tendenzen im englisch-amerikanischen Wortschatz des 20. Jahrhunderts*, Fremdsprachenunterricht 3, 1959, pp. 590 - 602.
(cf. ibid. 4, 1960, pp. 603 - 607, 728 - 731)

*363 WOOD, R. S.   : *Word-Building, Derivation and Composition*, (Books 1 - 7), London : MacMillan, 1885 - 1899.

*364   - : *Word-Building. Transcription & Composition. Simple Exercises*, 6 parts, London : MacMillan & Co., 1895-1898.

365 WRENN, C. L.   : *The English Language*, London : Methuen & Co., 1949, vi, 236 p..
(= Home Study Books)
(esp. pp. 118 - 120)

'366 WURTH, L. : *Das Wortspiel bei Shakespeare*, Diss. Vienna, Leipzig, 1895 .
(= Wiener Beiträge , Vol. 1)
(Vienna 2, p. 166; 1921)

367 WYATT, A. J. : *An Elementary Old English Grammar (Early West Saxon)* , Cambridge : University Press, 1921, ix, 173 p..
(esp. pp. 153 - 160)
(first ed., 1897)

368 YAMAGUCHI, H. : *A Lexical Note on the Language of Sir Gawain and the Grene Knight*, PhP 8, 1965, pp. 372 - 380.
(On the interaction between native English words and lexical elements derived from French and Scandinavian)

'369 YORDAN, E. L. and others : *Make Your Words : A Manual for Vocabulary Building* , New York : Contemporary Press, 127 p..

370 ZANDVOORT, R.W. : *A Handbook of English Grammar* , 2nd ed., London : Longmans, 1962, xii, 349 p..
(esp. pp. 265 - 325)
(first ed., 1957)

371   and ass. : *War-Time English. Materials for a Linguistic History of World War II*, Groningen Studies in English 6, Groningen - Djakarta : J. B. Wolters, 1957, ix, 254 p..

'372 ZEISE, A. : *Der Wortschatz der Ancrene Riwle*, Diss. Jena 19.1. 1923, Jena, 1923, 117 lvs..
(Germany 31, p. 563)

373 ZIESENIS, O. : *Der Einfluss des Rhythmus auf Silbenmessung, Wortbildung, Formenlehre und Syntax bei Lyly, Greene und Peele*, Diss. Kiel 15.10.1915, Heidelberg : Carl Winters Universitätsbuchhandlung, 1915, 118 p. vita.

374 ZUR MEGEDE, G.　　: *Wort- und Gestaltungskunst bei I. B. Priestley,*
Diss. Marburg 21.11.1938, Gelnhausen : Disserta-
tionsdruckerei F. W. Kalbfleisch, 1938, 76 p., vita.
(esp. pp. 18 - 20, 27 - 35)
(Germany 54, p. 496)

A) FORMATION OF NOMINALS

375 RAAB, E.   : *Mittelenglische Nominalbildung*, Diss. Erlangen 9.1.
                                1937, Coburg : Rossteutscher, 1936, viii, 57 p..
                                (Germany 53, p. 193)

358 WIGZELL, R. J.   : *Nominalization and Compounding in Modern English.*

B) FORMATION OF SUBSTANTIVES

376 BRUGGENCATE, K. ten : *On the Use and Formation of Substantives*, Taalstu-
                                die 7, 1886, pp. 348 - 352.

'377 HEMKEN, E. W.   : *Das Aussterben alter Substantiva im Verlaufe der
                                englischen Sprachgeschichte*, Diss. Kiel, 1906.

'377 a HUCKO, M.   : *Bildung der Substantiva durch Ableitung und Zusam-
                                mensetzung im Angelsächsischen*, Diss. Strassburg,
                                1904.

378 SCHLEPPER, E.   : *Die Neubildung von Substantiven in den Übersetzun-
                                gen König Alfreds mit einem Ausblick auf Chaucer*,
                                Diss. Münster 15.4.1936, Gütersloh i. Westf. : Buch
                                druckerei Thiele, vi, 136 p., vita.

379 WAGNER, K. H.   : *Zur Nominalisierung im Englischen*, in Schriften zur
                                Linguistik 3, Beiträge zur generativen Grammatik,
                                Referate des 5. Linguistischen Kolloquiums, Regens-
                                burg, 1970, ed. by A. v. Stechow, Braunschweig :
                                Vieweg, 1971, (vi), 295 p.; pp. 264 - 272.

'380   - : *A Proposal on Nominalizations I*, in PAKS-Arbeits-
                                bericht No. 3/4, October 1969, pp. 27 - 58.

C) FORMATION OF ADJECTIVES

'381 AICHINGER, G. : *Das Adjektiv in Chaucers Knightes Tale*, Diss. Innsbruck, 1911.
(Vienna 4, p. 207)

382 BARTH, H. : *Das Epitheton in den Dramen des jungen Shakespeare und seiner Vorgänger*, Halle: M. Niemeyer, 1914, xi, 203 p. (= Studien zur engl. Philologie, Vol. 52).

'383 BECKERS, G. : *Die kausative Kraft des Adjektivums in Shakespeares Sprachgebrauch*, Diss. Marburg 16.12.1947, 94 lvs.n.. (Germany 61-64, p. 640)

'384 DIEZ, H. : *Das Adjektiv in Shakespeares Macbeth*, Diss. Innsbruck, 1910.
(Vienna 4, p. 207)

385 HELMS, G. : *The English Adjective in the Language of Shakespere*, Diss. Bremen, Bremen : F. C. Dubbers, 1868, 56 p..
Reviews :
Asher, D. : ASNS 45, 1869, 214 - 216

'386 KUFFNER, E. : *Die Verwendung des Adjektivs bei Swinburne*, Diss. Vienna, 1931.
(Vienna 2, p. 183; 2154)

387 MAYR, K. : *Das Adjektiv in Cynewulfs Elene*, Diss. Innsbruck, 1913.
(Vienna 4, p. 208)

388 NEUNER, K. : *Untersuchungen zur Stilistik des Adjektivs in Tennysons epischen Dichtungen*, Diss. Innsbruck, 1911.
(Vienna 4, p. 207)

389 NOTTROTT, M. : *Der formale Gebrauch des Epithetons in Shakespeares Dramen 'Othello', 'King Lear', 'Macbeth' und 'Coriolanus'*, Diss. Leipzig, 1922 (unpublished manuscript).

244 OBERDÖRFFER, W. : *Das Aussterben altenglischer Adjektive und ihr Er-*
satz im Verlaufe der englischen Sprachgeschichte.

'390 QUENTIN, E. : *Die Form des Epithetons in den Gedichten Coleridges*
nach ihrem sprachlichen Ursprung und ihrem psycho-
logisch-ästhetischen Wert betrachtet, Diss. Leipzig
27.11.1920 (1922), 139 lvs..
(cf. Jahrbuch der Phil. Fakultät Leipzig, 1921, 1.S.
pp. 58 - 60)
(Germany 38, p. 679)

391 SCHEINERT, M. : *Die Adjectiva im Beowulf als Darstellungsmittel,*
Diss. Leipzig, Halle, 1905.
(= *Die Adjectiva im Beowulfepos als Darstellungs-*
mittel, PBB 30, 1905, pp. 345 - 430)

'392 SCHMITZ, Ch. : *Die schmückenden Beiwörter in den poetischen Werken*
von Algernon Charles Swinburne, Diss. Innsbruck,
1955, 584 p..

393 SCHÖN, E. : *Die Bildung des Adjektivs im Altenglischen,* Diss.
Kiel 4.8.1905, Kiel : Lüdtke & Martens, 1905, 29 p.,
(2), vita.
(= Kieler Studien zur englischen Philologie, N. F.
2)
(Germany 20, p. 301; 81)
Reviews :
Barnouw , A. J. : ASNS 119, 1907, 448 - 449
Jordan, R. : Anglia B 18, 1907, 36 - 37
Kock, E. A. : ESt 44, 1911/12, 387 - 388
Pogatscher, A. : DLZ 27, 1906, col. 1060

394 STEIN, G. : *Primäre und sekundäre Adjektive im Französischen*
und Englischen, Diss. Tübingen 26.5.1971, Tübinger
Beiträge zur Linguistik 22, 1971, viii, 284 p..
(DNB C 1972, 10; p. 14; 156)
Reviews :
Rettig, W. : ZFSL 82, 1972, 74 - 78

395   - : *Primäre und sekundäre Adjektive im Französischen und Englischen (Primary and Secondary Adjectives in French and in English)*, in English and American Studies in German, Summaries of Theses and Monographs. A Supplement to Anglia 1971, (1972), pp. 16 - 19.

396 VOGT, R.   : *Das Adjektiv bei Christopher Marlowe*, Diss. Berlin, Berlin : Mayer & Müller, 1908, viii, 68 p..

'397 WIETELMANN, I.   : *Die Epitheta in den ' Caedmonschen Dichtungen'*, Diss. Göttingen, 1952.

'398 WOLFF, H.   : *Die Epitheta in den " Cynewulfischen" Dichtungen*, Diss. Göttingen 9.2.1955, Göttingen, 1954, 216, iv lvs.n. (Masch. verv.). (Germany 71, p. 259)

D) FORMATION OF VERBS

399 BRUGGENCATE, K. ten : *Stray Notes on the Use and Formation of Verbs*, Taalstudie 7, 1886, pp. 279 - 285.

4(0 BURGSCHMIDT, E.   : *Studien zum Verbum in englischen Fachsprachen (Cricket)*, Diss. Erlangen, 1971, Nürnberg, 1971, 516 p..

401   - : *Studien zum Verbum in englischen Fachsprachen (Cricket) (Studies on the Verb in English Specialist Languages (Cricket)*, in English and American Studies in German, Summaries of Theses and Monographs. A Supplement to Anglia 1971, (1972), pp. 21 - 23.

402 MENCKEN, H. L.   : *New Verbs*, Words 1, 1934, p. 5.

403   - : *Verbs New and Old*, AS 21, 1946, pp. 303 - 305.

404   - : *The Birth of New Verbs*, in Philologica : The Malone
Anniversary Studies, ed. by Th. A. Kirby and H. B.
Woolf, Baltimore : The Johns Hopkins Press, 1949,
x, 382 p.; pp. 313 - 319.

'246 OFFE, J.   : *Das Aussterben alter Verba und ihr Ersatz im Verlaufe der englischen Sprachgeschichte.*

E) COMPOUNDS AND DERIVATIVES WITH SPECIFIC WORDS

405 ANON.   : *'Ace' and Its Progeny*, AS 18, 1943, pp. 71 - 72.
(ace-high, - hook, - note, acer, aceroo, ace-slug)

406 DICK, E. S.   : *Ae. Dryht und seine Sippe. Eine wortkundliche, kul-
tur- und religionsgeschichtliche Betrachtung zur
altgermanischen Glaubensvorstellung vom wachstüm-
lichen Heil*, Diss. Münster 24.7.1961, Münster, 1961,
xv, 579 p..
(= Neue Beiträge zur englischen Philologie 3)
(Germany 81, p. 1016)

407 LUGINBILL, B.   : *Variations on a German Theme*, AS 15, 1940, pp. 445
- 446.
(to hitlerize, - ian, - land, -ist, -ism)
(Naziland, - dom, - fy, - ification, - ate, - atio
- tic, - est, - ism)

'408 SACHOVA, N. I.   : *Smyslovoe razvitie imeni suscestvitel'nogo <u>work</u>
i glagola to <u>work</u> i obrazovannych ot ich osnov
proizvodnych i sloznych slov v anglijskom jazyke*
(The semantic development of the substantive *work*
and the verb *to work* and their derivatives and compounds from their stems), Diss. Moscow, 1965.

II. GENERAL STUDIES ON COMPOUNDING IN ENGLISH

'409 ACHMANOVA, O. S. : *K voprosu o slovosočetaniji v sovremennom anglijs-*
kom jazyke (On the question of word-combination
in English) , Izv AN 9, 1950, pp. 476 - 491.

'410   - : *K voprosu ob otličij složnych slov ot frazeologi-*
českich edinic. (*Na materiale anglijskogo i šveds-*
kogo jazykov) (On the difference between compounds
and phraseological units (On the material of English and Swedish), J - Institut jazykoznanija
(Akademija Nauk SSSR., Moskva), Trudy ... Tom 4,
1954, pp. 50 - 73.
(On the types cannon ball and to give up)

'411 AVRAMENKO, O. P. : *Sostavnye slova gibridnogo narečnomodal'nogo zna-*
čenija. (*Na materiale sovremennogo anglijskogo ja-*
zyke) (Compound words with hybrid adverbial and
modal meaning (Using material of the English language), Kiev IFK 1961, pp. 9 - 12.

'412 AZARCH, N. A. - NOVAKOVIČ, A. S. : *Nekotorye voprosy analiza složnych*
slov (Some problems of the analysis of compounds;
English examples), UZIMO 11, 1963, pp. 3 - 14.

'413 AZARCH, N. A. : *K voprosu ob otgraničenii složnych slov v slovo-*
sočetanij v sovremennom anglijskom jazyke (On
the segregation of compounds from word-combinations
in contemporary English) , Voen I 6, 1954, pp. 3
- 12.
(Structure, semantics, and orthography of compounds)

414 BALL, A. M. : *Uncle Sam and the Compounding of Words*, AS 13,
1938, pp. 169 - 174.

415   - : *Compounding in the English Language. A Comparative*
Review of Variant Authorities With a Rational System
for General Use and a Comprehensive Alphabetic List

of Compound Words, New York : The H. W. Wilson Co., 1939, x, 226 p. (reprint 1941).

416   - : *The Compounding and Hyphenation of English Words*, New York : Funk & Wagnalls Company, 1951, 246 p.. (A ready reference guide)

417 BARRETT, C. E.   : *A Graphemic Analysis of English Nominal Complexes*, Ph.D. The University of Texas, 1963, 241 p.. (DAb 24, 12, 1964, 5396) cf. Linguistics 11, 1965, pp. 92 - 93.

'418 BARRS, J. T.   : *Saying it Twice* , Word Study 29,3, 1954, p. 6. (Tautological compounds)

419 BARTLETT, A. C.   : *Full - Word Compounds in Modern English*, AS 15, 1940 pp. 243 - 249.

'420 BAUMANN, H.   : *Über Neubildungen von Wortzusammensetzungen in Tennysons epischen und lyrischen Gedichten*, Diss. Vienna, 1913. (Vienna 2, p. 175; 2037)

'421 BRANTNER, G.   : *Prosaakzent und metrisches Schema in englischen Kompositen*, Diss. Graz (unpublished manuscript), 47 p..

'422 BREITINGER, F.   : *Die Wortzusammensetzung in S. T. Coleridge's poetischen Werken*, Diss. Graz, 1913, 216 lvs.. (Graz 1, 2729)

423 BRINKMAN, E. A.   : *Attitudes and Practices in the Writing of Compound Words in Contemporary American English*, Ph. D. University of Wisconsin, 1967, 182 p.. (DAb 28, 2, 1967, 618 - A)

'424 BROWNE, M. W.   : *Confounded Compound*, New York : Braun, 1949.

425 BRYAN, W. F.   : *Epithetic Compound Folk Names in Beowulf*, in Studies in English Philology. A Miscellany in Honor of Frederick Klaeber, ed. by K. Malone and M. B.

Ruud, Minneapolis, 1929, pp. 120 - 134.

'426 BRYANT, M. M.   : *A Selected List of Compounds from Present-Day Reading*, PADS 48, November 1967 (1969), pp. 1 - 32.

'427 BYERLY, G.   : *Compounds and Other Elements of Poetic Diction Derived from an Oral Formulaic Poetic Diction, a Comparison of Aeschylus and the Beowulf Poet*, Diss. Pennsylvania University, 1966.

'428 CARR, E. B.   : *Trends in Word Compounding in American Speech*, Speech Monographs 21, 1954, p. 143. (= Abstract of the Ph.D. thesis, St. Louis University 1953)

'429   - : *Word-Compounding in American Speech*, Speech Monographs 26, 1959, pp. 1 - 20.

430 CASTELO, L. M.   : *An Inquiry into Compounds and Syntactic Phrases*, ZAA 11, 1963, pp. 265 - 268.

'431 ČEKMAZOVA, N. A.   : *Fonetičeskaja redukcija v anglijskom jazyke. (Na materiale oproščenija složnych slov i obrazovanija slabych form služebnych slov)* (Phonetic reduction in the English language. (Concerning weakened forms of compounds and the formation of weak-stressed forms of function words)), MGor Ped I , 1958, t.80, FiJa KLPA Ja, vyp. 3, pp. 185 - 239.

'432   - : *Fonetičeskaja redukcija v anglijskom jazyke. (Na materiale oproščenija složnych slov i obrazovanija slabych form služebnych i vspomogatel'nych slov)* (Phonetic reduction in the English language.(Concerning weakened forms of compounds and the formation of weak-stressed forms of function and auxiliary words), Diss. Moscow, 1959.

'433 ČIDEKEL, S. S.   : *O složnoprojizvodnych slovach v sovremennom anglijskom jazyke* (Compound derivatives in present-day English), Trudy vojennogo instituta inostrannych jazykov 2, 1953, pp. 46 - 64.

Reviews :

Passek, V. V. : VJa 1955, No. 1, 133

434 COOPER, L. : *Pleonastic Compounds in Coleridge*, MLN 19, 1904, pp. 223 - 224.

'435 DUBOVAJA, S. I. : *O nekotorych stilističeskich osobennostjach složnych slov v proizvedenijach Dž. Golssuorsi " Saga o Forsajtach" i " Sovremennaja komedija"* (On some stylistic features of compounds in John Galsworthy': " The Forsyte Saga" and " A Modern Comedy"), TKonf, pp. 30 - 31.

436 FENZL, R. : *To Hyphen or Not to Hyphen*, Idioma 3, 1966, pp. 266 - 267.

'437 GLIKINA, E. A. : *Akcentnoe stroenie složnogo slova v sovremennom anglijskom jazyke* (The accentual structure of the compound in modern English), UZ 1 - MPed I, 1960, t. 18, pp. 246 - 278.

'438 HAMILTON, F. W. : *Compound Words : A Study of the Principles of Compounding, the Components of Compounds, and the Use of the Hyphen*, Committee on Education, United Typothetae of America, 1918 (5).

439 HANSEN, K. : *Zur Analyse englischer Komposita*, in Wortbildung, Syntax und Morphologie, Festschrift zum 60. Geburts tag von Hans Marchand am 1. Oktober 1967, ed. by Herbert E. Brekle and Leonhard Lipka, The Hague - Paris : Mouton, 1968, 250 p.; pp. 115 - 126.

440 HATCHER, A. G. : *Modern Appositional Compounds of Inanimate Reference*, AS 27, 1952, pp. 3 - 15.

'441 HEIDER, E. : *Das analytische Kompositum im Neuenglischen*, Diss. Vienna, 1942, 139 lvs.. (Vienna 1937 - 1944, 2197)

442 HEMPL, G.   : *The Stress of German and English Compounds in Geo-graphical Names*, MLN 11, 1896, pp. 232 - 239.

443 HILL, L. A.   : *' Compounds' and the Practical Teacher*, ELT 12, 1957-1958, pp. 13 - 21.

444 HOOPS, J.   : *Altenglisch EALUSCERWEN, MEODUSCERWEN. Otto Jesper-sen zum 70. Geburtstag*, ESt 65, 1930/31, pp. 177 - 180.

445 HULBERT, J. R.   : *A Note on Compounds in Beowulf*, JEGP 31, 1932, pp. 504 - 508.

'446 KENNEDY, A. G. : *Hyphenation of Compound Nouns*, Words 4, 1938, pp. 36 - 38.

'447 KIVIMJAGI, L.   : *K voprosu izučenija slovosočetanij v sovremennom anglijskom jazyke* (On the study of word-combina-tions in present-day English), Tartu U , vyp. 77, 1959, pp. 137 - 164.
                     (in Estonian; Russian summary on pp. 165 - 166; English summary on pp. 167 - 168)

448 KOZIOL, H.   : *Shakespeares Komposita in deutschen Übersetzungen*, NS, N.F., 6, 1957, pp. 457 - 463.

*449 KRAAN, F.   : *Analytical Compounds*, De Drie Talen 65, 1949, pp. 74 - 76.

*450 KRAMSKÝ, J.   : *Složeniny v angličtine* (Compound Words in English), Zprávy Státního ústavu jazykového September - October 1954, pp. 8 - 16.

*451 KUKOLSCIKOVA, L. E.: *Fonetičeskaja karakteristika složnych slov i atri-butivnych slovosočetanija v sovremennom anglijs-kom jazyke* (The phonetic character of compound words and predicative word groups in modern English), Izvest. Akad. Nauk SSSR, Ser. Lit. Jazyka 1968, 27 (1), pp. 38 - 46.

452 LEES, R. B.   : *On a Transformational Analysis of Compounds : A Reply to Hans Marchand*, IF 71, 1966/67, pp. 1 - 13.

'453 LEONT'EVA, S. F.   : *Nekotorye osobennosti struktury slovosočetaniji charakternye dlja anglijskoj naučnoj leksiki. (Sintaksis i slovosloženie)* (Some structural pecularities of the word combinations that are characteristic of the learned vocabulary of English. (Syntax and Compounding)), MObl Ped I 1963, t. 136, IJa, vyp.13, pp. 73 - 80.

'454 LEVINSKIJ, N. N.   : *Dvučlennye terminy-slovosočetanija s prepozitivnym opredeleniem. (Na materiale amerikanskoj voenno-ustavnoj terminologii)* (Technical word combinations consisting of two components with a prepositive attribute. (On the material of American military service vocabulary)), Diss. Moscow, 1955, (Voen I).

455 LINCKE, O.   : *Über die Wortzusammensetzung in Carlyles " Sartor Resartus "*, Diss. Jena 28.9.1904, Berlin : Mayer & Müller, 1904, vi, 52 p., vita.
(Germany 20, p. 281; 71)

456 LUMIANSKY, R. M.   : *The Contexts of O. E. 'ealuscerwen' and 'meoduscerwen'*, JEGP 48, 1949, pp. 116 - 126.

'457 LUTSTORF, H. Th.   : *The Stressing of Compounds in Modern English. A Study in Experimental Phonetics*, Diss. phil. I, Zürich, 1960, 159 p..
Reviews :
Arnold, R.   : ZAA 12, 1964, 59 - 64
Koziol, H.   : Anglia 79, 1961, 69 - 72
Lehiste, I.   : Phonetica 6, 1961, 246 - 248
Schubiger, M. : ES 44, 1963, 60 - 62

'458 MAKEY, H. O.   : *Compound Words*, The English Journal 40, 1951, pp. 567 - 569.

'459   - : *The Rhythm in Compounds?* Word Study, May 1959,
                                  pp. 6 - 7.

460 MARCHAND, H.   : *Die Länge englischer Komposita und die entspre-
                                  chenden Verhältnisse im Deutschen*, Anglia 78, 1960,
                                  pp. 411 - 416.

461   - : *Der Wortbildungstyp anti-aircraft (battery) und
                                  Verwandtes*, in Festschrift zum 75. Geburtstag von
                                  Theodor Spira, ed. by H. Viebrock and W. Erzgrä-
                                  ber, Heidelberg : Carl Winter-Universitätsverlag,
                                  1961, 405 p.; pp. 335 - 342.

462   - : *On the Description of Compounds*, Word 23, 1967,
                                  pp. 378 - 387.

463 MENNER, R. J.   : *Compounding*, AS 14, 1939, pp. 300 - 302.
                                  (refers to A. M. Ball)

'464 MUCHIN, A. M.   : *Slovosloženie i slovosočetanie (Na materiale
                                  drevanglijskogo jazyka)* (Word-composition and
                                  word group in Old English), Probl. sravnit. filol.
                                  pp. 35 - 44, tab..

465 NYQUIST, A.   : *Stress, Intonation, Accent, Prominence in Disyl-
                                  labic Double-Stress Compounds in Educated Southern
                                  English*, Proceedings of th 4th International Con-
                                  gress of Phonetic Sciences 4, 1961, pp. 710 - 713.
                                  (= Janua Linguarum, ser. maior, 10)

466 OVERHOLSER, L. Ch.   : *A Comparative Study of the Compound Use in Andreas
                                  and Beowulf*, Ph.D. Diss. The University of Michi-
                                  gan, 1971, Authorized Facsimile Xerography, (5),
                                  ix, 253 p..

467 PADELFORD, F. M. - MAXWELL, W. C. : *The Compound Words in Spenser's Poe-
                                  try*, JEGP 25, 1926, pp. 498 - 516.

468 RUFENER, J.   : *Studies in the Motivation of English and German
                                  Compounds*, Ph.D. Thesis, Zurich I, 1969, Zurich:
                                  Juris Druck + Verlag, 1971, 222 p..

469 SALOMON, L. B.   : *The Game of Words*, Harper's 223, November 1961, pp.
40 - 43.
(On the semantic problems created by compound words)

470 SALUS, P. H.   : *Syntactic Compounds in Modern English*, ES 45, 1964,
pp. 462 - 464.
(Jack-in-the-pulpit ...)

471 SCHMITZ, A.   : *Bindestrich-Kombinationen im britischen Englisch*, Lebende Sprachen 17,2, 1972, pp. 38 - 39.

291 SCHNEIDER, D. B.   : *Wordsworth's "Prelude" and the O.E.D. : Word-Combinations*.

472 SCHUBIGER, M.   : *Zum sog. Level Stress bei englischen Composita*, NS 40,
1932, pp. 360 - 365.

473 SPECTOR, R. D.   : *Compound Words in Baseball*, AS 30, 1955, p. 153.

'474 STIASNY, M.   : *Ueber neue Composita bei Keats*, Diss. Vienna, 1917,
(unpublished manuscript).
(Vienna 2, p. 175; 2043)

475 STORMS, G.   : *Compounded Names of Peoples in Beowulf. A Study in the*
Diction of a Great Poet, Utrecht - Nijmegen : Dekker
en van de Vegt N. V., 1957, 26 p..
Reviews :
Malone, K.   : ES 41, 1960, 200 - 205
Matthes, H. Ch. : Anglia 80, 1962, 168 - 170
Wijngaarden, A. van : LT 1958, 293 - 294

'476 ŠUBIN, E. P.   : *K voprosu o složnom slove i slovosočetanij v anglijs-*
kom jazyke (On the question of the compound and the
word-combination in English), Poltavskij Institut Inženerov sels'kochozjaistvennogo stroitel'stva. UZ, vyp
10, 1955, pp. 427 - 463.

'477 SWOBODA, W.   : *Die englische und deutsche Betonung der Composita*,
Zeitschrift für deutsches Realschulwesen 20 (2), 1895
(Germ. Jahresbericht).

111

478 TEALL, F. H.   : *The Compounding of English Words. When and Why Join-*
                          ing or Separation is Preferable, with Concise Rules
                          and Alphabetical Lists, New York : J. Ireland, 1891,
                          223 p..

479   - : *The Compounding of Words in Funk & Wagnall's Standard*
                      Dictionary of the English Language : Containing a
                      Brief Statement of Principles that Govern the Com-
                      pounding of Words, with a Comprehensive Alphabetical
                      List of 40000 Terms to Which these Principles are Ap-
                      plied, London - New York - Toronto : Funk & Wagnall's
                      Company, 1892, 82 p..

480   - : *English Compound Words and Phrases, a Reference List*
                      with Statement of Principles and Rules, New York -
                      London - Toronto : Funk & Wagnall's Company, 1892,
                      309 p., (2).
                      (esp. pp. 1 - 26)

481 VERHAAR, J. W. M.   : *Enkele problemen uit de theorie van het Modern-Engel-*
                          se compositum (Some problems from the theory on the
                          Modern English compound) (Summary), Hand NPh C 23,
                          1954, pp. 46 - 47.

482 VOITL, H.   : *Neubildungswert und Stilistik der Komposita bei Sha-*
                          kespeare, Diss. Freiburg 8.7.1955, Freiburg, 1954,
                          vi, 260 lvs., vita, Masch. verv..
                          (Germany 71, p. 220)

483   - : *Shakespeares Komposita. Ein Beitrag zur Stilistik*
                      seiner Wortprägungen, Jahrbuch der deutschen Sha-
                      kespeare-Gesellschaft West 1969, pp. 152 - 173.

A) NOMINAL COMPOUNDS

1) PRENOMINAL MODIFIERS AND COMPOUNDS BY PREMODIFICATION

484 Anon. : *Is " cannon" an Adjective?* ELT 2, 1947, pp. 112.

'410 ACHMANOVA, O. S. : *K voprosu ob otličij složnych slov ot frazeologičeskich edinic.* (*Na materiale anglijskogo i svedskogo jazykov)* (On the difference between compounds and phraseological units. (On the material of English and Swedish).

485 - : *Lexical and Syntactical Collocations in Contemporary English,* ZAA 6, 1958, pp. 14 - 21.

'486 BOBYLEVA, L. K. : *Stilističeskie vozmožnosti atributivnych imen suščestvitel'nych v anglijskom jazyke* (The stylistic possibilities of substantives used attributively in English), UZ DVost U 1962, vyp. 4, serija filologija, pp. 25 - 32.

487 BYINGTON, S. T. : *The Attributive Noun Becomes Cancerous,* AS 2, 1926/ 1927, pp. 34 - 38.

'488 CAMAIORA, L. L. : *A Description of Nominal Group Premodification in English and Italian, with a Brief Treatment of the Principal Structural Differences,* M.Phil. London. (England 17, p. 14; 303)

'489 ČAPNIK, E. I. : *Atributivnye sočetanija tipa* stone wall *v sovremennom anglijskom jazyke* (Attributive collocation: of the *stone wall* type in contemporary English), 1-M Ped I , 1953, 230 p..

'490 - : *K voprosu o sočetanijach tipa* stone wall, Moscow students *v sovremennom anglijskom jazyke* (On the word combinations of the type *stone wall, Moscow students* in modern English), UZ Rjazan Ped I, 1961 t. 22, pp. 27 - 43.

491 CURME, G. O.   : *The Attributive Noun Again*, AS 5, 1929/1930, pp. 490
                      - 492.

492 DAWKINS, J.   : *Noun Attributives in ' Webster's Third New Interna-
                      tional Dictionary',* AS 39, 1964, pp. 33 - 41.

493 DRAAT, Fijn van P. : *Cannon-ball*, ESt 67, 1932/1933, pp. 86 - 97.

'494 FRÖHLICH, A.   : *Adjektivisch-attributive Substantiva und Kettenwör-
                      ter im Englischen*, Praxis 4, 1957, pp. 85 - 87.

495 GOVE, Ph. B.   : *" Noun Often Attributive" and " Adjective",* AS 39,
                      1964, pp. 163 - 175.

496 GUTSCHOW, H.   : *Probleme des attributiven und prädikativen Substan-
                      tivs im Englischen*, Praxis, 1963, pp. 10 - 16.

'497 KRAVCUK, N. V. : *Stilističeskaja značimost'mnogo člennych atribu-
                      tivnych imennych slovosočetanij. (Na materiale
                      jazyka romanov Č. Dikkensa i K. Emisa)* (On the
                      stylistic effect of multicomponent attributive no-
                      minal collocations. (Using linguistic material from
                      the novels of Ch. Dickens and K. Amis)),Naučnaja kon-
                      ferencija " Problemy sinchronnogo izučenija gramma-
                      ticeskogo stroja jazyka" . Tezisy dokladov isoobšče-
                      nij, Moscow, 1965, pp. 106 - 107.

'498 LANCE, D. M.   : *Sequential Ordering of Prenominal Modifiers in En-
                      glish. A Critical Review*, Ph.D. Diss. University of
                      Texas 1968, 339 p..

499 LEE, D. W.   : *Close Apposition : Un Unresolved Pattern*, AS 27,
                      1952, pp. 268 - 275.

500 LEONHARD, R.   : *The Types and Currency of Noun+Noun - Sequences in
                      Prose Usage 1750 - 1950*, M. Phil. London, 1968,
                      411 lvs..

501 MOESSNER, L.   : *Automatische syntaktische Analyse englischer nomi-
                      naler Gruppen (Automatic Syntactic Analysis of En-*

glish Nominal Groups), Diss. Freiburg, 1968, 150 p.
(unpublished typescript), English and American
Studies in German, Summaries of Theses and Monographs. A Supplement to Anglia 1970, pp. 4 - 5.

'502   - : *Automatische syntaktische Analyse englischer nomi-
naler Gruppen*, Janua ling. ser. practica (forthcoming).

503 MORČINIEC, N.   : *Attributive Word-Groups in English*, KNf 8, 1961,
pp. 279 - 288.

'504 MUTT, O.   : *A Contribution to the Historical Study of the Attributive Use of Substantives in English*, Tartu, 1955,
(unpublished diss.).

'505   - : *Substantiivide atributiivsest tarvitamisest ja
selle vastastikustest suhetest adjektiivide kate-
gooriaga inglise keeles*, Tartu Riikliku Ülikooli
Toimetised, vihik, no. 43, Ajaloo-Keeleteadnskonna
töid, Talliun, 1956.

506   - : *K voprosu ob atributivnom upotreblenii suščestvitel'nych i ego vzaimootnošenijach s kategoriei
prilagatel'nych v anglijskom jazyke* (On the attributive use of substantives and its relations with
the category of adjectives in English), Tartuskijj
Universitet. UZ, vyp. 43, 1956, pp. 205 - 220.
(In Estonian; Russ. summary on pp. 221 - 222)

'507   - : *The Use of Common-Case Forms of Substantives as
Premodifiers in Early Modern English*, Tartu Riik-
liku Ülikooli Toimetised,vihik 260. Töid Romaani-
Germaani Filoloogia Ahalt, III, Tartu : Romaani -
Germaani Filoloogia 63, 94 p..

'508   - : *K voprosu o vozniknovenii razvitii atributivnogo
upotreblenija suščestvitel'nych v anglijskom jazyke. (Suščestvitel'nye v forme obščego padeža*

v funkcii prepozitivnogo opredelenija) (On the origin and development of the adjectival use of substantives in English. Substantives in the common case in the function of a prepositive attribute), Diss. Leningrad, 1960, Leningradskij gosudarstvennyj universitet im. A. A. Ždanova, Leningrad.

'509   - : *Suščestvovanie v drevneanglijskom jazyke predposylki dlja razvitija atributivnogo upotreblenija suščestvitel'nych* (On the preconditions in Old English that facilitated the subsequent development of the use of substantives in the common case as prepositive attributes), UZ Tartu U , 1962, vyp. 117, Trudy po filologii no. 1, pp. 229 - 245.

510   - : *The Adjectivization of Nouns in English*, ZAA 12, 1964, pp. 341 - 349.

511   - : *Some Recent Developments in the Use of Nouns as Premodifiers in English*, ZAA 15, 1967, pp. 401 - 408.

512   - : *The Use of Substantives as Premodifiers in Early English*, NphM 69, 1968, pp. 578 - 596.

'513 ROEY, J. v.   : *Vergelijkende studie van de structuur der substantief groepen in het Engels en het Nederlands*, Diss. Louvain, 1957 (unpublished).

514 ROZENBERG, R. S.   : *K voprosu ob analize atributivnogo člena v opredelitel'nych sočetanijach tipa a sit-down strike, a pin-up girl v sovremennom anglijskom jazyke* (The analysis of the attributive member in constructions of the type *a sit-down strike, a pin-up girl* in modern English), UZ Rjaz P I , 31, 1962, pp. 39 - 50.

515 SARKISJAN, E. I.   : *Atributivnye imena sobstvennye ličnye v sovremennom anglijskom jazyke* (Proper personal attributive nominal words in modern English), Poltavskij Insti-

116

tut Inženerov Sels'kochozjaistvennogo stroitel'stva
UZ , vyp. 17, 1958, pp. 197 - 278.

516 SEARS, D. A.   : *The Noun Adjuncts in Modern English*, Linguistics 72,
1971, pp. 31 - 60.

'517 ŠIRVANSKAJTE, D. A. : *Složnye opredelitel'no-adjektivnye slovosočetanija
v sovremennom anglijskom jazyke* (Compound attribu-
tive-adjectival word combinations in modern English)
UZ VUZ 1965, No. 12, pp. 91 - 98.

'518 SMIRNICKIJ, A. I. - ACHMANOVA, O. S. : *Obrazovanija tipa stone wall, speec
sound v anglijskom jazyke* (Formations of the type
stone wall, speech sound in modern English), Institu
jazykoznanija (Akademija Nauk SSSR. Moskva), doklady i soobščenija, vyp. 2, 1952, pp. 97 - 116.

'519 ŠUBIN, E. P.   : *Atributivnye imena v jazyke Šekspira i ich genezis*
(Attributive nominal words in the language of Sha-
kespeare and their origin), Poltavskij Institut Inženerov Sels'kochozjaistvennogo stroitel'stva. UZ
vyp. 14, 1957, pp. 77 - 284; vyp. 17, 1958, pp. 347
- 504.
(Type : summer day, gold watch)

'520 TURNER, G. J.   : *A Linguistic Description and Comparison of the Nominal Group in Two Varieties of Contemporary Writ-
ten English*, MA London , (U. C.).
(England 16, p. 11; 223)

'521 VITONITE, I. P.   : *Sočetanija slov v funkcii prepozitivnogo opredelenija i vopros ob ich leksikalizacii* (Word groups
as prepositive attributes and the problem of their
lexicalization), L Ped I UZ , tom. 253/45, 1959,
pp. 35 - 49.

'522 VITONITE - GEGENE, I. P. : *Prepozitivnye atributivnye sočetanija slov
tipa pay-as-you-go (system), mud and straw (fish-
ing villages), off-the-record (briefing) v sovremennom anglijskom jazyke* (Prepositive attri-

butive word combinations of the type *pay-as-you-go*
(*system*), *mud-and-straw* (*fishing villages*), *off-
the-record* (*briefing)* in modern English, Diss. Leningrad, 1964 (LU).

'523 VLASENKO, S. N.　: *Slovosočetanija s atributivnymi geografičeskimi naz-
vanijami v sovremennom anglijskom jazyke* (Word
combinations with attributive geographical names in
present-day English), Poltavskij Institut Inženerov
Sels'kochozjaistvennogo stroitel'stva. UZ, vyp. 18,
1959, pp. 59 - 104.

'524 ŽLUKTENKO, Ju. A.　: *Grammatičeski oformlennye suščestvitel'nye v atri-
butivnoi funkcij v sovremennom anglijskom jazyke*
(Grammatically structured nouns in the attributive
function in present-day English), Kievskij finansovo
- zkonomičeskij institut. Naučnye zapiski No. 10,
1958, pp. 53 - 60.

2) NOMINAL COMPOUNDS

417 BARRETT, C. E.　　: *A Graphemic Analysis of English Nominal Complexes.*

525 BODE, W.　　　　: *Die Kenningar in der angelsächsischen Dichtung. Mit
Ausblicken auf andere Literaturen,* Diss. Strassburg
1886, Darmstadt & Leipzig : E. Zernin, 1886, 100 p..
(Germany 1, p. 188; 8)
Reviews :
   $\mathcal{Y}_{\mathcal{X}}\,\hbar$　　: Litcblatt 1887, col. 187 - 188
Bischoff, F.: ASNS 79, 1887, 115 - 116
Gummere, F. B. : MLN 2, 1887, 17 - 19
Kluge, F.　: ESt 10, 1887, 117
Meyer, R. M. : Anzeiger f. dt. Altertum u. dt. Li-
　　　　　　teratur 13, 1887, 136 - 138
'Nader, E.　: Litblatt für germ. und rom. Philolo-
　　　　　　gie 8, 1887, col. 10 - 12

526 BOROWSKI, B.   : *Zum Nebenakzent beim altenglischen Nominalkomposi-*
tum, Halle : Max Niemeyer, 1921, viii, 162 p..
(= Sächsische Forschungsinstitute in Leipzig, For-
schungsinstitut für neuere Philologie, III. Anglistische Abteilung unter Leitung v. Max Förster, Vol.
2).

Reviews :

Bradley, H.   : MLR 18, 1923, 341

Ehrentreich, A. : ASNS 148, 1925, 110 - 112

Eichler, A.   : Zeitschrift für frz. und engl. Unterricht 22, 1923, 139 - 140

Flasdieck, H. : ESt 57, 1923, 257 - 263

'527 BRAND, F.   : *Die Betonung der Nominalkomposita im Neuenglischen,*
Diss. Marburg 21.5.1918, (1922), 132 lvs..
(Germany 38, p. 706)

528 BREKLE, H. E. : *Generative Satzsemantik und transformationelle Syn-*
tax im System der englischen Nominalkomposition,
München : Wilhelm Fink Verlag, 1970, 221 p..
(= Internationale Bibliothek für allgemeine Linguistik / International Library of General Linguistics, ed. by E. Coseriu, Vol. 4.
(Habilitationsschrift Tübingen)

Reviews :

Bartsch, R.   : BLI 21, 1971, 50 - 57

Bauer, G.   : Sprache 18, 1972, 65 - 66

529   - : *Generative Satzsemantik und transformationelle Syntc*
im System der englischen Nominalkomposition (Ge-
nerative Sentence-Semantics and Transformational Syr
tax Applied to the System of English Nominal Com-
position), English and American Studies in German,
Summaries of Theses and Monographs. A Supplement
to Anglia 1969, pp. 3 - 6.

530 BUCKHURST, H. Th. McMILLAN : *Terms and Phrases for the Sea in Old English Poetry*, in Studies in English Philology : A Miscellany in Honor of Frederick Klaeber, ed. by K. Malone and Martin B. Ruud, Minneapolis, 1929, pp. 103 - 119.

'531 GLEITMAN, L. R. : *An Experiment Concerning the Use and Perception of Compound Nominals by English Speakers*, Ph.D. Diss. University of Pennsylvania, 1967, 176 p..
(DAb 28, 9 - 10, 1968, 4157-A)

'532 GLIKINA, E. A. : *Udarenie v složnych suščestvitel'nych i prilagatel'-nych anglijskogo jazyka* (Stress in compound substantives and adjectives in English), IJaS 3, 1955, pp. 33 - 40.

'533 GORGADZE, L. D. : *Sostavnoe imennoe skaznemoe v sovremennom anglijskom jazyke i ego ekvivalenty v gruzinskom jazyke* (The compound nominal predicate in contemporary English and its counterparts in Georgian), Tbilisskij Universitet 1956, 204 p. (in Georgian).

'534 GRAND, F. : *Die Betonung der Nominalkomposita im Neuenglischen*, Jahresbericht der philosophischen Fakultät der Philipps-Universität zu Marburg, 1922 - 1923, I. Philol. - historische Abteilung, Marburg, 1924.

535 HATCHER, A. G. : *Modern English Word-Formation and Neo-Latin. A Study of the Origins of English (French, Italian, German) Copulative Compounds*, Baltimore : The Johns Hopkins Press, 1951, ix, 226 p..
Reviews :
Benveniste, E. : BSL 47, 1951, 182 - 185
Bolinger, D. L. : Word 9, 1953, 83 - 85
Brunner, K. : DLZ 73, 1952, 431 - 432
Householder, F. W. : Lg 27, 1951, 597 - 601
Lee, D. W. : AS 27, 1952, 121 - 123
Liljegren, S. B. : SNPh 25, 1952/1953, 55 - 56
Migliorini, B. : AGI 36, 1951, 90 - 91
Nurmela, T. : NphM 57, 1956, 60 - 68

Pons, E. : Erasmus 5, 1952, col. 359 - 362

Sandmann, M.: RF 63, 1951, 416 - 418

Schick, C. : AGI 36, 1951, 87 - 90

Whatmough, J.: Classical Philology 49, 1954, 63

'536 HIETSCH, O.   : *A Contribution to the Study of Nominal Compound and Compound Elements in the Vocabulary of Old English Poetry*, M. Litt. Durham.
(England 1, p. 17; 353)

537 HILL, B.   : *Four Anglo-Saxon Compounds*, RES 8, 1957, pp. 162 166.
(all-efne, fifteig-daeg, hwit-corn, larcnaeht)

538 ISSHIKI, M.   : *The Kennings in Beowulf* , in Studies in English Grammar and Linguistics. A Miscellany in Honour of Takanobu Otsuka, ed. by K. Araki, T. Egawa, T. Oyama, M. Yasui. Tokyo : Kenkyusha Ltd., 1958, x, 419 p.; pp. 257 - 273.

539 KILIAN, F.   : *Shakespeares Nominalkomposita. Ein Beitrag zur Erforschung seiner Neuprägungen*, Diss. Münster 18.12.1953, 1953, (1), iv, (1), 218 lvs., vita.
(Germany 69, p. 64)

540 KLÖHN, G.   : *Die nominalen Wortverbindungen in der Dichtung von Gerard Manley Hopkins*, Diss. Mainz 16.11.1968, Mainz, 1968, vi, (1), 203 p.,vita.
(DNB C 1970, 4; p. 21; 231)

541 KRACKOW, O.   : *Die Nominalcomposita als Kunstmittel im altenglischen Epos*, Diss. Berlin 16.5.1903, Weimar : Druck von R. Wagner Sohn, 1903, 48 p..
(Germany 18, p. 20; 185)
Reviews :
Björkman, E. : ASNS 117, 1906, 189 - 190

542 KÜNZEL, G.   : *Das zusammengesetzte Substantiv und Adjektiv in der englischen Sprache*, Diss. Leipzig 19.10.1910,

Borna-Leipzig : Buchdruckerei R. Noske, 1911; vi,
64 p., (4), vita.

'543 LEES, R. B.   : *Generation of Nominal Compounds in English*, Linguistic
Society of America : Winter 1957, unpublished paper.

544   - : *The Grammar of English Nominalizations*, Bloomington,
Indiana University, Research Center in Anthropology,
Folklore, and Linguistics, Publication 12, 1960, xxvi,
205 p..
Reviews :

Gleason, H. A.   : AmA 62, 1960, 1110 - 1111
Hill, A. A.   : Lg 38, 1962, 434 - 444
Householder, F. W. : Word 18, 1962, 326 - 353
Matthews, P. H.   : ArchL 13, 1961, 196 - 209
'Nikolaeva, T. M.   : Issledovanija po strukturnoj tipo-
logii, Moscow, Iz. d. ANSSR (Inst.
slavjanovedenija), 1963, 244 - 247
'Oliverius, Z. F.: SPFUK-Ph 4, 1969, 225 - 230
Rohrer, Ch.   : IF 71, 1966/1967, 161 - 170
Schachter, P.   : IJAL, 28, 1962, 134 - 146
Standop, E.   : Kratylos 7, 1962, 77 - 81
Vintu, I.   : RRLing 11, 1966, 112 - 115

545   - : *Problems in the Grammatical Analysis of English No-*
minal Compounds, in Progress in Linguistics. A Collection of Papers selected and edited by Manfred Bierwisch and Karl Erich Heidolph, The Hague - Paris :
Mouton, 1970, 344 p.; pp. 174 - 186.

545 a MAGOUN, F. P. jr. : *Recurring First Elements in Different Nominal Com-*
pounds in Beowulf and the Elder Edda, in Studies in
English Philology. A Miscellany in Honor of Frederick
Klaeber, ed. by Kemp Malone and Martin B. Ruud, Minneapolis : University of Minnesota Press, 1929, x,
486 p.; pp. 73 - 78.

546 MALONE, K.	: *The Kenning in Beowulf 2220*, JEGP 27, 1928, pp. 318 - 324.

547 MARCHAND, H. : *Notes on Nominal Compounds in Present-Day English*, in Readings in Applied Linguistics ed. by H. B. Allen, New York, 1964, pp. 120 - 129.
(1958 edition : pp. 118 - 127)
(also in Word 11, 1955, pp. 216 - 227)

548 MARQUARDT, H. : *Die altenglischen Kenningar. Ein Beitrag zur Stilkunde altgermanischer Dichtung*, Halle : Max Niemeyer Verlag, 1938, xvi, 103 - 340 p.
(= Schriften der Königsberger Gelehrtengesellschaft, 14. Jahr, Geisteswissenschaftliche Klasse, Vol. 3)
Reviews :
Hamel, A. G. v. : ES 21, 1939, 12 - 15
Klaeber, F. : Anglia B 49, 1938, 321 - 326
Linke, G. : ASNS 174, 1938, 251 - 252
Malone, K. : MLN 55, 1940, 73 - 74
Potter, S. : MLR 34, 1939, 128
Rankin, J. W. : JEGP 38, 1939, 282 - 285
Reed, D. W. : Names 6, 1958, 241 - 247
LGRP 62, 1941, 196 - 197

549 MARTON, W. : *English and Polish Nominal Compounds. A Transformational Contrastive Study*, Studia Anglia Posnaniensia 2, 1969, 1 - 2, pp. 59 - 72.
(cf. Linguistics 61, 1970, p. 126)

550 RANKIN, J. W. : *A Study of the Kennings in Anglo-Saxon Poetry*, JEGP 8, 1909, pp. 357 - 422; 9, 1910, pp. 49 - 84.

'551 RÖMER, L. : *Zur strukturell - syntaktischen Beschreibung und algorithmischen Darstellung produktiver Nominalkomposita im britischen und amerikanischen Englisc* *Versuch einer synchron- linguistischen Untersuchung*

des englischen Wortbildungsmechanismus beim Vorgang des Compounding, Diss. Leipzig 2.12.1966, Leipzig, 1966, viii, 208 lvs.n., Masch. verv..
(DNB B 1967, 17; p. 1860; 167)

552 ROSS, A. S. C.   : *Aldrediana XV. On the Vowel of Nominal Composition*, NphM 69, 1968, pp. 361 - 374.

*553 RUBKE, H.   : *Die Nominalkomposita bei Aelfric. Eine Studie zu Aelfrics Wortschatz in seiner zeitlichen und dialektischen Gebundenheit*, Diss. Göttingen 24.5.1954, Göttingen, 1953, 171 lvs., Masch. verv..
(Germany 70, p. 273)

554 SCHOLTZ, H. van der MERWE : *The Kenning in Anglo-Saxon and Old Norse Poetry*, Utrecht - Nijmegen : N. V. Dekker & van de Vegt en J. W. van Leeuwen, 1928, 180 p., (1).

555 SMITH, G. G.   : *Recurring First Elements of Anglo-Saxon Nominal Compounds : a Study in Poetic Style*, Summaries of Theses 1931, Harvard University, pp. 244 - 246.

556 STEPHAN, K.   : *Das Aussterben und Fortleben der Nominalkomposita im altenglischen Beowulfepos und ihr Ersatz im Neuenglischen*, Diss. Graz, 1937, 216 lvs..
(Graz 1, p. 160; 2688)

557 STORCH, Th.   : *Angelsächsische Nominalcomposita*, Diss. Jena, Strassburg : K. J. Trübner, 1886, iv, 72 p..
Reviews :
            : Litcblatt 1887, col. 187

558 WANDRUSZKA, M.   : *Englische und deutsche Nominalkomposition*, in Wortbildung, Syntax und Morphologie, Festschrift zum 60. Geburtstag von H. Marchand am 1. Oktober 1967, ed. by Herbert E. Brekle and Leonhard Lipka, Janua Linguarum Series maior 36, The Hague - Paris : Mouton, 1968, 250 p.; pp. 242 - 250.

124

3) SUBSTANTIVAL COMPOUNDS (Sb-Sb, Adj.-Sb, ...)

'559 ACHMETOVA, S. G.   : *Sočetanie " prilagatel'noe + suščestvitel'noe "*
v anglijskom i russkom jazykach (The combina-
tion " adjective + substantive in English and
Russian), V Ja Met, pp. 3 - 6.

560 ALDRICH, R. I.   : *The Extension of ' Coffee Break'*, AS 33, 1958,
pp. 300 - 301.

561 BERGSTEN, N.   : *A Study on Compound Substantives in English,*
Diss. Uppsala : Almqvist & Wiksells Boktryckeri
A.-B., 1911, viii, 166 p..

Reviews :

Franz, W.   : ESt 47, 1913/1914, 235 - 236
Koeppel, E.   : Anglia B 23, 1912, 241 - 247

562 BREKLE, H. E.   : *Syntaktische Gruppe (Adjektiv + Substantiv) vs.*
Kompositum im modernen Englisch. Versuch einer
Deutung auf klassen- und relationslogischer Basis,
Linguistics 23, 1966, pp. 5 - 29.
(Ling. Abstract : Linguistics 40, 1968, p. 143)

'563 BURANOV, D.   : *O charaktere tak nazyvaemoj soedinitel'noj mor-*
femy " s " v anglijskom jazyke (On batman / bats-
man etc. in the history of English), UZ Taš P IIn,
VI, 1, 1962, pp. 124 - 137.

'564   - : *Osobennosti zvukovoj struktury slov, obrazovannych*
pri pomošči polusuffiksa -man v sovremennom an-
glijskom jazyke (The characteristics of the phono]
gical sound structure of words with the semi-suffi>
-man in modern English), UZ Tašk Ped I, 1962, vyp.

125

6, c. 1, pp. 118 - 123.

'565   - : *Leksičeskoe značenie slov so vtorym komponentom -men v anglijskom jazyke* (The lexical meaning of words with -men as second component in English), Voprosy jazykoznanija, kn. 1, Taškent 1965, pp. 48 - 57.

'566 CROFT, K.   : *English Noun Compounds. An Introductory Study for Students of English as a Second Language*, Institute of Languages and Linguistics, Georgetown University, 1964.

'567 DUMERIL, H.   : *Quelques anomalies de la grammaire anglaise : 'man' et ' woman' (esp. in compounds)*, RLaV, November pp. 396 - 399.

568 EINARSSON, S.   : *Kyning-wuldor and mann-skratti*, MLN 75, 1960, pp. 193 - 194.

'569 EYESTONE, M. A.   : *Tests and Treatment of Compound Substantives in Modern American English with Special Emphasis on Stress and Intonation Patterns*, Ph.D. Diss. Michigan State College, 1954, 140 p.. (DAb 15,3, 1955, 407 - 408)

'570 FOMENKO, N. V.   : *K voprosu o substantivnych sočetanijach* (On the question of substantival word-combinations) , UZ Taškentskij pedagogičeskij Institut inostrannych jazykov, vyp. 2, 1957, pp. 159 - 176.

571 GARDNER, Th. J.   : *Semantic Patterns in Old English Substantival Compounds*, Diss. Heidelberg 15.2.1967, Hamburg 1968, 366 p., vita.
(DNB C 1969, 6; p. 19; 216)

'532 GLIKINA, E. A.   : *Udarenie v složnych suščestvitel'nych i prilagatel'nych anglijskogo jazyke* (Stress in compound substantives and adjectives in English)

'572 GRUDINKO, B. I.   : *O strukturnoj prirode obrazovanij tipa woman doctor v anglijskom jazyke* (On the structural character of formations of the type woman doctor in English), UZ LU 1961, No. 283, serija filologičeskich nauk, vyp. 56, pp. 35 - 47.

'573   - : *K voprosu o sojazi komponentov v strukture slovosočetanija. (Na materiale obrazovanij tipa woman doctor v sovremennom anglijskom jazyke)* (On the structural relationship of the components of word combinations. On the material of formations of the type woman doctor in modern English), Issl AFil 3, 1965, pp. 44 - 60.

574 HATCHER, A. G.   : *Twilight Splendor, Shoe Colors, Bolero Brilliance,* MLN 61, 1946, pp. 442 - 447.

575   - : *An Introduction to the Analysis of English Noun Compounds*, Word 16, 1960, pp. 356 - 373.

576 KOBAN, Ch.   : *Substantive Compounds in Beowulf*, Ph.D. Diss. University of Illinois, 1963, 329 p..
(DAb 24, 10, 1964, 4175 - 4176; Linguistics 9, 1964, pp. 110 - 111)

577 KOEPPEL, E.   : *Tautological Compounds of the English Language*, in An English Miscellany Presented to Dr. Furnivall in Honour of His Seventy-Fifth Birthday, Oxford: Clarendon Press, 1901, viii, (2), 500 p.; pp. 201 - 204.

578 LIVANT, W. P.   : *Productive Grammatical Operations : I : The Noun-Compounding of 5-Year-Olds*, LL 12, 1962, pp. 15 - 26.

579 MARCHAND, H.   : *The Analysis of Verbal Nexus Substantives*, IF 70, 1965/1966, pp. 57 - 71.

580   - : *On the Analysis of Substantive Compounds and Suffixal Derivatives Not Containing a Verbal Element*, IF 70, 1965/1966, pp. 117 - 145.

581 OLIPHANT, R.   : *Two Questionable Old English Compounds : Dungraéd and Tidscriptor*, PhQ 43, 1964, pp. 123 - 125.

582 REIBEL, D. A.   : *A Grammatical Index to the Compound Nouns of Old English Verse (Based on the Entries in Grein-Köhler, Sprachschatz der Angelsächsischen Dichter)*, Ph.D. Diss. Indiana University, 1963, 212 p.. (DAb 25, 1, 1964, 465 - 466; Linguistics 12, 1965, pp. 117 - 118)

583 REPPERT, J. D.   : *Tautological Compounds*, Word Study 30, 1, 1954, pp. 8. (greyhound, yardstick ...)

584 ROEY, J. van   : *A Note on Noun + Noun Combinations in Modern English*, ES 45, 1964, pp. 48 - 52.

585 SANKIN, A. A.   : *O charakternych čertach sostavnych terminov tipa ' prilagatel'noe + suščestvitel'noe'v anglijskom jazyke* (On the characteristics of compounded technical terms of the type ' adjective + substantive in English), 1-M Ped I, 1956, t. 9.

'586 VLADIMIROVA, E. S. : *Kontekstno neraz ložimye slovosočetanija struktur-*
nogo tipa ' prilagatel'noe + suščestvitel'noe ' v
sovremennom anglijskom jazyke (Contextually un-
analysable word collocations of the structural
type 'adjective + substantive ' in modern English)
UZ Tul Ped I, 1964, Fil S, pp. 113 - 139.

4) ADJECTIVAL COMPOUNDS (Adj-Adj, Sb-Adj....)

'587 ACHMETOVA, S. G.   : *K voprosu o sočetanijach suščestvitel'nych s prila-*
gatel'nymi v anglijskom jazyke (On the combination
of substantives with adjectives in English), Resp
Konf pp. 11 - 12.

588 BINGHAM, M.   : *The Terms ' Accident-Prone' and ' Accident-Prone-*
ness', N & Q 204, July - August 1959, pp. 287 - 288.
(The terms date from 1926 and have been in general
use since 1929)

'589 BIRENBAUM, Y.   : *Obraznye sravnitel'nye oboroty* (Metaphorical comparisons), VObšč, vyp. 2, pp. 90 - 93.

590   - : *English Compound Adjectives Consisting of a Noun*
Stem Plus an Adjective Stem, ZAA 15, 1967, pp. 279
- 286.

591 CARSTENSEN, B.   : *Weltweit und world-wide*, Mu 72, 1962, pp. 341 -
342.

'592 DONY, A.   : *Über einige volkstümliche Begriffsverstärkungen*
bei deutschen und englischen Adjektiven , Pro-
gramme der Spremberger Realschule 1862 - 1872,
Spremberg, 1865,
(cf. ASNS 39, 1866, pp. 340 - 341)

593 EICHHORN, E.   : *Das Partizipium bei Gower im Vergleich mit Chaucers Gebrauch*, Diss. Kiel 7.10.1912, Kiel : Druck von H. Fiencke, 1912, viii, 99 p., vita.
(esp. pp. 11 - 16 : compound participles, pseudo-participles (type pearled, rooted), participles prefixed by un-)
(Germany 28, p. 225)

594 GERIKE, F.   : *Das Participium Präsentis bei Chaucer*, Diss. Kiel 19.5.1911, Potsdam : Biermann & Co., 1911, x, (2), 75 p., (1), vita.
(Germany 26, p. 442)

595 GROOM, B.   : *The Formation and Use of Compound Epithets in English Poetry from 1579*, Oxford : Clarendon Press, 1937, pp. 293 - 322. (= S. P. E. Tract No. 49).
Reviews :
Brand, A. H.   : ES 23, 1941, 25 - 27
Havens, R. D.   : MLN 53, 1938, 550

596 HELLINGER, M.   : *Die adjektivischen Partizipialkomposita vom Typus ' computer-making' und ' state-controlled'. Eine syntaktisch-semantische Analyse im Rahmen der generativen Transformationsgrammatik*, Diss. Hamburg 28.8.1969, Hamburg : Fotodruck, Dissertationsdruck Lüdke bei der Uni, 1969, (vi), 175 p., vita.
(DNB C 1970, 11; p. 25; 278)

597   - : *Die adjektivischen Partizipialkomposita vom Typus ' computer-making' und ' state-controlled'. Eine syntaktisch-semantische Analyse im Rahmen der generativen Transformationsgrammatik (Adjectival Participial Compounds of the Type ' Computer-Making' and 'State-Controlled'. A Syntactic-semantic Analysis Within the Frame-Work of Generative transformational Grammar)*, Diss. Hamburg, 1969, (vi), 175 p., in English and German Studies in German, Summaries of Theses and Monographs. A Supplement

to Anglia 1969, pp. 6 - 8.

598 HOFFMANN, F. : *Das Partizipium bei Spenser. Mit Berücksichtigung*
Chaucers und Shakespeares, Diss. Berlin 28.5.1909,
Berlin : Mayer & Müller, 1909, vi, 48 p., vita.
(Germany 24, p. 34)

599 HÜTTMANN, E. : *Das Partizipium Präsentis bei Lydgate im Vergleich*
mit Chaucer's Gebrauch, Diss. Kiel 28.4.1914, Kiel:
Schmidt & Klaunig, 1914, 92 p., vita.
(Germany 30, p. 673)

600 LIENHART, M. : *Aufkommen der zusammengesetzten Epitheta in der*
englischen Literatur, Diss. Freiburg 8.11.1927,
Freiburg : Druck W. Wiemken, 1927, 70 p., vita.
(Germany 43, p. 135)

601 LIPKA, L. : *Die Wortbildungstypen WATERPROOF und GRASS-GREEN*
und ihre Entsprechungen im Deutschen, Diss. Tübin-
gen 10.3.1966, Bamberg, 1966, ix, 173 p., vita.
(Germany 82, p. vii, 55 (7. Lieferung))
(cf. Linguistics 30, 1967, p. 99)
Reviews :
Braun, F. : Mu 77, 1967, 180 - 182
Gester, F. W. : Anglia 85, 1967, 433 - 437
Hansen, K. : ZAA 15, 1967, 297 - 300
Koziol, H. : ASNS 206, 1969/1970, 457 - 458
Standop, E. : IF 72, 1967/1968, 367 - 368

602 MASSEY, B. W. A. : *The Compound Epithets of Shelley and Keats, Con-*
sidered from the Structural, the Historical, and
the Literary Stand Points with Some Comparisons,
from the Greek, the Old English and the German,
Poznań, 1923 (NPT), xv, 256 p..
Reviews :
Jespersen, O. : MLR 19, 1924, 386 - 387

603 - : *The O.E.D. and Some Adjectives of Shelley and Keats*
N & Q 12, 1923, pp. 243 - 244.

'604   - : *Browning's Vocabulary : Compound Epithets*, Poznań
(Poznanskie Towarzystwo Przy jaciół Nauk), 1931,
272 p..
Reviews :
Liljegren, S. B. : Anglia B 44, 1933, 245 - 246

605 MÜLLER-SCHOTTE, H. : *A Moon-bound Rocket. Erläuterungen zur englischen
Wortkomposition Substantiv + Participium praeteri-
ti*, NS, N. F., 16, 1967, pp. 178 - 182.

'606 NEËLOV, A. A.   : *K voprosu o častotnosti nekotorych morfologičeskich struktur v jazyke " Beowul'fa"* (On the fre-
quency of compound two-stem and simple one-stem
adjectives in Beowulf (English summary), Probl
Morf , pp. 199 - 203.

607 PELTOLA, N.   : *The Compound Epithet and Its Use in American Poetry
from Bradstreet Through Whitman*, Suomalaisen Tiede-
akatemian Toimituksia AASF, Sarja - Ser. B, Nide
Tom. 105, Helsinki : Akateeminen kirjakauppa, 1956,
Wiesbaden : O. Harrassowitz, 299 p..
Reviews :
Ahnebrink, L. : MSpråk 54, 1960, 135 - 136
Francis, W. N. : ArchL 10,1958, 147 - 149
Galinsky, H. : Erasmus 11, 1958, 479 - 483
Hilen, A.   : SNPh 30, 1958, 127 - 128
Riese, T.   : ASNS 196, 1960, 93 - 94

'608 ROCHOWANSKÁ, I. : *Anglická adjektivní kompozita končicína - ing* a
-ed (The English compound adjectives in *-ing*
and *-ed*), ČMF 50, 1968, pp. 97 - 105.

'609 ROSENDORN, T. P. : *Rol' pričastija I v popolnenii slovarnogo sostava
anglijskogo jazyka* (The role of participle I in
the enrichment of the English vocabulary) , 1 - M
Ped I, UZ, tom. 23, 1959, pp. 377 - 392.

610 SACHS, E. : *On steinalt, stock-still, and Similar Formations,* JEGP 62, 1963, pp. 581 - 596.

'611 ŠIRVINSKAJTE, D. A. : *O razgraničenii slovosočetanij i složnych prilagatel'nych tipa ' suščestvitel'noe ⌐ prilagatel'noe v sovremennom anglijskom jazyke* (On the differenciation of word combinations and compound adjectives of the type substantive + adjective in modern English), VKyjiv U 1964, No. 6, pp. 106 - 111.

612 SPITZBARDT, H. : *Präfigierte Verstärkungselemente im Englischen,* WZUJ 11, 1962, pp. 135 - 143.

'613 - : *Usilitel'nye pristavočnye elementy v sovremennom anglijskom jazyke* (On prefixed intensive elements of the type : *stone-*(deaf); *bran(d)-, clock-, cock-, rip-, rock-, stock-, etc.* in present-day English) (German summary), Probl Morf, pp. 155 - 163.

614 WHITESELL, J. E. : *Logic and Analogy in Some Adjectival Compounds,* College English 20, 1958/1959, pp. 368 - 369.

615 WOJTASIEWICZ, O. A. : *A Type of Compound Adjective in Present-Day English,* KNf 16, 1969, pp. 171 - 175. (Type : oil-rich, power-greedy, snow-white, world-famous)

'616 WOODWARD, E. H. : *Adverbial Adjectives,* Word Study 34, December 1958, pp. 6 - 7.

'617 YANG, Shu - hsün : *Chin-tai Ying-yü chung te fu-ho hsing-jung-tz'u,* (Compound adjectives in present-day English), HFYW 11, 1958, pp. 158 - 165.

5) COMPOUNDS WITH SPECIFIC WORDS

ĀER :

618 BRYAN, W. F.   : *Āergōd in Beowulf, and Other English Compounds of aer*, MPh 28,1930/ 1931, pp. 157 - 161.

BREAK :

560 ALDRICH, R. I.   : *The Extension of ' Coffee-break'* .

COW :

'619 HAMILTON, A. P.   : *Compounds of the Word ' Cow'. A Study in Semantics*, Ph.D. Diss. University of Pennsylvania, 1923, iv,1, 59 p..

CURTAIN :

620 FEUERLICHT, I.   : *A New Look at the Iron Curtain*, AS 30, 1955, pp. 186 - 189.

621   - : *More 'Curtains'*, AS 34, 1959, pp. 75 - 76.

622 ROGERS, F. R.   : *' Iron Curtain ' Again*, AS 27, 1952, pp. 140 - 141.

'623 ZONOV, V. M.   : *Iron Curtain*, New York Times, March 18, 1952, p.'4.
(Attributes ' iron curtain ' to J. Goebbels)

EXPLOSION :

'624 Anon.   : *Notes and Comment*, New Yorker 37, 28 October 1961, p. 43.
(On the phrase *population explosion* and its

proliferation of explosion compounds)
(homerun - , rental - , value - , piety - , cul-
ture - , reading - , paperback - , stockowner - ,
ballet - , rurban -)

HORSE :

'625 FOULKROD, E.   : *Compounds of the Word " Horse". A Study in Semantics*
                            Ph.D. Diss., University of Pennsylvania, 1919, 83 p.

JOCKEY :

626 ALDRICH, R. I.   : *The Burgeoning of ' Jockey'*, AS 35, 1960, pp. 158
                            - 159.
                            (cf. Editor's note on p. 159 - 160)

627 LYMAN, J.   : *' Jockey' Compounds*, AS 37, 1962, p. 72.

628 RANDLE, W.   : *' Disc-Jockey ', ' Record-Jockey'*, *1941*, AS 36,
                            1961, p. 151.

MASTER :

629 REESE, G. H.   : *The Word ' Master' in Trade-Names*, AS 12, 1937,
                            pp. 262 - 266.

PROOF :

630 E., R.   : *Compounds with ' Proof'*, N & Q 125, 1938, pp. 369.

601 LIPKA, L.   : *Die Wortbildungstypen WATERPROOF und GRASS-GREEN
                            und ihre Entsprechungen im Deutschen.*

SELF :

'631 FUTERMAN, Z. Ja   : *Slovo self i self-formy sovremennogo anglijskogo
                            jazyka* (The word self and *self*-forms in present-
                            day English), UZ Ukrainskaja Akademija sel' sko-

chozjajstvennych nauk), Kiev 1959, KIJa, t. 1, pp.
62 - 70.

'632   - : *Slovo self i složnye slova s morfemoj self v anglijs-*
kom jazyke (The word *self* and words formed with *self*
in English), Diss. Leningrad (L Ped I), 1963.

633 LUDWIG, H.-W.   : *Die Self-Komposita bei Thomas Carlyle, Matthew Ar-*
nold und Gerard Manley Hopkins. Ein Beitrag zum Ver-
hältnis von Sprache und Geist, Diss. Tübingen 3.7.
1962, Tübingen, 1962, 304 lvs..
(Germany 78, p. 793)

634   - : *Die Self-Komposita bei Thomas Carlyle , Matthew Ar-*
nold und Gerard Manley Hopkins. Untersuchungen zum
geistigen Gehalt einer sprachlichen Form , Tübingen:
Max Niemeyer Verlag, 1963, xvi, 243 p..
(= Studien zur englischen Philologie, N. F., 2)
Reviews :
Gläser, R.   : ZAA 15, 1967, 74 - 76
Zettersten, A. : MSprak 60, 1966, 408 - 411

635 WAENTIG, K.   : *Die Self-Komposita der Puritanersprache,* Diss. Leipzig 21.4.1932, Leipzig : Druckerei der Werkgemein-
schaft G.m.b.H. 1932, viii, 123 p., vita.
(Germany 48, p. 522)

TYPE :

636 BIRD, D. A.   : *Type Compounds,* College English 17, 1955, pp. 178
- 179.

'637 RICE, L. H.   : *A Garland of Type's,* Word Study 41, October 1965,
pp. 3 - 4.
(On the " wanton use" of the suffix *-type* among
various professional groups)

638 SHELDON, E. K.   : *A Very Nice-Type Girl,* AS 23, 1948, pp. 251 - 256.

B) VERBAL COMPOUNDS

639 MARCHAND, H. : *Compound and Pseudo-Compound Verbs in Present-Day English*, AS 32, 1957, pp. 83 - 94.

C) COMPOUNDS WITH LOCATIVE PARTICLES

640 MARCHAND, H. : *Compounds with Locative Particles as First Elements in Present-Day English*, Word 12, 1956, pp. 391 - 398.

'641 GURS'KYJ, S. : *Spolučnist' pryslovnikiv up, down u su časnij anhlijs'kij movi* (*Up* and *down* as prefixes in present-day English), ZbR 1962, pp. 103 - 120.

D) OBSCURED COMPOUNDS

'642 AMOSOVA, N. N. : *Slova s oproščennym morfologičeskim sostavnom v sovremennom anglijskom jazyke* (Words with obscured morphological elements in modern English), UZ LU 1955, No. 180, SFilN, vyp. 21.

643 GÖTZ, D. : *Studien zu den verdunkelten Komposita im Englischen*, Diss. Erlangen, Erlanger Beiträge zur Sprach- und Kunstwissenschaft Vol. 40, Nürnberg : Verlag Hans Karl, 1971, x, 137 p..

644 - : *Studien zu den verdunkelten Komposita im Englischen (Studies on the Obscuration of English Nominal Compounds)*, , Diss. Erlangen - Nürnberg, Erlanger Beiträge zur Sprach- und Kunstwissenschaft 40, Nürnberg : Hans Carl, 1971, 139 p., in English and American Studies in German. Summaries of Theses and Monographs. A Supplement to Anglia 1971, Tübingen : Max Niemeyer, pp. 26 - 28.

645 HANKEY, C. T.　　　　: *" Cranberry" and Composition*, AS 42, 1967, pp. 234.

646 KLEIN, E.　　　　　　: *Die verdunkelten Wortzusammensetzungen im Neu-englischen*, Diss. Königsberg 29.3.1911, Königsberg : Druck von Karg und Manneck, 1911, 81 p., vita.
　　　　　　　　　　　　　Reviews :
　　　　　　　　　　　　　Koeppel, E. : Anglia B 23, 1912, 247 - 249

647 KRUEGER, J. R.　　　: *The Morphemes of " Cranberry"*, AS 38, 1963, pp. 155 - 156.

648 SWEET, H.　　　　　　: *Disguised Compounds in Old-English*, Anglia 3, 1880, pp. 151 - 154.
　　　　　　　　　　　　　(fultum, sulung, látteow, láreow, intinga)

E) PHRASAL VERBS

'649 ACHMANOVA, O. S.　: *" Ekvivalenty slov" i ich klassifikacija v sovre-mennom anglijskom jazyke* (" Word equivalents" and their classification in modern English), Moskovskij Universitet M. V. Lomonosova. Filologičeskij fakultet. Doklady i soobščenija, vyp. 6, 1948, pp. 5 - 11.

'410　　　　　　　　　　- : *K voprosu ob otličij složnych slov ot frazeolo-gičeskich edinic. (Na materiale anglijskogo i švedskogo jazykov)* (On the difference between compounds and phraseological units. (On the material of English and Swedish).

'650　　　　　　　　　　- : *Uto predstavljajut soboi obrazovanija tipa* stand up, go out *i.t.p. v anglijskom jazyke? Možno li objasnit'ich, ischodja iz obščeprinjatych ling-vistističeskich ponatij - slovo i slovosočetanie - ili dlja etogo trebnetsja vvedenie novych ponjatij*

138

(*naprimev, " analitičeskogo slova"?* (What are the formations of the *stand up, go out* etc. type in English? Can one explain them proceeding from the conventional linguistic concepts - word and word combination - or is the introduction of new concepts, for instance, that of the " analytical word" required?), IJaŠ 1955, 1, pp. 121 - 122.

'651 ADDISON, W. C. : *Prepositional Verbs,* The English Journal 16, 7, September 1927.

652 ANASTASIJEVIĆ, K. : *Adverbial Modifiers up, down, in, out, on, off in Contemporary English,* MA London, 1954, (4), 343 lvs..

'653 - : *Dvočlani glagol u savremenom engleskom jeziku* (The two-word verb in contemporary English),Filološki Fak. Univerziteta u Beogradu, Monografije 17; Beograd, 1968, 187 p..
Reviews :
Kalogjera, D. : SRAZ 25/26, 1968, 183 - 185

'654 ANIČKOV, I. E. : *Anglijskie adverbialvnye poslelogi* (English adverbial postpositions), Diss. Moscow, 1947.

'655 - : *Adverbial'nye poslelogi v sovremennom anglijskom jazyke* (Adverbial postpositions in modern English), UZ Pjat Ped I, 24, 1961, pp. 221 - 254.

656 ANTHONY, E. M. Jr. : *Test Frames for Structures with up in Modern American English,* Ph.D. Diss. University of Michigan, 1954, 135 p..
(DAb 14,4, 1954, p. 677)
(Authorized facsimile produced by microfilm - xerography 1969, Ann Arbor, Michigan, 2, 129 p.)

'657 ARCHANGEL'SKAJA, A. M.: *Predložnye sočetanija v sostavnom skaznemom* (Preposition groups in the compound predicate), 1 - MPed I, 1960, 353 p..

'658 BANDIK, A. N.   : *Vidy sočetanija tipa to be up* (The kinds of collocation of the type *to be up*), UZ M Ped I, 1964,
No. 210, pp. 143 - 160.

'659 BERLIZON, S. B.   : *Glagol'no - narečnye sočetanija i ich rol' v obo-
gaščenii slovarnogo sostava sovremennogo anglijsko-
go jazyka* (Verb - Adverb collocations and their
role in the enrichment of contemporary English lexicon), M Gor Ped I, 1955, 434 p..

'660   - : *Sočetanija tipa to go in, to cry out, to speed up,
to give up v sovremennom anglijskom jazyke* (Collocations of the type *to go in, to cry out, to
speed up, to give up* in modern English), IJaŠ 1958,
6, pp. 9 - 24.

'661   - : *Semantičeskije osobennosti predložnych narečij v
sovremennom anglijskom jazyke* (The semantic features of the prepositional adverbs in modern English), Magnit Ped I, UZ, vyp. 7, 1958, pp. 319 -
344.

'662   - : *Ustoičivost' formy glagol'no - narečnych frazeologičeskich edinic i slučai ee narušenija* (The
stability of the form of verb - adverb phraseological units and its violations), Sbornik Statei po
germanskoi filologii kafedry inostrannyсh jazykov
(Magnit Ped I), 1959, pp. 3 - 24.

'663   - : *Strukturnye osobennosti glagol'no - narečnych frazeologičeskich edinic v sovremennom anglijskom jazyke* (Structural characteristics of verb - adverb
phrases in modern English), UZ M Ped I, 1961, No.
166, KLFAJa, pp. 191 - 200.

'664   - : *Sočetanie tipa make up, make for v sovremennom
anglijskom jazyke (Posobie dlja studentov ped. in-
stitutov)* (The syntagmas of the type *make up*

make for in modern English), Moskva - Leningrad : Izd. " Prosveščenie", 1964, 416 p..

665 BOLINGER, D.   : *The Phrasal Verb in English*, Cambridge, Mass. : Harvard University Press, 1971, xviii, 187 p..

'666 BURAKOVA, S. I.   : *Časticy v sovremennom anglijskom jazyke* (Particles in modern English), 1 LPed I, 1946, 369 p..

667 BURGESS, O. N.   : *Particle Verb Transformations in Australian English* AUMLA 33, 1970, pp. 61 - 66.

'668 BUŠINA, G. V.   : *Frazovyi glagol v sovremennom anglijskom jazyke* (The phrasal verb in modern English), Kiev Ped I, 1955, 220 p..

669 CARSTENSEN, B.   : *Zur Struktur des englischen Wortverbandes*, NS, N.F. 13, 1964, pp. 305 - 328.

'670 CRUZ, FERNANDEZ, J. M. de la : *Origins and Development of the Phrasal Ver to the End of the Middle English Period*, Ph. D. Dis Queen's University Belfast, 1968/1969. (England 19, p. 14 ; 341)

'671 DEVITT, N. A.   : *Upotreblenie pri glagolade slov tipa up, out v anglijskom jazyke. (V istoričeskom plane)* (The use of words of the up,out type with verbs in English. (In a historical perspective), Leningradskij inženerno - ekonomičeskij institut. Trudy. / Vyp. 15, 1957, pp. 38 - 52.

672 DIETRICH, G.   : *Die Akzentverhältnisse im Englischen bei Adverb und Präposition in Verbindung mit einem Verb und Verwandtes*, in Strena Anglica, Otto Ritter zum 80. Geburtstag am 9.Januar 1956, ed. by Gerhard Dietrich and Fritz W. Schulze, Halle : VEB Max Niemeyer Verlag, 1956, vii, 263 p.; pp. 1 - 67.

673   - : *Adverb oder Präposition? Zu einem klärungsbedüftigen Kapitel der englischen Grammatik* , Halle : VEB

Max Niemeyer Verlag, 1960, 173 p..

674 DONGEN, W. A. van : *He put on his hat and he put his hat on*, Nph 4, 1919, pp. 322 - 353.

'675 EGOROVA, T. A. : *K istorii tak nazyvaemych sostavnych glagolov v anglijskom jazyke* (On the history of the so-called compound verbs (phrasal verbs) in English), UZ LPed I, 1958, t.157, FAJa.

676 EITREM, H. : *Stress in English Verb + Adverb Groups*, ESt 32, 1903, pp. 69 - 77.

'677 ELLINGER, J. : *Über die Betonung der aus Verb + Adverb bestehenden Wortgruppen*, (Published with) 35. Jahresbericht der k.k. Franz-Joseph-Realschule in Wien, 19o9 - 1910, Vienna : Verlag der k.k. Franz-Joseph-Realschule, 1910, 3 - 16 p..
Reviews :
'Eichler, A. : Zeitschrift für österr. Gymnas. 64, 185

678 ERADES, P. A. : *Points of Modern English Syntax XL* (continued), ES 42, 1961 pp. 56 - 60.
(deals also with phrasal verbs)

'679 ERŠOVA, I. A. : *K istorii razvitija v anglijskom jazyke sočetanij glagola s prostrantsvennym narečiem (v svjazi s problemoi skandinavskogo vlijanija na anglijskij jazyk* (On the historical development of the combinations verb + locative adverb in English (In connection with the problem of the Scandinavian influence on English)), Lomonossow State University of Moscow Diss. 1951, 13 p..
Reviews :
: IJaš v.s. 3, 1952, 124

680 FAIRCLOUGH, N. L. : *Studies in the Collocation of Lexical Items With Prepositions and Adverbs in a Corpus of Spoken and*

Written Present-Day English, MA London, 1965,
258 lvs..

681 FOLTINEK, H.   : Die Wortverbindung Verbum + up oder out im modernen Englisch, Moderne Sprachen 8, 3-4, 1964, pp.
94 - 104.

'682 FRASER, B.   : An Examination of the Verb-Particle Construction
in English, unpublished MIT Doctoral Diss., Cam-
bridge, Mass., 1965.

683   - : Some Remarks on the Verb-Particle Construction in
English, in Report of the Seventeenth Annual Round
Table Meeting on Linguistics and Language Studies
No. 19, 1966, Francis P. Dinneen, S. J. editor,
Georgetown University Press, Washington, 1966, x,
258 p.; pp. 45 - 61.

'684 GELASVILI, M. V.   : Sopostavitel'nyi analiz gruzinskich preverbov i
anglijskich poslelegov (A comparative analysis of
English postverbs and Georgian preverbs), Tbilisskij
pedagogičeskij inostrannych jazykov. Trudy...Tom.2,
1959, pp. 125 - 136.
(In Georgian; Russian summary on p. 136)

'685   - : Sopostavitel'nyi analiz anglijskich postverbov i
gruzinskich preverbov (A comparative analysis of
English postverbs and Georgian preverbs), Tbilisski
pedagogičeskij inostrannych jazykov. Trudy ... Tom.
3, 1960, pp. 67 - 92.
(In Georgian; Russian summary on pp. 92 - 93)

'686 GRINBLAT, A. F.   : Sočetanie glagola s postpozitom v sovremennom anglijskom jazyke (The modern English verb-postposit-
collocation), Latvijskij Universitet IM.P., UZ,
Tom./ Filologičeskie nauki vyp. 25, 1958, pp. 259
- 315.
(In Lettish; Russian summary on p. 315)

'687   - : *Omonimija postpozitivnych sočetanij v sovremennom anglijskom jazyke* (The homonymy of the collocations with postposition in modern English), UZ Latv U, 1959, t. 30, Fil N , vyp. 4 A, pp. 123 - 137. (Russian summary)

'688   - : *Glagol'nye postpositivnye sočetanija v sovremennom anglijskom jazyke i ich ekvivalenty v latysskom jazyke* (Modern English verbal postpositive collocations and their Lettish counterparts), Latvijskij Universitet im. P. Stučki (Riga), 1960, 324 p..

'689 GRJAZNOVA, L. A.   : *K voprosu ob opredelenii antonimov glagol'nych frazeologičeskich edinic i ich klassifikacii* (On the definition of the antonyms of verbal phraseological units and their classification), UZ Bašk U, Ufa, 1964, vyp. 21, SFil N No. 9, pp. 243 - 249.

'690   - : *Sposoby vyraženija antonimičnosti glagol'nych frazeologičeskich edinic*, (The means of expressing antonymy in verbal phraseological units), MatTD, pp. 52 - 53.

'691 GURS'KYJ,S. O.   : *K voprosu o slovosočetanijach tipa stand up v sovremennom anglijskom jazyke* (On word-combinations of the *stand up* type in modern English), Sbornik rabot aspirantov kafedr filologičeskich nauk (L'vovskij Universitet), 1960, pp. 139 - 148. (In Ukrainian)

'692   - : *O tak nazyvaemych "slitnych" glagolach v sovremennom anglijskom jazyke* (On the so-called " merged" verbs in modern English), Sbornik rabot aspirantov kafedr filologičeskich nauk (L'vovskij Universitet), 1960, pp. 149 - 161. (In Ukrainian)

'693   - : *Glagol'no - narečnye sočetanija v sovremennom jazyke* (The verb-adverb combinations in modern English), Ak. Diss. L'vov, 1962.

'694 HAMMARBERG, V.   : *The Particle up as Used in Transferred Senses with Verbs in Modern English*, (Published with) Inbjudning till öfvervarande af årsexamen vid Kararina all männa läroverk, Vårtarminen, 1905, Stockholm : Haegg ström, 1905, 1 - 32 p..

'695 HARRIS, B.   : *Towards Recognizing English Phrasal Verbs for Machin Translation*, Cetadol. Rech. Trad. Automatique 6, 196 pp. 48 - 74, BBG. (9).

696 HARRISON, Th. P.   : *The Separable Prefixes in Anglo-Saxon*, Diss. The Johns Hopkins University, Baltimore : John Murphy & Co., 1892, 59 p., vita.

'697 HEATON, J. B.   : *Prepositions and Adverbial Particles*, London : Longmans, 1965, vii, 160 p..
Reviews :
Anon.   : ELT 23, 1968/69, 90 - 91

698 HENDRICKSON, J. R.   : *Old English Prepositional Compounds in Relationship to Their Latin Originals*, University of Pennsylvania Diss., Language Diss. No. 43 (Supplement to Language Vol. 24, No. 4), 1948, 73 p..

699 HILL, L. A.   : *Prepositions and Adverbial Particles, an Interim Classification, Semantic, Structural, and Graded*, London : Oxford University Press, 1968, xxvi, 403 p.

'133 HUECKEL, W.   : *Einige Fragen des Wortverbandes im Englischen*.

700 JOWETT, W. P.   : *On Phrasal Verbs*, ELT 5, 1950/1951, pp. 152 - 157.

701 KENNEDY, A. G.   : *The Modern English Verb-Adverb Combination*, Stanford University Publications University Series, Language and Literature, Vol. 1, No. 1, Stanford University, California, published by the University, 1920, 51 p..
(Reprinted 1967 by arrangement with Stanford University Press)
Reviews :
B(right), J. W.   : ' Brief Mention', MLN 36, 1921, 252 - 256

'702 KERLIN, A. A. - KUZNEC, M. D. : *Sostavnye glagoly v sovremennom anglijs-kom jazyke* (Composite verbs in modern English), 2nd ed. abridged, Moscow (Učpedgiz), 1959, 88 p.. (1rst ed. 1956)

703 KIFFER, Th. E.   : *A Diachronic and Synchronic Analysis and Description of English Phrasal Verbs*, Ph. D. Diss. The Pennsylvania State University, 1965, 152 p.. (DAb 26,8, 1966, 4632 - 4633)

704 KONOSHI, T.   : *The Growth of the Verb-Adverb Combination in English - a Brief Sketch*, in Studies in English Grammar and Linguistics. A Miscellany in Honour of Takanobu Otsuka, ed. by K. Araki, T. Egawa, T. Oyama, M. Yasui, Tokyo : Kenkyusha Ltd., 1958, x, 419 p.; pp. 117 - 128.

'705 KRASIL'NIKOVA, O. S. : *K voprosu razvitija glagol'nonarečnych slovosočetanij v anglijskom jazyke (Issledovanie na materiale pamjatnikov sredne - anglijskogo perioda XII - XIV vekov)* (On the development of the verb-adverb combinations in English (On the material of ME. documents of the XII - XIV centuries)), UZ Gork Ped I, 1958, vyp. 4, pp. 155 - 184.

'706   - : *K voprosu o leksičeskich značenijach narečij, vystupajuščich v roli vtorych komponentov glagol'no - narečnych ustojčivych slovosočetanij v sovremennom anglijskom jazyke* (On the lexical meaning of the adverbs as second components in fixed verb-adverb combinations in modern English), UZ Gork Ped I, 1959, vyp. 14, FAJa, pp. 45 - 75.

'707 LEGUM, S. E.   : *The Verb-Particle Construction in English, Basic or Derived?* in Papers from the Fourth Regional Meeting, Chicago Linguistic Society, April 19-20, 1968, ed. by B. J. Darden, Ch.-J. N. Bailey & A. Davison, Chicago, Ill., University of Chicago, Department of Linguistics, 1968, (iv), 254 p.; pp. 50 - 62.

708 LIPKA, L.   : *Ein Grenzgebiet zwischen Wortbildung und Wortseman-*
                       tik : die Partikelverben im Deutschen und Englischen,
                       in Interlinguistica, Sprachvergleich und Übersetzung,
                       Festschrift zum 60. Geburtstag von Mario Wandruszka,
                       ed. by Karl-Richard Bausch and Hans-Martin Gauger,
                       Tübingen : Max Niemeyer, 1971, pp. 180 - 189.

709   - : *Semantic Structure and Word-Formation. The Verb-Par-*
                      ticle Construction in Contemporary English, München :
                      W. Fink Verlag, (= Internationale Bibliothek für All-
                      gemeine Linguistik/ International Library of General
                      Linguistics, ed. by E. Coseriu, Vol. 17), 1972, 251 p.
                      (A Tübingen Habilitationsschrift 1971)

710 LIVE, A. H.   : *The Discontinuous Verb in English,* Word 21, 1965,
                       pp. 428 - 451.

'711 MAKEENKO, V. N. : *Sočetanija glagolov s predložnymi narečiyami v sovre-*
                       mennom anglijskom jazyke (Combinations of verbs with
                       prepositional adverbs in modern English), Diss. Mos-
                       kva, 1951, 99 p..

'712   - : *K voprosu o sočetanijach glagolov s predlogami i nare-*
                      čijami v sovremennom anglijskom jazyke (On the pro-
                      blem of verb-preposition and verb-adverb combinations
                      in modern English), Voen I, Trudy...N. n.s. 9, 1955,
                      pp. 68 - 82.

'713 MALIŠEVSKAJA, E. V. : *K voprosu o glagolach tipa give up v jazyke tech-*
                       ničeskoj literatury (On verbs of the type *give up*
                       in the language of technical literature), LIAv P,
                       1960, vyp. 32, Vtoroj Sb. statej KIJa (kafedra ino-
                       strannych jazykov), pp. 17 - 25.

'714 MAMONOVA, S. E. : *Predlogi v anglijskom jazyke (Spravočnik)* (Refer-
                       ence book on the use of prepositions in English),
                       Moscow, 1940, 144 p..
                       (Part III : Short list of commonly used verb-ad-
                       verb combinations)

715 MECHNER, M.   : *Some Problems of Collocations of Verb and Particle in the Teaching of English as a Foreign Language,* MA London, 1956, (5), 222 lvs., App. 216 lvs., tabl..

'716 MEYER, H. J.   : *Semantische Analyse der modern englischen Verbalpartikel up im Vergleich zu verwandten englischen und deutschen Verbalpartikeln,* Diss. Berlin, Humboldt Univ., 21.12.1970, Berlin, 1970, 182 lvs.n., lvs.n. 183 - 391.
(DNB C 1971, 9; p. 20, 215)

717   : *Die Richtungsvarianten von up im Kontext mit Verben,* ZAA 19, 1971, pp. 387 - 408.

718 MITCHELL, T. F.   : *Syntagmatic Relations in Linguistic Analysis,* Transactions of the Phil. Society 1958, pp. 101 - 118.
(esp. pp. 103 - 106)

719   - : *Some English Phrasal Types,* in In Memory of J. R. Firth, ed. by C. E. Bazell, J. C. Catford, M. A. K. Halliday and R. H. Robins, London, 1966, pp. 335 - 358.

720 MÜLLER-SCHOTTE, H. : *Pleonastische Verberweiterungen im Englischen,* NS, N. F., 4, 1955, pp. 363 - 367.

721 PALMER, F. R.   : *A Linguistic Study of the English Verb,* London : Longmans, 1965, xi, 199 p..
(esp. pp. 180 - 191 : Phrasal verbs and prepositional verbs)

'722 PEPRNÍK, J.   : *Problematika složných sloves* (Problems of the compound verbs), Sbornik Vysoké školy pedagogické v Olomonci, jazyk a literatura 2, 1955, pp. 207 - 222.

723 POTTER, R.   : *Prepositions Which Are Really Part of the Verb,* Praxis 11, 1964, pp. 331 - 333.

262 POTTER, S.   : *Changes in Present-Day English.*

148

724   - : *English Phrasal Verbs*, PhP 8, 1965, pp. 285 - 289.

725 SHUMAN, R. B.   : *To 'daughter out' and to ' sheriff-out', Two New Coinages*, AS 36, 1961, pp. 80.

'726 SOSNOVSKAJA, V. B.   : *Tipy glagol'no-narečnych sočetanij i ich zavisimost' ot leksičeskogo značenija glagola* (The types of verb-adverb combinations and their dependency on the lexical meaning of the verb), Trudy Samarkandskij gosudarstvennyj universitet im. A. Navoi, Samarkand, 1961, n.s. vyp. 106, pp. 193 - 200.

'727   - : *O metodike identifikacija glagol'no-narečnych sočetanij v sovremennom anglijskom jazyke* (On the method to identify verb-adverb combinations in modern English), Materialy naučno-metodičeskoj konferencii prepodavatelej inostrannych jazykov vuzov kazachskoj SSR, Alma-Ata, 1962, pp. 68 - 88.

'728 SPASOV, D.   : *English Phrasal Verbs*, Sofia, 1966.

'729 SROKA, K.   : *English Phrasal Verbs*, The Hague, 1972 (= Janua linguarum ser. practica 129).

'730 STAUBACH, Ch. N.   : *Two Word Verbs. A Study in Idiomatic English*, Bogotá : Publicacioñ del Centro Colombo-Americano, 1945.

'731 STEPANOVA, T. N.   : *Sintaksičeskie funkcii priglagol'nych predloznych konstrucij v sovremennom anglijskom jazyke* (Syntactical functions of preposition groups refering to the verb in modern English), 1 - M Ped I, 1955, 174 p..

732 STUCKERT, K.   : *Untersuchungen über das Verhältnis von Präfix und postverbaler Partikel bei lateinischen Lehnverben im Englischen, dargestellt an den Gruppen der ad- und dis- Komposita*, Diss. Zürich (Philos. Fak. I)

Zürich : Juris Druck + Verlag, 1968, 185 p., vita.
Reviews :
Hansen, K.   : ZAA 18, 1970, 325 - 326
Lipka, L.   : Anglia 88, 1970, 352 - 354

'733 TAHA, A. K.   : *The Structure of Two-Word Verbs in English*, Ph.D. Diss. The University of Texas, 1958, 166 p..
(DAb 19, 10, 1959, 2609)

734   - : *The Structure of Two-Word Verbs in English*, LL 10, 1960, pp. 115 - 122.

735   - : *The Structure of Two-Word Verbs in English*, in Readings in Applied English Linguistics, ed. by H. B. Allen, New York : Appleton - Century Crofts, 1964, xii, 535 p., pp. 130 - 136.
(first edition 1958)

'736 THOMAS, W.   : *Etude sommaire des verbes composés anglais* , Revue de l'Enseignement des Langues Vivantes 10, 1893/94, pp. 482 - 486, 516 - 520.

737 TRAGER, E. C.   : *Superfix and Sememe. English Verbal Compounds*, GL 2,1, 1956, pp. 1 - 14.

'738 VESELITSKIJ, V. V. : *Opyt sopostavitel'nogo izučenija slovosočetanij* (Essai d'étude comparée de syntagmes. Examples : *stand up - aufstehen*, LSb 6, 1963, pp. 126 - 130.

'739 WENDE, F.   : *Über die nachgestellten Präpositionen im Angelsächsischen. Einleitung und Abschnitt 1 und 2 des 1. Hauptteils*, Diss. Berlin 5.8.1914, Berlin : Mayer & Müller, 1914, xiv, 63 p..
(Germany 30, p. 527)
(Complete ed. Berlin : Mayer & Müller, 1915, xviii, 294 p. (= Palaestra 70).

'740 WILLIS, C. A.   : *Prepositional Verbs*, The English Journal 16, 1927, pp. 543 - 545.

741 WOOD, F. T.   : *Verb-Adverb Combinations : The Position of the Adverb*, ELT 10, 1955/56, pp. 18 - 27.

742   - : *English Verbal Idioms*, London : MacMillan, 1964, vi, 325 p..
Reviews :
Anon.   : ELT 20, 1965/66, 91 - 92

'743 ZAJCEVA, L. P.   : *Glagol'no-narečnoe zameščenie v anglijskom jazyke* (The verb-adverb substitution in English), VObsc vyp. 3, pp. 23 - 24.

'744 ZAMUDIO, M.   : *A Study of Spanish Equivalents of English Phrasal Verbs*, Diss. Edinburgh 1960/1961.

'745 ZANDVOORT, R. W.   : *Varia Syntactica*, RLaV 35, 1969, pp. 473 - 510.
(4. Hyphened verb-adverb combinations)
(Another reference gives : *Varia Syntactica:*
III : On Hyphened Verb-Adverb Combinations, in Language and Society : Essays presented to Arthur M. Jensen on his Seventieth Birthday, Copenhague, 1961 pp. 200 - 202)

'746 ZIL'BERMAN, L. I.   : *Kategorija predel'nosti i semantika narečnych častic v glagol'nych obrazovanijach tipa to go out v sovremennom anglijskom jazyke* (The category of terminativeness and the semantics of verbal particles in verbal formations of the type *to go out* in modern English), Diss. Moskva, Institut jazykoznanija Moskva Akademija Nauk SSSR, 1956, 229 p

'747   - : *Semantika narečnoi casticy up v sostava glagol'nych obrazovanij tipa to stand up* (The semantics of the adverbial particle *up* in the structure of verbal formations of the *stand up* type), RGFil, Sbornik statei. Vyp. 2, 1958, pp. 110 - 131.

'748 ŽLUKTENKO, Ju. A.   : *O tak nazyvaemych " složnychglagolach" tipa stand up v sovremennom anglijskom jazyke* (Concerning

the so-called " composite verbs" of the *stand up*
type in modern English), VJa N. 1954, 5, pp. 105 -
113.
(German translation by G. Riegel, ed. by H.-H. Biel-
feldt : *Über die sogenannten " zusammengesetzten Verben" vom Typ* stand up *in der englischen Sprache der
Gegenwart*, Sowjetwissenschaft 8, 1955, pp. 223 - 235)

'749   - : *Postpozitivnye glagol'nye pristavki v sovremennom anglijskom jazyke* (Postpositive verbal prefixes in contemporary English), 1 - M Ped I, 1955, 327 p.. (Diss.)

'750   - : *Stepen' podvižnosti vtorogo komponenta anglijskich
glagol'nych edinic tipa* stand up (The degree of mo-
vability of the second component of English verbal
units of the *stand up* type), Kievskij finansovo-zkonomičeskij institut. Naučnye zapiski No. 10, 1958,
pp. 113 - 125.

'751   - : *Vzaimosvjazi sovremennych anglijskich postpozitivnych
pristavok (* " *poslelogov")* s narečijami i predlogami
(The interrelations of modern English postpositive
prefixes (" postpositions" with adverbs and prepositions), Kievskij finansovo-zkonomičeskij Institut
Naučnye zapiski No. 10, 1958, pp. 127 - 140.

III. GENERAL STUDIES ON DERIVATION IN ENGLISH
   (Affixation, prefixation and suffixation,...)

752 Anon.   : *Prefixes, Postfixes, and Principal Latin and Greek
                              Roots of the English Language for the Use of Schools
                              in the Madras Presidency*, Madras : The Tract and
                              Book Society : American Mission Press, 1849, iv,
                              pp. 277 - 351.

753 Anon.   : *Rules for Spelling, and Derivations from Latin and
                              Greek Roots*, London : The National Society's Depo-
                              sitory, Sanctuary Westminster, 48 p..
                              (esp. pp. 6 - 13)

'754 Anon.   : *Words Derived from Proper Names*, Word Study 16, 1,
                              October 1940, p. 6.

'755 A LITERARY ASSOCIATION : *A Hand-Book of Anglo-Saxon Derivatives*, in two
                              parts; Boston : F. Parker; New York : A. Montgo-
                              mery, 1853, x, 134 p..

756   - : *A Handbook of the Engrafted Words of the English
                              Language, Embracing the Choice Gothic, Celtic,
                              French, Latin, and Greek Words on the Basis of the
                              Hand-Book of the Anglo-Saxon Root-Words*, in three
                              parts; New York : D. Appleton and Company; London :
                              16 Little Britain, 1854, xiv, 355 p..

757   - : *A Hand-Book of Anglo-Saxon Derivatives, on the Ba-
                              sis of the Hand-Book of Anglo-Saxon Root-Words*, in
                              three parts; New York : D. Appleton & Company ,
                              1855, xv, 285 p..
                              (Earlier edition 1854)

7 ANDREWS, E.   : *A History of Scientific English. The Story of its
                              Evolution Based on a Study of Biomedical Termino-
                              logy. With a Foreword by A. B. Luckhardt.*

758 AYERS, D. M.   : *English Words from Latin and Greek Elements*, Tuc-
son : University of Arizona Press, 1965, xiii,
271 p..

'759 BENDER, T. K.   : *Some Derivative Elements in the Poetry of Gerard
Manley Hopkins*, Ph.D. Diss. Stanford, 1962

760 BERGMANN, K.   : *Die gegenseitigen Beziehungen der deutschen, englischen und französischen Sprache auf lexikologischem
Gebiete*, Dresden und Leipzig : C. A. Kochs Verlagsbuchhandlung (II. Ehlers), 1912, xi, (1), 151 p..
(= Neusprachliche Abhandlungen aus den Gebieten
der Phraseologie, Realien, Stilistik und Synonymik
unter Berücksichtigung der Etymologie, ed. by Professor Dr. Clemens Klöpper, Vol. 18)
(esp. pp. 79 - 81)

761 BEYER, E.   : *Gestaltende Kräfte bei den Wortbildungen des amerikanischen Sportslang*,Die lebenden Fremdsprachen
3, 1951, pp. 205 - 208.
(Blends, -ster, -ee, -eer, -ite, -itis)

762 BLACKLEY, W. L.   : *Minute English Etymology*, Contemporary Review 5,
1867, pp. 284 - 303.
(Refers to S. S. HALDEMAN : *Affixes in their Origin and Application...*, see No. 797)

763 BLOOMFIELD, L.   : *The Structure of Learned Words* (A Commemorative
Volume 1933), in The English Language, Vol. 2,
Essays by Linguists and Men of Letters 1858 - 1964,
selected and edited by W.F. Bolton and D. Crystal,
Cambridge : University Press, 1969, xiii, 325 p.;
pp. 157 - 162.

'764 BROWN, R. W.   : *Materials for Word Study; a Manual of Roots, Prefixes, Suffixes and Derivatives in the English Lan-
guage*, New Haven, Conn.; :van Dyck & Co.; 1927,
234 p..

— : *Composition of Scientific Words: A Manual of Methods and a Lexicon of Materials for the Practice of Logotechnics*, Washington : The Author, 1954, 882 p.. (Rev. ed. of 764)

766 BROWN, T. R. : *A Treatise on the English Terminations of Words; with a List of the Most Common Prefixes, and their Usual Significations: to which is Appended a Practical Vocabulary*, Oundle : Richard Toold; London : Simpkin, Marshall & Co.; Cambridge : Stevenson, 1838, 25 p..

'767 BUCHBERGER, R. : *Die polare Ausdrucksweise im Englischen*, Diss. Vienn. 1951, 122 lvs.. (Vienna 1950 - 1957, p. 67, 1329)

768 BURNHAM, J. M. : *An Imported Fashion*, AS 30, 1955, pp. 222 - 223.

769 CHAPIN, P. G. : *On Affixation in English*, in Progress in Linguistics A Collection of Papers Selected and Edited by Manfred Bierwisch and Karl Erich Heidolph, The Hague - Paris : Mouton, 1970, 344 p.; pp. 51 - 63.

770 CHARNOCK, R. S. : *Verba nominalia; or, Words Derived from Proper Names*, London : Trübner & Co., 1861, iv, 357 p..

'771 CHASKINA, E. M. : *Produktivnye sposoby slovoobrazovanija v sovremennom anglijskom jazyke (Suffiksacija i prefiksacija)*, IJaŠ 1953, 6, pp. 20 - 29.

'433 CHIDEKEL, S. S. : *O složnoprojizvodnych slovach v sovremennom anglijskom jazyke* (Compound derivatives in present-day English).

772 CHOMSKY, N. : *Remarks on Nominalization*, in Readings in English Transformational Grammar, ed. by R. A. Jacobs and P. S. Rosenbaum, Waltham, Mass. : Ginn and Co., 1970, x, 277.; pp. 184 - 221. (also in N. CHOMSKY : *Studies on Semantics in Generative Grammar*, The Hague - Paris : Mouton, 1972, 207 p.; pp. 11 - 61)

'773 COATES, R. M.   : *Effable, Scrutable English*, New Yorker 13, No. 31, September 18, 1937, pp. 22 - 23.
(Anomalities in the use of prefixes and suffixes in English)

'774 CURL, Th. D.   : *Word Building Through the Use of Greek and Latin Roots and Affixes*, Ph.D. Diss. Columbia University 1963.
(DAb 27, 3, 1966/67, 743 A)

'775 DANIELSSON, B.   : *Native, Classical, or Romance Etymology and Accentuation in English*, SMSpr 17, 1949, pp. 30 - 38.

776 DAVIES, W. R.   : refers to McGovern
N & Q, s. 12, 9, 1921, pp. 432 - 433.

777 DIKE, E. B.   : *Obsolete Words*, PhQ 12, 1933, pp. 207 - 219.
(Obsolete Words and Affixes : -aster, - logue, -ess, -age, -ment, - ate)

778 EARL, L. L.   : *Structural Definition of Affixes in Multisyllable Words*, Mechanical Translation 9, June 1966, pp.34 - 37.

779   - : *Part-of-Speech Implications of Affixes*, Mechanical Translation 9, June 1966, pp. 38 - 43.

780   - : *Automatic Determination of Parts of Speech of English Words*, Mechanical Translation 10, 1967, pp. 53 - 67.

781 EARLE, J.   : *An Unnamed Habit of Language*, Macmillan's Magazine 31, 1874, pp. 47 - 56.
(Reprinted in Living Age 123, pp. 600 - 608)
(On cumulation or the use of double derivative or inflectional endings)

782 FALTENBACHER, H.   : *Die romanischen, speciell französischen und lateinischen (bezw. latinisierten) Lehnwörter bei Caxton (1422 ? - 1491)*, Diss. München 23.7.1906, München : Mössl, 1907, (8), 224 p..
(Germany 22, p. 517, 156)

'783 FARGO, N. : *Some English Affix Classes*, Ph.D. Diss. Georgetown University, 1964.

784 FISCHER, E. L. : *Verba nominalia*, ESt 23, 1897, pp. 70 - 73.

785 FISIAK, J. : *Morphemic Structure of Chaucer's English*, Alabama: Alabama University Press, 1965, 125 p..
(= Alabama Linguistic and Philological Series 10)
(esp. pp. 57 - 73)

786 FLOOD, W. E. : *Scientific Words. Their Structure and Meaning. An Explanatory Glossary of About 1.150 Word Elements (Roots, Prefixes, Suffixes) which Enter into the Formation of Scientific Words*, London : Oldbourne, 1960, xviii, 220 p..

'787 FRANCK, Th. : *Wörter für Satzinhalte. Zur inhaltlichen Leistung abstrakter Wortstände im Deutschen und Englischen*, Diss. Bonn 30.7.1958; (1958), (3), 285 lvs.n..
(Germany 74, p. 98)

'788 FRANK, A. : *Das Kausativum bei Shakespeare*, Diss. Marburg 21. 4.1925, xiii, 215 p..
(Germany 41, p. 627)

789 FRIEDRICH, W. : *Spelling Rules*, ELT 17, 1962/63, pp. 20 - 26.

790 FUNKE, O. : *Die gelehrten lateinischen Lehn- und Fremdwörter in der altenglischen Literatur von der Mitte des X. Jahrhunderts bis um das Jahr 1066. Nebst einer einleitenden Abhandlung über die " Quaestiones Gram maticales" des Abbo Floriacensis*, Halle a. S. : M. Niemeyer, 1914, xviii, 209 p..
(esp. pp. 130 - 131)

791 GIBSON, T. A. : *Etymological Geography; Being a Classified List of Terms of Most Frequent Occurrence, Entering, as Prefixes or Postfixes, into the Composition of Geographical Names, Intended for the Use of Teachers*

and Advanced Students of Geography, and as a Reference-
Book in Geographical Etymologies, Edinburgh : Oliver
& Boyd, Stirling & Kennedy; and Alexander Macredie;
London : Simpkin, Marshall & Co.; Whitaker & Co.; Du-
blin : J. Cumming, 1835, viii, 76 p..

792 GIVON, T. : *Transformations of Ellipsis, Sense Development and
Rules of Lexical Derivation*, System Development Cor-
poration, SP 2896, 22 July, 1967, Santa Monica, Calif..

793 GRUMMEL, W. C. : *English Word Building from Latin and Greek*, Palo Alto:
Pacific Books, 1961.

794 GRZEBIENIOWSKI, T. : *Słownictwo angielskie od imion własnych* (English
words derived from proper names), Sprawozdania z
czynnosai i posiedzeń Łódzkiego Towarzystwa Naukowe-
go 16, 1961, No. 2, pp. 1 - 14.

795 GUILLEMARD, F. H. H. : *Verbalized Surnames*, N & Q s. 12, Vol. 9, 1921,
pp. 474.

796 GUNTER, R. : *English Derivation*, JL 8, 1, 1972, pp. 1 - 19.

797 HALDEMAN, S. S. : *Affixes in their Origin and Application, Exhibiting
the Etymologic Structure of English Words*, Philadel-
phia : E. H. Butler & Co., 1865, 271 p..
Reviews :
Anon.   : The Nation (N. Y.), 1, 1865, 283 - 284
Haldeman, S. S. : The Nation (N. Y.)1, 1865, 332 -
                    333
(Rev. ed. : 1871, 292 p.)
Reviews :
'Stowne, W. H. : Southern Magazine 8, 501 - 504
(See also No. 762)

798 HARRISON, H. G. : *(Verbalized Surnames)* refers to McGovern, N & Q ,
s. 12, Vol. 9, 1921, p. 432.

799 HENISZ, B. : *Derivation, Morphophonemic Alternation Patterns,
Generative Formation Rules and System for Computer*

Processing, Ph. D. Diss. Georgetown University 1965, 310 p..
(DAb 28,2, 1967, 653 A)

'800 HEROLD, C. P. : *The Morphology of King Alfred's Translation of the Orosius*, Ph.D. Diss. Indiana University, 1961, 170 p.
(DAb 22,9, 1962, 3196)

801 HIETSCH, O. : *Moderne englische Wortbildungslemente*, in Anglistische Studien, Festschrift zum 70. Geburtstag von Professor Frederick Wild, ed. by Dr. Karl Brunner, Dr. Herbert Koziol, Dr. Siegfried Korninger, Vienna IX - Stuttgart : Wilhelm Braumüller, 1958, (= Wiener Beiträge zur englischen Philologie 66), pp. 81 - 101.

'802 JACKL, E. : *Von lateinischen Partizipia perfecti abgeleitete Adjectiva, Substantiva und Verba im englischen Wortschatz*, Diss. Innsbruck 1952, 242 p..

803 JESPERSEN, O. : *Negation in English and Other Languages*, København : Bianco Lunos Bogtrykkeri, 1917, 151 p., (1) (= Det Kgl. Danske Videnskabernes Selskaab. Historisk - filologiske Meddelelser I, 5)
(2nd ed. 1966)

804 JONES, D. : *The Use of Syllabic and Non-Syllabic l and n in Derivatives of English Words Ending in Syllabic l and n*, ZPhon 12, 1959, pp. 136 - 144.

805 JOPP, G. : *Die Modifikation des Verbalbegriffes bei Galsworthy*, Diss. Marburg 16.4.1934, Marburg : Bauer, 1934, vi, 64 p., vita.
(Germany 50, p. 493)
(esp. pp. 3 - 12, 38 - 50)

806 JORDAN, R. : *Eigentümlichkeiten des anglischen Wortschatzes. Eine wortgeographische Untersuchung mit etymologischen Anmerkungen*, Heidelberg : Carl Winters Universitätsbuchhandlung, 1906, viii, 131 p.. (= Anglistische For-

schungen 17)
(esp. pp. 101)

'807 KARASČUK, P. M. : *Zakonomernosti upotreblenija otricatel'nych affik-
sov v sovremennom anglijskom jazyke* (Tendencies in
the use of negative affixes in present-day English),
UZ Dal U 4, 1962, pp. 101 - 113.

'808 - : *Affiksal'noe slovoobrazovanie v anglijskom jazyke*
(Word-formation by means of affixes in English),
Moskva, Vysšaja škola, 1965, 173 p..
(cf. Linguistics 30, 1967, pp. 110 - 111)

809 KILIAN, D. : *Homemade Words*, NS, N. S., 8, 1959, pp. 375 - 377.
(-ness, -able, -ability, -er, -ify, -manship,-acy,
-ama)

810 KIRCHNER, G. : *Die zehn Hauptverben des Englischen im Britischen
und Amerikanischen. Eine semasiologisch-syntakti-
sche Darstellung ihrer gegenwärtigen Funktionen mit
sprachgeschichtlichen Rückblicken*, Halle : M. Niemeyer, 1952, xl, 607 p..

811 KOCH, Ch. F. : *Die vocalischen Ableitungen im Angelsächsischen
und deren Verlauf. Ein Beitrag zur englischen Wortbildungslehre*, Jahrbuch für rom. und engl. Literatur
8, 1867, pp. 217 - 227.

812 KOZIOL, H. : *Zu englischen Präfix- und Suffixbildungen*, in Studien zur Sprachwissenschaft und Kulturkunde, Gedenkschrift für Wilhelm Brandenstein (1898 - 1967)
eb. by Manfred Mayrhofer in collaboration with F.
Lochner - Hüttenbach and Hans Schmeja, Innsbruck :
Amoe, 1968, 411 p. (= Innsbrucker Beiträge zur Kul-
turwissenschaft 14), pp. 69 - 76.

813 LANGENFELT, G. : *Toponymics or Derivations from Local Names in English. Studies in Word-Formation and Contributions*

to *English Lexicography*, Diss. Uppsala, Uppsala :
Appelbergs Boktryckeri Aktiebolag, 1920, xvi, 252 p..
Reviews :

Fischer, W.   : ESt 56, 1922, 408 - 410
'Hoops, J.   : Wissenschaftliche Forschungsberichte
                    9, 1923, 47 - 49
Hübener, G.   : Anglia B 32, 1921, 5 - 8
Mawer, A.   : MLR 16, 1921, 370

814 LEITNER, G.   : *Argumente für eine morphologische Ebene in einem TG-
                       Modell*, in Linguistik 1971, Referate des 6. Lingui-
                       stischen Kolloquiums 11. - 14. August 1971 in Kopen-
                       hagen, ed. by Karl Hyldgaard - Jensen, Frankfurt :
                       Athenäum-Verlag, 1972, (6), 379 p.; pp. 236 - 251.
                       (= Athenäum-Skripten, Linguistik 1)

815 M., G. M.   : *(Verbalized Surnames)* refers to McGovern, N & Q ,
                       s. 12, Vol. 9, 1921, p. 432.

816 McGOVERN, J. B. : *Verbalized Surnames*, N & Q, s.12, Vol. 9, 1921, pp.
                       370.
                       (to macadamize, to mercerize ...)

817 MARCHAND, H.   : *Über zwei Prinzipien der Wortableitung in ihrer An-
                       wendung auf das Französische und Englische*, ASNS 190,
                       1954, pp. 217 - 221.

580   - : *The Analysis of Verbal Nexus Substantives.*

818 MAUTNER, F. H.   : *Word-Formation by Shortening and Affixation : The
                       ' Sudetens' and the ' Yugos'*, AS 18, 1943, pp. 200
                       - 207.

819 METZGER, E.   : *Zur Betonung der lateinisch-romanischen Wörter im
                       Neuenglischen mit besonderer Berücksichtigung der
                       Zeit von c. 1560 bis c. 1660*, Diss. Tübingen 5.11.
                       1908, Heidelberg : Carl Winters Universitätsbuch-
                       handlung 1908, 96 p., vita.
                       (Germany 24, p. 656)

820 MEYNELL, A. : *An Article on Particles*, Living Age 303, 1919,
pp. 787 - 788.
(Reprint from The London Mercury)
(Chiefly about the affixes un- and -less)

821 MONROE, G. K. jr. : *Phonemic Transcription of Graphic Post-Base Affixes in English : A Computer Problem*, Ph.D. Diss.
Brown University, 1965, 235 p..
(DAb 26, 8, 1966, 4648 - 4649; cf. Linguistics
40, 1968, pp. 160 - 162)

822 MOTHERWELL, G. McCORMICK : *Old English Morphemic Structure : A Grammatical Restatement*, Ph.D. Diss. Indiana University,
1959.
(DAb 20, 1959, 1359)

823 NEUHAUS, H. J. : *Semantische und phonologische Beschränkungen in
der Grammatik der Wortableitungen*, in Beiträge zur
generativen Grammatik, ed. by Arnim v. Stechow,
Braunschweig : Vieweg, 1971, pp. 178 - 183.

824 - : *Beschränkungen in der Grammatik der Wortableitungen im Englischen*, Diss. Saarbrücken, Saarbrücken,
1971, vii, 227 p., 15 p. appendix).

825 - : *Beschränkungen in der Grammatik der Wortableitungen
im Englischen (Constraints in the Grammar of Word-
Derivations in English)*, Diss. Saarbrücken, 1971,
210 p. (Appendices), in English and American Studies in German, Summaries of Theses and Monographs.
A Supplement to Anglia 1971, Tübingen : Max Niemeyer,
ix, (1), 190 p.; pp. 30 - 31.

826 NIDA, E. : *Morphology, the Descriptive Analysis of Words*, 2nd
and completely new ed., Ann Arbor : University of
Michigan Press, 1949, 342 p..

827 NORMAN, F. B. : *English Synonyms with Etymologies and Examples and
an Appendix Containing an Alphabetical List of Pre-*

fixes and Affixes, 2nd ed., Vienna : Lechmer, 1889, vii, 126 p..

'828 PERL, E.   : *Die Bezeichnung der kausativen Funktion im Neuenglischen*, Diss. Breslau 8.7.1931, Breslau : Priebatsch, (1931), vii, 155 p..
(= Sprache und Kultur der germ.-rom. Völker, Anglistische Reihe 9)
(Germany 48, p. 137)

829 PIERCE, J. E.   : *The Morphemes of English : Major Morpheme Stem Classes*, Linguistics 36, 1967, pp. 29 - 51.

830   - : *The Morphemes of English : Theme Formers*, Linguistics 45, 1968, pp. 50 - 61.

831   - : *The Morphemes of English : Structural Outline*, Linguistics 64, 1970, pp. 50 - 59.

832 PILCH, H.   : *Nebenakzent und Wortableitung im Englischen*, in Phonologie der Gegenwart, Vorträge und Diskussionen anlässlich der Internationalen Phonologie-Tagung in Wien 30.8. - 3.9.1966, ed. by Josef Hamm with the assistance of Otto Back and Gebhard Neweklowsky , Graz - Vienna - Köln : Hermann Böhlaus Nachf., 1967, 391 p., (1), pp. 46 - 58.
(= Wiener Slavistisches Jahrbuch, Ergänzungsband 6)
Reviews :
Most, P. : Germanistik 9, 1968, 676 - 677

'833 PITTMAN, R.   : *Notes on Linguistic Analysis*, University of North Dakota, Summer Institute of Linguistics, 1963, 72 p. (esp. pp. 22 - 27)

834 PLATE, R.   : *Englische Wortkunde auf sprach- und kulturgeschichtlicher Grundlage. Ein Hilfsbuch für Studium und Unterricht*, München : Max Hueber Verlag, 1934, 137 p.. (2nd ed. 1957, viii, 115 p.)

262 POTTER, S.   : *Changes in Present-Day English*.

835 POUND, L.   : *Vogue Affixes in Present-Day Word-Coinage*, Dialect
Notes 5, 1, 1918, pp. 1 - 14.

836 PRICE, H. T.   : *A History of Ablaut in Class 1 of the Strong Verbs
from Caxton to the End of the Elizabethan Period*,
Diss. Bonn 23.2.1910, Halle : Karras, 1910, xv, 36 p..
(Germany 25, p. 68)
(Complete ed. under the title : *A History of Ablaut
in the Strong Verbs from Caxton to the End of the Eli-
zabethan Period*, Bonn : P. Hanstein, 1910, xvi, 200 p.
(= Bonner Studien zur engl. Philologie 3).
Reviews :
Gadow, W.   : ASNS 129, 1912, 249 - 251
Mařik, J.   : ESt 44, 1911/12, 97 - 101

837 RESNIKOFF, H. L. - DOLBY, J. L. : *The Nature of Affixing in Written English*, Mechanical Translation 8, 1965, pp. 84 - 89,
4 tab.; 9, 1966, pp. 23 - 33, 5 tab..

838 REVARD, C.   : *Affixal Derivation, Zero Derivation and " Semantic
Transformations"*, in Linguistic Society of America,
42nd Annual Meeting, December 28 - 30, 1967, Chicago.
Meeting Handbook, published by the C. A. L. Washing-
ton D.C., 1967, p. 52.
(Abstract of the Communication LLBA 2, 1968, 392)

278 RITCHIE, F.   : *Exercises in English Word-Formation and Derivation.*
(Derivation only)

339 ROCKINGHAM   : *Verbalized Surnames*, N & Q s.12, Vol. 10, 1922, p. 15.
(Refers to McGovern, Guillemard, Wood)

840 ROSE, J. H.   : *Relational Variation and Limited Productivity in
Some Indonesian and English Verbal Derivatives*, Ph.
D. Diss. University of Michigan, 1969, 108 p..

841 ŠACHOVA, N. I.   : *K voprosu o značenii proizvodnych slov v anglijskom
jazyke* (On the meaning of derivatives in English),
RGFil 3, 1961, pp. 148 - 182; 4, 1964, pp. 33 - 57.

284 SANNIKOV, N. G.   : *K voprosu o složnoproizvodnych slovach v anglijs-*
                           kom jazyke (On the question of derived compounds
                           in English).

842 SARGENT, E.   : *A School Manual of English Etymology, and Textbook*
                           of Derivations, Prefixes and Suffixes. With Numerou
                           Exercises for the Use of Schools, Philadelphia : J.
                           H. Butler & Co., (1873), 264 p. (The New America
                           Series).

'843 SCHAEFFER, R. F.   : *An English-Latin-Greek Derivative Lexicon*, Ph. D.
                           Diss. Columbia University, 1951, 842 p..
                           (DAb 11, 3, 1951, 672 - 674)

'844   - : *Latin-English Derivative Dictionary*, Oxford, Ohio,
                           1960, 48 p..
                           (= American Classical League. Pamphlet 62)
                           (A condensed and adapted version of the Latin-
                           English list in the author's doctoral diss.)

845 SCHÖNFELDER, K.-H.   : *Deutsche Wortbildungselemente im amerikanischen*
                           Englisch. Ein Beitrag zu Stalins Theorie über die
                           Sprachmischung, WZUL 5, 1951/52, pp. 8 - 18.

'846 SMOCK, J. C.   : *The Greek Element in English Words*, ed, by P. W.
                           Long
                           Reviews :
                           C., W. A.   : MPh 30, 1932/1933, 345 - 346

847 SPARKE, A.   : *(Verbalized Surnames)* refers to McGOVERN, N & Q,
                           s.12, Vol. 9, 1921, p. 432.

848 SWAN, W. D.   : *The Spelling-Book : Consisting of Words in Columns*
                           and Sentences for Oral and Written Exercises; To-
                           gether with Prefixes, Affixes, and Important Roots
                           from the Greek and Latin Languages, Philadelphia :
                           Thomas, Cowperthwait and Co., 1850, 148 p..
                           (also published in 1856)

'849 SWINTON, W. : *New Word-Analysis : or, School Etymology of English Derivative Words. With Practical Exercises in Spelling, Analyzing, Defining, Synonyms, and the Use of Words*, New York : American Book Company, c. 1879, 1907, 1921.

'850 SYKES, F. H. : *French Elements in Middle English. Chapters Illustrative of the Origin and Growth of Romance Influence on the Phrasal Power of Standard English in its Formative Period*, Oxford, 1899.

'851 TAULI, V. : *The Origin of Affixes*, FUF 32, 1956, pp. 170 - 225.

852 TCHEKHOFF, C. : *Les formations savantes gréco-latines en français, anglais, italien, espagnol, allemand et russe. Norme et déviations récentes*, Linguistique 7, 2, 1971, pp. 35 - 53 (to be continued).

853 THORNDIKE, E. L. : *Derivation Ratios*, Lg 19, 1943, pp. 27 - 37.

854 TOWN, S. : *An Analysis of the Derivative Words in the English Language; or, a Key to Their Precise Analytic Definitions, by Prefixes and Suffixes : Designed to Furnish an Easy and Expeditious Method of Acquiring a Knowledge of Their Component Parts*, 21rst ed., carefully rev., enlarged, and adapted to schools of all grades, Auburn: New York : H. & J. C. Ivison, Merrell & Hollett Printers, 1845, 164 p..
(1rst ed. 1835)

855 TRNKA, B. : *Principles of Morphological Analysis*, PhP 4, 1961, pp. 129 - 137.

856 VOL'FSON, I. I. : *Vtorostepennoe udarenie v prostych i proizvodnych slovach anglijskogo jazyka* (Secondary stress in simple and derived words in English), UZ Viln Ped I 1957, t. 3.

857 : *Slovesnoe udarenie v anglijskom jazyke. (Zakonomernosti raspredelenija udarenija v mnogoslożnych*

prostych i proizvodnych slovach) (Word stress in English. (The regularities of the distribution of accent in polysyllabic simple and derived words), Diss. Moscow, 1960.

858 WEHRLE, O.   : *Die hybriden Wortbildungen des Mittelenglischen (1050 - 1400). Ein Beitrag zur englischen Wortgeschichte,* Diss. Freiburg 1.5.1935, Freiburg : Weis, Mühlhans & Räpple, 1935, iii, 62 p..
(Germany 51, p. 421)

859 WESTERGAARD, E.   : *Studies in Prefixes and Suffixes in Middle Scottish,* Diss. Copenhague, 1924, Oxford University Press, 1924, xii, 135 p..
Reviews :
Anon.   : ASNS 148, 1925, 300
B., C.   : MLR 20, 1925, 497
G., J. H. G.   : RES 3, 1927, 119
Magoun, F. P. jr. : MLN 42, 1927, 196 - 197
Marik, J.   : Anglia B 37, 1926, 299 - 303

'860 WHEELER, G. C.   : *A Blast for Formicology (Comments and Communications,* Science 115, April 18, 1952, pp. 445 - 446.
(Hybrid derivatives)

861 WHITEBROOK, M.   : *(Verbalized Surnames)* refers to McGOVERN, N & Q, s. 12, Vol. 9, 1921, p. 432.

'862 WOLVERTON, R. E.   : *Classical Elements in English Words,* Totowa , N. Y.: Littlefield, Adams, 1965, vi, 85 p..

863 WOOD, F. L.   : *(Verbalized Surnames)* refers to McGOVERN, N & Q , s. 12, Vol. 9, 1921, p. 432.

368 YAMAGUCHI, H.   : *A Lexical Note on the Language of Sir Gawain and the Green Knight.*

864 ZIMMER, K. E.   : *Degrees of Productivity. Affixal Negation in English and Other Languages*, Ph.D. Diss. Columbia University, 1963, 152 p..

(DAb 24,7, 1964, 2902 - 2903)

A slightly revised version of the doctoral dissertation was published as

Affixal Negation in English and Other Languages : An Investigation of Restricted Productivity, Supplement to Word 20, 2, Monograph No. 5, New York : Linguistic Circle of New York, 1964, 105 p..

Reviews :

András, L. T.	: ALH 21, 1971, 241 - 243	
François, F.	: Linguistique 2,2, 1966, 147 - 151	
Marchand, H.	: Lg 42, 1966, 134 - 142	
Ney, J. W.	: LL 15, 1965, 95 - 99	
Price, G.	: ArchL 17, 1965, 38 - 40	

865   - : *Reply to Ney*, LL 15, 1965, pp. 100 - 101.

*866 ZVEREVA, E. A.   : *Razryv semantičeskoj svjazi meždu ischodnymii proizvodnymi slovami (suffiksal'noe obrazovanie)* (The rupture of the semantic tie between original words and their derivatives), RGFil 4, 1962, pp. 58 - 78.

ADDENDA :

757a ANNEAR, S. - ELLIOT, D. : *Derivational Morphology in Generative Grammar*, 1965.

A) PREFIXATION

(General studies, prefix groups ...)

867 BAREŠ, K.   : *Semantic Features of Quantitative Prefixes in Technical English*, PhP 12, 1969, pp. 152 - 158.

868 BECKER, D.   : *Shakespeares Präfixbildungen. Ein Beitrag zur Erforschung der sprachlichen Neubildungen Shakespeares*, Diss. Münster 8.5.1950; 1950, 144 lvs., vita. (Germany 66, p. 483)

869   - : *Shakespeares Englisch und seine Erforschbarkeit mit Hilfe des New English Dictionary*, Shakespeare-Jahrbuch 84-86, 1950, pp. 199 - 213. (A shortened and revised summary of the introduction of his dissertation)

870 COLLITZ, K. HECHTENBERG : *Accentuation of Prefixes in English*, ESt 43, 1910/11, pp. 252 - 260.

'871 DOLININA, I. G.   : *Leksiko-grammatičeskie funkcii glagol'nych pristavok anglijskogo jazyka* (The lexical-grammatical functions of the English verbal prefixes), Metodičeskij sbornik istoriko-filologičeskogo fakul'teta (Kabardino - Balkarskij Universitet), Nalčik, 1960 pp. 129 - 142.

'872 EGOROVA, G. A.   : *Die Rolle der Präfigierung als Möglichkeit der Wortbildung in der englischen Sprache im Lichte der historischen Entwicklung* (Russian diss. - Reference in German taken from ZAA 1, 1953, p. 246), Diss. Zdanow - Universitet Leningrad, Leningrad, 1951. (9th - 17th century)
Reviews :
'   : IJaŠ 4, 1952, 126

'873 FROLOVA, T. I.   : *Vlijanie romanskich jazykov na prefiksal'nuju sistemu anglijskogo jazyka* (Romance influence on the system of prefixes in English), VMU 16, 1961, No. 4, pp. 50 - 58.

'874   - : *Process vyčlenenija prefiksov romanskogo proischož-denija v anglijskom jazyke* (On prefixes of Romance origin in English), NDVS - F 6, 1963, No. 2, pp. 44 - 57, tab..

875 GIBBS, J. W.   : *English Prefixes Derived from the Greek,* The American Journal of Science and Arts, Second Series Vol. 6, 1848, pp. 206 - 209.

(amphi-, an-, ana-, anti-, apo-, cata-, dia-, dys-, ec-, en-, epi-, eu-, hama-, hyper-, hypo-, is- , meta-, para-, peri-, pro-, pros-, syn-)

696 HARRISON, Th. P.   : *The Separable Prefixes in Anglo-Saxon.*

876 HAYAKAWA, H.   : *Negation in William Faulkner,* in Studies in English Grammar and Linguistics. A Miscellany in Honour of Takanobu Otsuka, ed. by K. Araki, T. Egawa, T. Oyama, M. Yasui, Tokyo : Kenkyusha Ltd., 1958, x, 419 p.; pp. 103 - 116.

803 JESPERSEN, O.   : *Negation in English and Other Languages.*

877 MARCHAND, H.   : *Notes on English Prefixation,* NphM 55, 1954, pp. 294 - 304.

878   - : *The Negative Verbal Prefixes in English,* in Mélanges de linguistique et de philologie, Ferdinand Mossé in memoriam, Paris : Didier, 1959, 534 p.; pp. 267 - 276. (un-, dis-, de-)

879 PRINDLE, L. M.   : *Some Negative Prefixes in English,* The Classical Weekly 41, 1948, pp. 130 - 133.

880 SCHMIDT, K.   : *Präfixwandlungen im Mittelenglischen und Neuengli-schen bei Verben, Substantiven und Adjektiven,* Diss. Strassburg 27.2.1909, Sobernheim : G. Höhnen'sche

Buchdruckerei, 1909, x, 70 p., vita.
(Germany 24, p. 639)

881 SEALE, L. L.   : *The Rise and Decline of Negative Doublets in English*,
                          AS 35, 1960, pp. 206 - 209.
                          (un- / in-)

'882 ŠKARUPIN, V. I.   : *O specifike prefiksacii v anglijskom jazyke* (On
                          special prefixation in English), Probl Morf pp. 146
                          - 154.

'883 ZJATKOVSKAJA, R. G. : *Slovoobrazovatel'naja funkcija iskonno-anglijskich*
                          prefiksov v tečenie X - XV st (The word-forming funç
                          tion of OE. prefixes : 10th - 15th century), NZ Kiev
                          P II n 5, 1962, pp. 51 - 60.

A-   :

884 JACOBSSON, B.   : *An Unexpected Usage : ahead, alive, and the Like, be-*
                          fore Nouns, MSpråk 55, 1961, pp. 240 - 246.

885 KIRCHNER, G.   : *Attributive Verwendung der mit Präfix " a-" gebil-*
                          deten Adjektiva des Englischen. " An Unexpected Us-
                          age" ?, NS, N. F., 11, 1962, pp. 168 - 173.

'886 LINDNER, F.   : *Über das Präfix a im Englischen*, Habilitationsschrift
                          Jena, Jena : E. Frommann, 1874, 25 p..
                          Reviews :
                          Asher, D. : ASNS 53, 1874, 119 - 120

887 NEUMANN, J. H.   : *A Nineteenth Century ' Poetic' Prefix*, MLN 58, 1943,
                          pp. 278 - 283.

'888 PALMGREN, C.   : *A Chronological List of English Formations of the*
                          Types alive, aloud, aglow, Norrköpings Högre Allm.

Läroverks Redogörelse, Norrköping : A.-B. Trycksaker, 1923, 38 p..

'889   - : *A Study on the History of English Words Formed by the Prefix a- < on (in)-*, Norrköpings Högre Allm. Läroverks Redogörelse, 1924, Norrköping : A.-B. Trycksaker, 1924, 22 p..

890 PILTZ, O.   : *Zur englischen Wortbildungslehre. Vom Standpunkte der englischen Sprachforschung.*
2. *Ueber die Vorsilbe a im Englischen*, ASNS 8, 1851, pp. 40 - 58.

'891 RAYSOR, C.   : *An Unexpected Usage : ' Ahead', ' Alive', and the Like, before Nouns*, AS 34, 1959, pp. 302 - 303.
(cf. editorial note p. 304)

'892 REGEL, K.   : *De syllabae a ad formanda adverbia substantivis vel adiectivis in lingua Anglica praefixae origine ac natura*, Programm des Gymnasiums in Gotha, 1855, 14 p..
Reviews :
Anon.   : ASNS 17, 1855, 323 - 324

893 SKEAT, W. W.   : *On the Prefix A- in English*, The Journal of Philology 5, 1874, pp. 32 - 43.

AERO- :

894 JACKSON, J. L.   : *Aerospace*, AS 41, 1966, pp. 158 - 159.

AND- :

895 MAISENHELDER, K. : *Die altenglische Partikel " and".* (*Mit Berücksichtigung anderer germanischer Sprachen)*, Diss. Heidelberg 4.7.1935, Königsfeld (Schwarzwald) : Herbert Stolz, 1935, 87 p., vita.
(esp. pp. 20 - 23, 31 - 39)
(Germany 51, p. 463)

BE-   :

'896 BEEK, P. van   : *The Prefix be in King Alfred's Translation of Boethius' De Consolatione Philosophiae*, University of
Iowa Doctoral Dissertation Abstracts and References
(1900 - 1937) I, 1940, pp. 161 - 175.

897 PILTZ, O.   : *Zur englischen Wortbildungslehre. Vom Standpunkt
der geschichtlichen Sprachforschung.
1. Ueber die Vorsilbe be.*
ASNS 6, 1849, pp. 371 - 389; 8, 1851, pp. 36 - 40.

BI-   :

898 LENZE, J.   : *Das Präfix bi- in der altenglischen Nominal- und
Verbalkomposition mit gelegentlicher Berücksichti-
gung der anderen germanischen Dialekte*, Diss. Kiel
11.1.1910, Kiel : H. Fiencke, 1909,149 p., vita.
(Germany 25, p. 417)
Reviews :
Dittes, R.   : Anglia B 22, 1911, 144 - 148
Fehr, B.   : Est 43, 1910/1911, 105 - 109

CO-   :

899 MINTON, A.   : *Co- Signifying Subordinate Rank*, AS 33, 2, 1958,
pp. 97 - 100.

DE-   :

'900 Anon.   : ' *Debunk' out of ' delouse'* , Word Study, December
1944, p. 5.

'901 Anon.   : *Denazification*, New York Times Magazine, October,
8, 1944, p. 2.
(A sudden new word in the language)

902 HENCH, A. L.   : *Two More ' De- ' Verbs*, AS 10, 1935, pp. 78.
(to deflea, to detooth)

903 MARCHAND, H.   : *Die deadjektivischen reversativen Verben im Deut-*
schen, Englischen und Französischen : entmilitari-
sieren, demilitarize, démilitariser, in Interlin-
guistica, Sprachvergleich und Übersetzung, Festschrift zum 60. Geburtstag von Mario Wandruszka,
ed. by Karl-Richard Bausch and Hans-Martin Gauger,
Tübingen : Max Niemeyer Verlag, 1971, pp. 208 -
214.

DIS- :

732 STUCKERT, K.   : *Untersuchungen über das Verhältnis von Präfix und*
postverbaler Partikel bei lateinischen Lehnverben
im Englischen, dargestellt an den Gruppen der ad-
und dis- Komposita.

EX- :

904 HAGEN, S.   : *Note on the Pronunciation of EX in English*, MSprak
55, 1961, pp. 247 - 252.

FOR- / FORE- :

905 SCHRADER, W.   : *For- und fore- Verbalkomposita im Verlauf der en-*
glischen Sprachgeschichte, Diss. Greifswald 19.7.
1914, Greifswald : J. Abel, 1914, 102 p., vita.
(Germany 30, p. 618)

906 SIEMERLING, O.   : *Das Präfix " for(e)-" in der altenglischen Verbal-*
und Nominalkomposition, Diss. Kiel 21.10.1909,134 p.,
vita.
(Germany 25, p. 421)

174

Reviews :
Dittes, R. : Anglia B 22, 1911, 128 - 144

'907 WILHELMSEN, L. J. : *On the Verbal Prefixes for- and fore- in English*,
Avhandlinger utgitt av Det Norske Videnskaps-Akademi
i Oslo, II Hist.-filos. klasse, 1938, No. 2, 32 p..
Reviews :
Koziol, H. : Anglia B 51, 1940, 124 - 125

GE- :

908 BELDEN, H. M. : *Perfective ge- in O.E. bringan and gebringan*, ESt 32,
1903, pp. 366 - 370.

909 BLOOMFIELD, L. : *Notes on the Preverb ge- in Alfredian English*, in
Studies in English Philology : A Miscellany in Honor
of Frederick Klaeber, ed. by K. Malone and M. B. Ruu
Minneapolis, 1929, pp. 79 - 102.

910 DRAAT, P. F. van : *The Loss of the Prefix ge- in the Modern English Verb
and Some of its Consequences*, ESt 31, 1902, pp. 353
384; 32, 1903, pp. 371 - 388.

911 FRANZ, W. : *Grammatisches*, Zeitschrift für franz. und engl. Unte
richt 20, 1921, pp. 120 - 123.
(esp. pp. 122 - 123 : ge- in OE)

'912 GÖTZL, J. : *Die Aktionsarten des Verbums in König Alfreds Uber-
setzung des Orosius*, Diss. Vienna, 1930.
(Vienna 2, p. 182, 2139)

913 HESSE, H. : *Perfektive und imperfektive Aktionsart im Altenglischen*, Diss. Münster 25.7.1906, Münster : Westfäli-
sche Vereinsdruckerei, 1906, 100 p., vita.
(Germany 21, p. 497, 22)

'914 HOPPER, H. P. : *A Study of the Function of the Verbal Prefix ge- in
the Lindisfarne Gospel of Saint Matthew*, Ph. D. Diss

175

George Washington University 1956.
(American Doctoral Dissertations 1955/ 1956, p. 146)

915 JOLY, A.   : *Ge- préfixe lexical en vieil anglais*, CJL 12, 2, 1967,
                      pp. 78 - 89.

916 LENZ, Ph.   : *Der syntaktische Gebrauch der Partikel ge- in den Wer-
                      ken Alfred des Grossen*, Diss. Heidelberg, Darmstadt :
                      G. Ottos Buchdruckerei, 1886, 80 p..

*917 LINDEMANN, J. W. R. : *Ge- as a Preverb in Late Old English Prose : its
                      Meaning and Function as Suggested by a Collection of
                      West-Saxon, Mercian, and Northumbrian Versions of the
                      Gospel According to Saint Matthew*, Ph. D. Diss. Uni-
                      versity of Wisconsin, 1957, Publ. No. 22, 385, 460 p..
                      (DAb 17, 9, 1957, 2004 - 2005)

918   : *Old English Preverbal ge- : A Reexamination of Some
                      Current Doctrines*, JEGP 64, 1965, pp. 65 - 83.

919 LORZ, A.   : *Aktionsarten des Verbums im Beowulf*, Diss. Würzburg
                      10.12.1908, Würzburg : C. J. Beckers Universitäts -
                      Buchdruckerei, 1908, 86 p., vita.
                      (Germany 24, p. 691)
                      (esp. ge-)

*920 PILCH, H.   : *Der Untergang des Präverbs ge- im Englischen*, Diss.
                      Kiel 9.1.1952, Kiel, 1951, xx, 227 lvs.n..
                      (Germany 68, p. 444)
                      Reviews :
                      Waldo, G. S. : Word 11, 1956, 488 - 491

921   - : *Das AE. Präverb ʒe-* , Anglia 71, 1952/ 1953, pp.
                      129 - 139.

922   - : *Der Untergang des Präverbs ʒe- im Englischen*, An-
                      glia 73, 1955, pp. 37 - 64.

923   - : *Me. I- beim Participium Präteriti*, Anglia 73, 1955,
                      pp. 279 - 291.

924 SAMUELS, M. L.   : *The ge- Prefix in the Old English Gloss to the Lindisfarne Gospels*, Transactions of the Phil. Soc., 1949 (1950), pp. 62 - 116.

925 SCHERER, Ph.   : *The Theory of the Function of the Preverb GA*, Proceedings of the Ninth International Congress of Li¬ guistis, Cambridge, Mass., August 27 - 31, 1962, e by Horace G. Lunt, The Hague, 1964, pp. 859 - 861.

'926 STROHMEYER, H.   : *Aktionsarten der Verba in den alt- und mittelengli schen Prosaversionen der Benediktinerregel*, Diss. Graz, 1933, xiv, 181 lvs.. (Graz 1, p. 160, 2689)

927 WEICK, F.   : *Das Aussterben des Präfixes ge- im Englischen*, Dis Heidelberg 30.10.1911, Darmstadt : C. F. Winter- sche Buchdruckerei, 1911, vi, 149 p., vita. (Germany 27, p. 392)

'928 WUTH, A.   : *Aktionsarten der Verba bei Cynewulf*, Diss. Leipzig 28.7.1915, Weida i. Thür. : Thomas & Hubert, 1915, 123 p.. (Germany 31, p. 361)

'929 ZATOČIL, L.   : *Ge- bei den sogenannten perfektiven und imperfekti ven Simplizien*, Sborník Filozofickej Fakulty Uni- verzity Komenského, Philologica 8, A 7, 1959, pp. 50 - 64.

IN-   :

881 SEALE, L. L.   : *The Rise and Decline of Negative Doublets in En- glish.*

KA-, KE-, KER- :

930 SADILEK, E. A.   : *American Intensives in ka-, ke-, and ker-*, AS 7, 1931/32, p. 142.

MINI- :

931 FENZL, R.   : *Der Minirock und seine Folgen*, Idioma 4, 1967, pp.
145 - 151.
(Mini- in English, French, and German)

OFER- :

932 RÖHLING, M.   : *Das Präfix ofer in der altenglischen Verbal- und*
Nominalkomposition mit Berücksichtigung der übrigen
germanischen Dialekte, Diss. Kiel 24.10.1914, Heidelberg : Carl Winters Universitätsbuchhandlung,
1914, xviii, 106 p., vita.
(Germany 30, p. 675)

ON(D)- :

933 LÜNGEN, W.   : *Das Präfix "on(d)-" in der altenglischen Verbalkom-*
position mit einem Anhang über das Präfix "oš-
(uš-) ", Diss. Kiel 28.8.1911, Kiel, 1911, 85 p.,
vita.
(Germany 27, p. 457)

Od- (Uct-) :

933 LÜNGEN, W.   : *Das Präfix "on(d)-" in der altenglischen Verbalkom-*
position mit einem Anhang über das Präfix "oct -
(uct-) ".

PAN- :

934 ARMSTRONG, T. P.   : *Words Compounded with ' Pan',* N & Q 176, 1939, pp.
337.

935 IGNORAMUS   : *Words Compounded with " Pan "*, N & Q 176, 1939, pp.
280.

RE-   :

936 CELANDER, Th.   : *Om uttalet av prefixet re- i engelskan*, MSpråk 25,
1931 , pp. 24 - 25.

SUPER-   :

937 Anon.   : *Superpower*, AS 14, 1939, pp. 79 - 80.

'938 ADAMS, L.   : *Weakening the English Language*, Words 7, December
1941, pp. 87 - 90.
(A discussion of over-emphasis in the use of such
words as super-service-station)

TO-   :

939 ALBERS, J.   : *Der syntaktische Gebrauch der Präposition to in der*
altenglischen Poesie, Diss. Kiel 17.12.1907, Kiel :
H. Fiencke, 1907, 54 p., (1), vita.
(Germany 23, p. 348, 46)
(esp. pp. 52 - 53)

940 BECHLER, K.   : *Das Präfix to im Verlaufe der englischen Sprachge-*
schichte, Diss. Königsberg 12.8.1909, Königsberg :
Hartungsche Buchdruckerei, 1909, 91 p., vita.
(Germany 24, p. 396)

UN-   :

941 CYGAN, J.   : *On the Systems of Negation in English and Polish*,
LL 15, 1965, pp. 17 - 27.

876 HAYAKAWA, H.   : *Negation in William Faulkner*.

942 KIRCHNER, G.   : *Past Participles Prefixed by ' un- '* , ES 32, 1951,
pp. 218 - 219.

881 SEALE, L. L.   : *The Rise and Decline of Negative Doublets in English.*

943 SHUMAN, R. B. - HUTCHINGS, H. Ch. II : *The un-Prefix : A Means of Germanic Irony in Beowulf*, MPh 57, 1959/1960, pp. 217 - 222.

944 W., E.   : *The Stress of the Uns*, The Academy 56, 1899, p. 385.

945 WESTERGAARD, E.   : *Präfix un i Engelsk rigssprog og Engelske dialekter*, NTS (s. 4), 8, 1919, pp. 41 - 49.

946 WONG, S.   : *A Linguistic Study of the Prefix un- in the Derivation of English Adjectives*, M. Phil. (Arts), London, 1969, 148 lvs..

UZ-   :

*947 LEHMANN, W.   : *Das Präfix uz- im Altenglischen. Ein Beitrag zur germanischen Wortbildungslehre. 1. Teil : Nominal-Komposition*, Diss. Kiel 4.11.1905, Hamburg : Schroeder & Jeve, 1905, iii, 54 p..

(Germany 21, p. 316, 81)

Complete edition under the title:
Das Präfix uz- besonders im Altenglischen mit einem Anhang über das präfigierte westgerm. $^{x}\bar{o}$- *(*$^{x}\bar{a}$- *).*
Ein Beitrag zur germanischen Wortbildungslehre,
Kiel : Cordes, 1906, viii, 193 p..
(= Kieler Studien zur englischen Philologie, N. F. 3)

WITH(ER)- :

948 HOHENSTEIN, C.   : *Das altenglische Präfix wi ð (er)- im Verlauf der englischen Sprachgeschichte mit Berücksichtigung der andern germanischen Dialekte*, Diss. Kiel 24.7. 1912, Kiel : Chr. Donath, 1912, 123 p., vita.
(Germany 27, p. 456)

B) SUFFIXATION

(General studies, suffix groups ....)

'949 ANON.
: *New Words Coined by Use of Suffixes*, New York Times 24 November 1926.

950 ADOLPHI, P.
: *Doppelsuffixbildung und Suffixwechsel im Englischen mit besonderer Rücksicht auf das lateinisch-romanische Element*, Diss. Marburg 21.5.1910, Marburg : Verlag von Franz Fues,Tübingen, 1910, xii, 43 p., vita.
(Germany 25, p. 554)

951 BAREŠ, K.
: *On the Transformation of Morphemes in Present-Day English*, PhP 8, 1965, pp. 124 - 131.
(Concentrates on that part of suffixes which are u dergoing a development i. e. the suffixes arising in present-day technical style)

952 BURNHAM, J. M.
: *Three Hard-Worked Suffixes*, AS 2, 1926/1927, pp. 244 - 246.
(-dom, -ster, -itis)

953 CHAPIN, A. B.
: *An Inquiry into the Origin and Meaning of English Suffixes*, New Haven : Stanley & Chapin, 1843, 44 p.

954 CHAPIN, P. G.
: *On Suffixation in English*, Xème Congrès International des Linguistes. Résumés des Communications, Bucarest, 1967, p. 58.

772 CHOMSKY, N.
: *Remarks on Nominalization*.

'955 EDMONDS, J.
: *A Study on Some Very Confusing Suffixes; or, Phonetic Regularities in Some Words Derived from Romance Tongues*, Unpublished paper, Mimeograph, Cambridge, Mass., M. I. T., 1966.

956 FRIEDRICH, W.
: *Orthographic Peculiarities of Certain Suffixes*, Idioma 3, 1966, pp. 58 - 62 (to be continued)

(-able, -ible, -uble, -ant, -ent, -ance, -ence, re-,
-er, -or)
Idioma 3, 1966, pp. 270 - 273.
(-ify, -efy, -ity, -ety, -our, -or, -ation, -age,
-ction, -xion, -ise, -ize)

957 HENCH, A. L. : *Irradiating Suffixes*, AS 21, 1946, pp. 155 - 156.
(esp. -rama, -cade, -mobile, -genic)

958 HILLS, E. C. : *Irradiation of Certain Suffixes*, AS 1, 1925/1926, pp.
38 - 39.
(esp. -teria, -torium, -ery)

959 LEJNIEKS, V. : *The System of Suffixes*, Linguistics 29, 1967, pp.
80 - 104.

'960 McCUTCHEON, J. T. : *Love that Suffix*, Chicago, Daily Tribune, June 2,
1955, p. 20.
(Seven popular suffixes)

961 McMILLAN, J. B. : *Doubling Consonants before Suffixes*, AS 42, 1967,
pp. 235 - 236.

962 MALONE, K. : *The Suffix of Appurtenance in ' Widsith'* , MLR 28,
1933, pp. 315 - 325.

963 MARCHAND, H. : *Notes on English Suffixation*, NphM 54, 1953, pp.
246 - 272.

579 - : *On the Analysis of Substantive Compounds and Suffixal
Derivatives Not Containing a Verbal Element.*

964 MENCKEN, H. L. : *The Current Suffixes*, AS 21, 1946, pp. 67 - 69.
(-ability, -burger, -cide, -ee, -eria, -eteer,
-ette, -ist, -ium, -ogenic, -olator, -orium, -ster)

965 NEWMAN, S. S. : *English Suffixation : a Descriptive Approach*, Word
4, 1948, pp. 24 - 36.

'966 NICHOLSON, G. A. : *English Words with Native Roots and with Greek, La-*

182

tin or *Romance Suffixes,* University of Chicago Press
1916, (1), 55 p..
Reviews :
'Prick van Wely, F. P. H. : Ling. Museum 23, 266 - 268

967 POUND, L.　　　: *Trade-Name Irradiations,* AS 26, 1951, pp. 166 - 169.

968 PRENNER, M.　　: *More Notes on Neo-Suffixes,* AS 18, 1943, p. 71.
(-aroo, -orium)

969 SCHWARTZ, A.　: *On Interpreting Nominalizations,* in Progress in Linguistics. A Collection of Papers Selected and Edited
by Manfred Bierwisch and Karl Erich Heidolph, The Hague - Paris : Mouton, 1970, 344 p.; pp. 295 - 305.

'970 STAHL, H. E.　: *Studien zum Problem der sprachlichen Neuschöpfungen
bei Shakespeare. Die Suffixbildungen,* Diss. Freiburg
18.12.1953; (1953), 231 lvs.n., tab., (Masch. verv.)
(Germany 69, p. 229)

971 STEIN, G.　　　: *Zur Typologie der Suffixentstehung. (Französisch,
Englisch, Deutsch),* IF 75, 1970, pp. 131 - 165.

'972 THORNDIKE, E. L.　: *The Teaching of English Suffixes,* Teachers College,
Columbia University, Contributions to Education, No.
847, New York, 1941, 81 p..
Reviews :
Pooley, R.　　: AS 17, 1942, 189 - 191

'973 VENDLER, Z.　　: *Nominalizations,* University of Pennsylvania, Transfor
mations and Discourse Analysis Papers, No. 55, 1964.

974　　　　　　- : *Adjectives and Nominalizations,* The Hague - Paris :
Mouton, 1968, 134 p..
(= Papers on Formal Linguistics No. 5)

'975 WHITAKER, H.　: *Unsolicited Nominalizations by Aphasics : the Plausibility of the Lexicalist Model,* Paper read at the
Winter Meeting of the LSA.

183

'976 WHITNEY, W. D.   : *Primary and Secondary Suffixes of Derivation and their Exchanges*, TAPA 15, 1884

1) DERIVATION OF SUBSTANTIVES

a) DIMINUTIVES   (General studies)

977 ECKHARDT, E.   : *Die angelsächsischen Deminutivbildungen*, Habilitationsschrift Freiburg 1903, Altenburg : Pierer, 1903, 42 p..
(Germany 18, p. 102, 169)
(= ESt 32, 1903, pp. 325 - 366)

978 HÖGE, O.   : *Die Deminutivbildungen im Mittelenglischen*, Diss. Heidelberg 1906, Heidelberg : E. Geisendörfer, 1906, 55 p., vita.
(Germany 22, p. 291, 207)

979 KEY, T. H.   : *On Diminutives. I. English*, Trans. Phil. Soc. 1856, pp. 219 - 250.
(-ock, -el, -er, -em/-om, -ing, -kin, -ling)

980 L(EWIS), G. C.   : *On English Diminutives*, The Philological Museum 1, 1832, pp. 679 - 686.

981 ROTZOLL, E.   : *Das Aussterben alt- und mittelenglischer Deminutivbildungen im Neuenglischen*, Diss. Heidelberg 18.2. 1908, Heidelberg : Carl Winters Universitätsbuchhandlung, 1909, vii, (1), 56 p., vita.
(Germany 24, p. 333)
Complete edition under the title :
Die Deminutivbildungen im Neuenglischen unter besonderer Berücksichtigung der Dialekte, Heidelberg :
Carl Winters Universitätsbuchhandlung, 1910, x, (2), 329 p..
(= Anglistische Forschungen 31)

184

Reviews :

Bastide, Ch. : Revue Critique d'Histoire et de Littérature n.s. 72, 1911, 20 - 21

Björkman, E. : ASNS 127, 1911, 226
ESt 43, 1910/1911, 442 - 445

Draat, P. F. van : Museum 19, 1912, col. 135 - 137

Schröer, A. : DLZ 32, 1911, 2730 - 2731

-EROO :

982 WENTWORTH, H. : *The Neo-Pseudo-Suffix '-eroo '* , AS 17, 1942, pp. 10 - 15.

-ETTE₁ :

'983 ADAM, H. P. : *The Kitchenette Age*, Spectator No. 5698, September 10, 1937, pp. 417 - 418.
(On the rise and significance of 'kitchenette' and 'flatlet')

984 M., F. : *Tanksterettes*, AS 8, 1933, p. 73.

985 RAU, M.-L. : *Das -ette-Suffix im Englischen*, NS, N. F., 13, 1964, pp. 501 - 512.

-INCEL :

986 TRNKA, B. : *K staroanglické deminutivní připoně -incel* (The Old English diminutive suffix -incel)(with summary in English), ČMF 38, 1956, pp. 1 - 5.

-INE₁ :

987 BEHRE, F. : *Middle English rochine*, SNPh 11, 1938/39, pp. 251 - 256.

Reviews :

Delbouille, M. : RBPh 18, 1939, 777

Gougenheim, G. : BSL 40, 1939, 73

-LET :

'983 ADAM, H. P.   : *The Kitchenette Age*.

988 COLERIDGE, H.   : *On Diminutives in ' LET '*, Trans.Phil. Soc., 1857,
                          pp. 93 - 115.

989 KEY, T. H.   : *Reconsideration of Substantives in -let*, Trans. Phil.
                          Soc. 1862 - 1863, pp. 220 - 231.

-S$_1$:

990 LANGENFELT, G.   : *The Hypocoristic English Suffix -s*, SNPh 14, 1941/42,
                          pp. 197 - 213.

991 THIELKE, K.   : *Neuenglische Kose- und Spitznamen auf -s*, ESt 73,
                          1938/39, pp. 315 - 316.

-SKI, -SKY :

992 POUND, L.   : *Domestication of a Suffix*, Dialect Notes 4, 4, 1916,
                          p. 304.

993   - : *Odd Formations*. Dialect Notes 4, 5, 1916, p. 354.
                          (Addenda to Dialect Notes 4, 4, 1916, p. 304)

-Y$_1$:

994 LANGENFELT, G.   : *-y in Billy etc.*, SMSpr 15, 1943, pp. 67 - 92.

995 SUNDÉN, K. F.   : *On the Origin of the Hypochoristic Suffix -y (-ie,
                          -ey) in English*, in Sertum philologicum Carolo Fer-

dinando Johansson oblatum. Festskrift tillegnad Karl
Ferdinand Johansson paa hans 50-aars-dag den 16 Sept.
1912, Göteborg, pp. 131 - 170.

b) AGENT NOUNS   (General studies)

996 BENGTSSON, E.   : *Studies on Passive Nouns with a Concrete Sense in En-*
glish, Lund : Håkan Ohlsson, 1927, 164 p..   (Diss.)
Reviews :
Collinson, W. E.   : Litteris 6, 1928, 38 - 39
Dekker, A.   : Nph 23, 1938, 65 - 66
Fischer, W.   : Anglia B 41, 1930, 77 - 80
Flom, G. T.   : Lg 6, 1930, 94 - 96
Stern, G.   : SNPh 2, 1929, 101 - 104

997 BEST, K.   : *Die persönlichen Konkreta des Altenglischen nach ihrer*
Suffixen geordnet, Diss. Strassburg 1.8.1905, Strass-
burg : M. DuMont - Schauberg, 1905, ix, 46 p., vita.
(Germany 21, p. 550, 50)
Reviews :
Pogatscher, A.   : DLZ 27, 1906, col. 1060

998 BOTH, M.   : *Die konsonantischen Suffixe altenglischer Konkreta*
und Kollektiva, Diss. Kiel 13.3.1909, Kiel : Schmidt
& Klaunig, 1909, xii, 99 p., vita.
(Germany 24, p. 382)

999 DOBBIE, E. V. K. : *Agent-Noun Neologisms*, AS 18, 1943, pp. 310.
(Farmatroopers, gardeneers, cookie pushers, adven-
turist, alibist, governmentalist)

1000 GÜTE, J.   : *Die produktiven Suffixe der persönlichen Konkreta im*
Mittelenglischen, Diss. Strassburg 25.1.1908, Strass-
burg : M. DuMont - Schauberg, 1908, ix, (1), 103 p.,
vita.
(Germany 23, p. 604, 63)

Reviews :
M(ann), M. F. : Anglia B 19, 1908, 384

1001 KÄRRE, K.   : *Nomina agentis in Old English*. Part I, Diss. Uppsala,
Uppsala Universitets Årsskrift 1, Filosofi, Språkveten-
skap och Historiska Vetenskaper 3, Uppsala : A.-B. Aka-
demiska Bokhandeln, 1915, 243 p..
Reviews :
Bloomfield, L.   : JEGP 15, 1916, 143 - 144
'Hoops, J.   : Wissenschaftliche Forschungsberichte
9, 1923, 101 - 103
Koeppel, E.   : Anglia B 26, 1915, 353 - 357
Schröer, A.   : DLZ 40, 1919, col. 370 - 371

1002 KLUMP, W.   : *Die altenglischen Handwerkernamen sachlich und sprach-
lich erläutert*, Heidelberg : Carl Winters Universitätsbuchhandlung, 1908, viii, 129 p..
(= Anglistische Forschungen 24)

1003 LINDELÖF, U.   : *English Agent-Nouns with a Suffixed Adverb*, NphM 36,
1935, pp. 257 - 282.

1004 LINDHEIM, B. von : *Die weiblichen Genussuffixe im Altenglischen*, Anglia
76, 1958, pp. 479 - 504.

1004 a   - : *Die weiblichen Genussuffixe im Altenglischen. Korrek-
turen und Nachträge*, Anglia 87, 1969, pp. 64 - 65.

1005 LINSKIJ, S. S.   : *Neologizmy s obščim značeniem " dejstvujuščego lica "
(nomina agentis) v slovarnom sostave anglijskogo
jazyka XVI veka* (Agent noun neologisms in 16th century English vocabulary), UZ DVost U, 1962, vyp. 5,
Serija filologiceskaja, pp. 57 - 68.

1005 a OTTO, G.   : *Die Handwerkernamen im Mittelenglischen*, Diss. Berlin
29.6.1938, Bottrop i. W. : Postberg, 1938, vii, 99 p..
(Germany 54, p. 55)

1006 PROCTOR, J. W.   : *New Agent Nouns Suggested*, AS 1, 1925/1926, p. 564.

'1007 SHELDON, E. K.   : *Peacemonger*, Word Study 24, 1, 1950, pp. 1 - 2.

1008 SHULMAN, D.   : *More on Adding the Suffix of Agency*, AS 12, 1937, p. 243.
(giver-upper, pin-putters-in...)

-ATOR :

1009 DANIELSSON, B.   : *Studies on the Accentuation of Polysyllabic Latin, Greek, and Romance Loan-Words in English with Special Reference to those Ending in -able, -ate, -ator -ible, -ic, -ical, and -ize*, Stockholm Studies in English 3, Stockholm : Almqvist & Wiksell, 1948, xvi, 644 p..

Reviews :

Anon.	: N & Q 194, 1949, 555
'Anon.	: Classical Journal 47, 1951, 140
'Anon.	: Durham Univ. Journal 42, 1949/5o, 39 - 40
Boleo, M. P.	: RPF 3, 1949/50, 422
Davis, N.	: ArchL 3, 1951, 79 - 82
'Derolez, R.	: RBPh 29, 1951, 190 - 194
'	Scriptorium 5, 1951, 165 - 166
Dobson, E. J.:	MAe 21, 1952, 56 - 59
Eliason, N. E.:	MLR 45, 1950, 360 - 362
Ewert, A.	: FS 4, 1950, 71 - 72
'Giertler, E. K.:	Antonianum 26, 1951, 176 - 177
Lausberg, H.	: RF 64,1952, 458 - 459
Mosse, F.	: BSL 46, 1950, 152 - 153
Pisani, V.	: Paideia 6, 1951, 161 - 162
Price, H. T.	: JEGP 50, 1951, 537 - 538
Prins, A. A.	: ES 34, 1953, 173 - 175
	Museum 58, 1953, 122 - 124
Pyles, T.	: MLN 67, 1952, 266 - 267

Reed, D. W.   : Lg 28, 1952, 140 - 144
Reuter, O.   : NphM 50, 1949, 254 - 259
Sandmann, M.   : ZRPh 68, 1952, 102 - 104
Scherer, G.   : Anglia 70, 1951, 123 - 126
Scheurweghs, G.: LB Bijbl 41, 1951, 32 - 33
Schubel, F.   : SNPh 22, 1949/50, 214 - 217
Wilson, R. M.: YW 29, 1948, 37

-EE :

'1009 a ANON.   : ' Draftee','Trainee', ' Selectee', etc., New Yorker
                      16, No. 43, December 7, 1940, p. 21.

'1010 GAFFNEY, W. G. : As to Standee, Word Study 33, October 1957, p. 7.

1011 HARDER, K. B.   : 1. The Suffix " -ee,"AS 39, 1964, pp. 294 - 296.

'1012 KOSTOMAROV, V. G.: Zametki po anglijskomu slovoobrazovaniju : suffiksy
                      suščestvitel'nych ee i ful (Notes on English word-
                      formation : the substantival suffixes -ee and -ful),
                      Problemy obščego i častnogo jazykoznanija, Moscow,
                      1966, pp. 117 - 140.

1013 McATEE, W. L.   : Irradiations of the Suffixes ' -ee ' and ' -eer ',
                      AS 20, 1945, pp. 75 - 76.
                      (giftee, forgettee, furlonghee, pigeoneer, bargain-
                      eer, donuteer)

1014 ODELL, R.   : More ' Sitter ' Progeny, AS 25, 1950, pp. 316 - 317.

'1015 PERSON, H. A.   : Ware the Escapee, Word Study 34, October 1958, pp.
                      6 - 8.
                      (Growth of the suffix -ee)

'1016 PHILLIPS, A.   : In Defence of English, Spectator, January 7, 1944,
                      p. 8.
                      (cf. January 14, 1944, p. 33)
                      (Against evacuee ...)

'1017 ROCKWELL, L. L. : Extraordinary Efflorescence of -ee, Benedictine Review

6, 1956, pp. 24 - 30.

(Growth of the suffix -ee)

-EER :

1018 DAVIS, E. B. : *Patrioteer*, AS 2, 1926/27, p. 491.

1013 McATEE, W. L. : *Irradiations of the Suffixes ' -ee ' and ' -eer '.*

-ER :

'1018 a ANON. : ' *Backer-uppers*', New York Times Magazine, October 21, 1948, p. 7.

1019 BRINK, B. ten : *Das altenglische Suffix ere*, Anglia 5, 1882, pp. 1 - 4 (refers to Stratmann, No. 1030)

1020 COULTER, V. C. : *The -er Suffix of Agency*, AS 12, 1937, p. 82.

1021 KASTOVSKY, D. : *The Old English Suffix -ER(E)*, Anglia 89, 1971, pp. 285 - 325.

1022 KELLNER, L. : *Das Suffix -er in passiver Bedeutung*, Bausteine 1, 4, 1906, p. 327.

'1023 McDAVID, R. I. jr. : *Adviser and Advisor : Orthography and Semantic Dif* *ferenciation*, SIL 1, 7, 1942.

1024 MEREDITH, M. J.: ' *Eaters' and ' Cookers*', AS 8, 1933, p. 80.

'1025 PERVAZ, D. : *Agentivni sufiks -er u savremenom engleskom jeziku*, GFFNS 12, 1969, pp. 473 - 485. (English summary)

1026 R., A. W. : *Watch-Stuffer*, AS 16, 1941, pp. 230 - 231.

'1027 ŠACHRAJ, O. B. : *K voprosu o suffiksal'noj polisemii i omonimii (na materiale substantivnogo suffiksa -er v sovremennom anglijskom jazyke)*, NDVS - F 1969, 6, 54, pp. 131 - 136.

1028 STRANG, B. M. H. : *Swift's Agent-Noun Formations in -ER*, in Wortbildung, Syntax und Morphologie, Festschrift zum 60. Geburtstag von Hans Marchand am 1. Oktober 1967, ed. by Herbert E. Brekle and Leonhard Lipka, The Hague - Paris : Mouton, 1968, 250 p., pp. 217 - 229.

1029   - : *Aspects of the History of the -ER-Formative in English*, TPS 1969, (1970), pp. 1 - 30.

1030 STRATMANN, F. H. : *Altenglisch -ere (-aere, -are)*, ESt 3, 1880, pp. 273.

1031 SYTEL', V. V. : *K istorii suffiksa ličnych imen suščestvitel'nych -er v anglijskom jazyke* (On the history of the suffix -er in English, nouns denoting persons), UZ P P II Ja 25, 1962, pp. 209 - 214.

1032 WENTWORTH, H. : *On Adding the Suffix of Agency -er to Adverbs*, AS 11, 1936, pp. 369 - 370.

-ESS :

1033 COARD, R. L. : *When Women Were Women with -ess*, Georgia Review 14, Winter 1960, pp. 385 - 388.

1034 DIKE, E. B. : *The Suffix -ess etc.*, JEGP 36, 1937, pp. 29 - 34.

1035 LEWIS, R. G. : *A Needed Word*, AS 3, 1928, p. 128. (athletess)

1036 MEREDITH, M. J. : *' Doctoresses ', ' Authoresses', and Others*, AS 5, 1930, pp. 476 - 481.

1037   - : *' Amanda the Administratress' and Other Woman Workers*, AS 27, 1952, pp. 224 - 225.

1038 WISE, C. M. : *' Chiefess ' - a Hawaiian Word*, AS 26, 1951, pp. 116 - .21.

-ETTE₂ :

984 M., F.   : *Tanksterettes.*

1038 a MEREDITH, M.   : *Be a Cabette*, AS 27, 1952, pp. 74 - 76.

985 RAU, M.-L.   : *Das -ette-Suffix im Englischen.*

-I   :

1039 MARCHAND, H.   : *Political History and the History of the Suffix / i / in English*, NS, N. F., 19, 1970, pp. 353 - 358.

-ICGE :

1040 MEZGER, F.   : *Der germanische Kult und die ae. Feminina auf -icg und -estre*, ASNS 168, 1935, pp. 177 - 184.

1041 PLATT, J.   : *Angelsächsisches*, Anglia 6, 1883, pp. 171 - 178. (p. 178 : 7. Ags. fem. Bildung -icge)

1042 SCHABRAM, H.   : *Bemerkungen zu den ae. Nomina agentis auf -estre und -icge*, Anglia 88, 1970, pp. 94 - 98.

-INE₂ :

1043 BARRY, Ph.   : *Dudine*, AS 4, 1929, p. 206.

1044 D., J.   : *'Dude', 'Dudine', 'Duding'*, AS 10, 1935, p. 158.

1045 DRESEN, M. H.   : *Dudine*, AS 3, 1928, p. 447.

1046 POUND, L.   : *Chorine*, AS 3, 1928, p. 368. (actorine, knitterine, doctorine, batherine, booberine, soldierine)

-IST :

1047 AUBIN, R. A.   : *Tourist*, MLN 59, 1944, pp. 334 - 335.
(The word dates from 1780)

1048 MALONE, K.   : ' *Anglist*' *and* ' *Anglicist* ', in Studies in Honor of Hermann Collitz. Presented by a Group of his Pupils and Friends on the Occasion of his Seventy - Fifth Birthday, February 4, 1930, Baltimore : The Johns Hopkins Press, 1930, xii, 331 p., pp. 325 - 329.

-ITE :

1049 ANON.   : *Socialite*, The Saturday Review of Literature, January 4, 1941, p. 9.

1050 GRAHAM, W.   :*Timecrime*, The Saturday Review of Literature, January 4, 1941, p. 9.
(Discussion of ' socialite ')

1051 ZAIC, F.   : *Zur Geschichte der Bedeutung des Suffixes -ite im Englischen und Amerikanischen*, Orbis 10, 1961, pp. 516 - 526.

-LING :

1051 a MORRIS, R.   : *On the Words Groveling and Grovelling, and the Connection of the Syllable -ling in Groveling with the -long in Headlong, Sidelong, etc.*, TPS 1862 - 1863, pp. 85 - 113.

-OR :

1052 KRAPP, G. P.   : *Insurors*, AS 3, 1928, p. 432.

1023 McDAVID, R. I. jr.   : *Adviser and Advisor : Orthography and Semantic*

Differenciation.

1053 MASON, C. P.　: *More Words in -or*, AS 4, 1929, p. 329.
(Resistors, inductors, capicitors, lightning arre-
stors)

-STER　:

'1054 HEKKET, B. J.　: *De uitgang -ster*, Driemaandelijkse Bladen 14, 1962,
pp. 49 - 50.

1055 JESPERSEN, O.　: *The Ending -ster*, MLR 22, 1927, pp. 129 - 136.

1056　　　　- : *A Supposed Feminine Ending*, in Linguistica, Selected
Papers in English, French and German, Copenhague :
Levin & Munksgaard, 1933, pp. 420 - 429.

1057 LUBBERS, K.　: *The Development of ' -ster ' in Modern British and
American English*, ES 46, 1965, pp. 449 - 470.

1040 MEZGER, F.　: *Der germanische Kult und die ae. Feminina auf -icge
und -estre*.

1042 SCHABRAM, H.　: *Bemerkungen zu den ae. Nomina agentis auf -estre und
-icge*.

1058 SCHRÖDER, E.　: *Die Nomina agentis auf -ster*, Niederdeutsches Jahrbuch Vol. 48, Norden und Leipzig : H. Soltau, 1922,
pp. 1 - 8.

c) GRADATION NOUNS, ABSTRACT NOUNS, CONCRETE NOUNS OTHER THAN DIMINUTIVES
AND AGENT NOUNS
(General studies....)

1059 BERGENER, C.　: *A Contribution to the Study of the Conversion of Adjectives into Nouns in English*, Diss. Uppsala, Lund :
H. Ohlsson, 1928, xvi, 222 p..

Reviews :

K., A. G.   : AS 5, 1930, 247 - 249

998 BOTH, M.   : *Die konsonantischen Suffixe altenglischer Konkreta*
                     und Kollektiva.

1060 BOWERS, F.   : *The Deep Structure of Abstract Nouns*, FL 5, 1969, pp.
                     520 - 533.

1061 BRAME, M. K. - LASNIK, H. : *A Derived Nominal Requiring a Nonsentential*
                     Source, Ling I 4, 1970, pp. 547 - 549.
                     (availability)

'1062 BRISKIN, R. U. : *Semantičeskaja struktura otvlečennych imen suščest-*
                     vitel'nych v sovremennom anglijskom jazyke (The se-
                     mantic structure of modern English abstract nouns),
                     Ussurijskij pedagogičeskij Institut. UZ Tom./Vyp. 3,
                     1, 1960, pp. 93 - 118.

1063 CLARK, J. W.   : *The Gawain-Poet and the Substantival Adjective*, JEGP
                     49, 1950, pp. 60 - 66.

*1064 DAHL, L.   : *Nominal Style in the Shakespearean Soliloquy, with*
                     Reference to the Early English Drama, Shakespeare's
                     Immediate Predecessors and his Contemporaries, Annales
                     Universitatis Turkuensis, Series B, Tom. 112, Diss.
                     Turku, 1969, 270 p..

*1065 DORSKIJ, S. L. : *Slovobrazovanie otvlečennych imen suščestvitel'nych*
                     v drevanglijskom jazyke (Word-formation of abstract
                     substantives in OE), Minsk, 1960.

* 787 FRANCK, Th.   : *Wörter für Satzinhalte. Zur inhaltlichen Leistung ab-*
                     strakter Wortstände im Deutschen und Englischen.

1066 FRASER, B.   : *Some Remarks on the Action Nominalization in English*,
                     in Readings in English Transformational Grammar, ed.
                     by R.A. Jacobs and P. S. Rosenbaum, Waltham, Mass.,
                     Toronto, London : Ginn and Company, 1970, x, 277 p.,
                     pp. 83 - 98.

'1067 FRENCH, M. A.   : *The Selection of Noun-Forming Suffixes in Contemporary English*, M. A. Manchester, 1966/ 1967. (England 17, p. 15, 310)

1068 FRY, D. P.   : *On the Last Syllable in the Words KNOWLEDGE and WEDLOCK : Further Remarks*, TPS 1862 - 1863, pp. 33 - 47.

1069 GARDNER, Th. J.   : *ʔreaniedla and ʔreamedla : Notes on Two Old English Abstracta in -la(n)*, NphM 70, 1969, pp. 255 - 261.

1070 GARNER, E. R.   : *The Derived Nominal in The Sea Around Us* (Carson) Ph. D. Diss. Georgetown University, 1971; Authorize Facsimile Xerography,(7), iv, 163 p..

1071 GERBER, E.   : *Die Substantivierung des Adjektivs im XV. und XVI. Jahrhundert mit besonderer Berücksichtigung des zu Adjektiven hinzutretenden one*, Diss. Göttingen 31.8 1895, Göttingen : Druck der Dieterich'schen Universitäts-Buchdruckerei (W. Fr. Kaestner), 1895, 59 p vita. (Germany 11, p. 97, 81)

'1072 GORBAČEVIC, V. A.   : *Iz istorii razvitija leksičeskoj gruppy glagolov znanija i proizvodnych ot nich imen suščestvitel'- nych v anglijskom jazyke* (On the historical development of the lexical group of verbs of knowledg and their derived substantives in English), Diss. 1 - L Ped I , 1956.

1073 HERTRAMPF, A.   : *Die Entstehung von Substantiven aus Verben im Neuenglischen*, Diss. Breslau 27.7.1932, Breslau : Fran kes Verlag und Druckerei / Otto Borgmeyer, 1932, 84 p., 2 tab., vita. (Germany 48, p. 134)

' 127 HOFFMANN, A.   : *Nominale Ausdrucksweise im modernen Englisch.*

1074   - : *Zur nominalen Ausdrucksweise im Englischen* (Me-

thodologische Überlegungen und Versuch einer Analyse),
WZPhP 11, 1967, pp. 211 - 214.

1075   - : *Die verbo-nominale Konstruktion - eine spezifische
Form der nominalen Ausdrucksweise im modernen Englisch,*
ZAA 20, 1972, pp. 158 - 183.

1076 HUNTER, E. R. : *Verb + Adverb = Noun,* AS 22, 1947, pp. 115 - 119.

1077 IRMER, R. : *Die mit Nullmorphem abgeleiteten deverbalen Substantive des heutigen Englisch,* Diss. Tübingen 1970, Tübingen, 1972, 203 p., vita.

141 JENSEN, J. : *Die I. und II. Ablautsreihe in der altenglischen Wortbildung.*

1078 KASTOVSKY, D. : *Old English Deverbal Substantives Derived by Means
of a Zero Morpheme,* Diss. Tübingen 5.7.1968, Esslin-
gen a. N. : Bruno Langer Verlag, 1968, xv, (1), 639 p.,
vita.
Reviews :
Standop, E. : IF 75, 1970, 356 - 359

1079 KENNEDY, A. G. : *On the Substantivation of Adjectives in Chaucer,* The
University Studies of the University of Nebraska,Vol.
5, No. 3, 1905, pp. 251 - 269.

1080 KOO, ZUNG-FUNG WEI : *Old English Living Noun Suffixes Exclusive of Personal and Place-Names,* Ph. D. Diss. Cambridge, Mass.,
Radcliffe College, 1947.

1081 KOTOVA, Z. I. : *Imena suščestvitel'nye sobiratel'nye v drevneanglijskom jazyke* (Collective nouns in Old English), UZ
LP I, 226, 1962, pp. 135 - 145.

1082 LAKOFF, G. - ROSS, J. R. : *A Derived Nominal Requiring a Sentential
Source,* Ling I 1,2, 1970, pp. 265 - 267.
(availability)

1083 LINDELÖF, U.   : *English Verb-Adverb Groups Converted into Nouns*,
Societas Scientiarum Fennica : Commentationes Humanarum Litterarum 9, 5, 1938, 41 p..

1084 MARTIN, F.   : *Die produktiven Abstraktsuffixe des Mittelenglischen*,
Diss. Strassburg 16.6.1906, Strassburg : M. DuMont
Schauberg, 1906, vi, (preface), 79 p., vita.
(Germany 21, p. 552, 66)

'1085 MATHESIUS, V. : *O nominálních tendencích v slovesné predikaci novoanglické*, Sbornik filologický 4, Prague, 1913, pp.
325 - 339.
(On to have a look ...)

'1086 MAZO, B. V.   : *Dead'ektivnoe obrazovanie imen suščestvitel'nych v
sovremennom anglijskom jazyke* (Deadjectival substantives in present-day English), Diss. Moscow, 1963.

'1087 NEDOŠIVINA, K. S.: *Nekotorye osobennosti kornevych suščestvitel'nych
sovremennogo anglijskogo jazyka* (Some particularities of the root substantives in modern English),
UZ IMO 1958, KZJa, vyp. 1, pp. 5 - 30.

1088 NEWMEYER, F. J. : *The Derivation of the English Action Nominalization*,
in Papers from the 6th Regional Meeting of the Chicago Linguistic Society, 1970, pp. 408 - 415.

1089   - : *The Source of Derived Nominals in English*, Lg 47,
1971, pp. 786 - 796.

1090 NICKEL, G.   : *Complex Verbal Structures in English*, IRAL 6, 1968,
pp. 1 - 21.
(On to have a look ...)

1091 OLSSON, Y.   : *On the Syntax of the English Verb with Special Reference to have a look and Similar Complex Structures*,
Gothenburg Studies in English 12, Göteborg : Elanders Boktryckeri Aktiebolag, 1961, 246 p..

1092 PALMGREN, C.

: *English Gradation-Nouns in their Relation to Strong Verbs*, Diss. Uppsala, Uppsala : K. W. Appelberg, 1904, 92 p..
Reviews :
Fehr, B. : ESt 43, 1910/1911, 261 - 263

'1093 PEREL'MAN, M. M.

: *Sobiratel'nye suščestvitel'nye v sovremennom anglijskom jazyke* (Collective nouns in present-day English), UZ LP I, 272, 1965, pp. 162 - 174.

1094 PHOENIX, W.

: *Die Substantivierung des Adjektivs, Partizips und Zahlwortes im Angelsächsischen*, Diss. Berlin 15.11. 1918, Berlin : Mayer & Müller, 1918, 82 p..
(Germany 34, p. 238)
Reviews :
Anon. : ASNS 140, 1920, 311 - 312
Ekwall, E.: ESt 54, 1920, 288 - 292
Fischer, W. : Anglia B 31, 1920, 10 - 12

1095 POSTON, L. III.

: *' Happy ', ' Merry ', and ' Jolly ' as Nouns*, AS 37, 1962, pp. 289 - 290.

1096 POWELL, A. F.

: *Forms and Uses of Nouns of Nationality*, ELT 21, 1966/1967, pp. 159 - 165.

1097 PREUSS, F.

: *Substantivische Neologismen aus Verb und Adverb*, Lebende Sprachen 7, 1, 1962, pp. 1 - 3.

836 PRICE, H. T.

: *A History of Ablaut in Class 1 of the Strong Verbs from Caxton to the End of the Elizabethan Period.*

1098 PRIESS, M.

: *Die Bedeutungen des abstrakten substantivierten Adjektivs und des entsprechenden abstrakten Substantivs bei Shakespeare*, Diss. Göttingen 1.9.1906, Halle : E. Karras, 1906, x, 57 p..
(= Studien zur englischen Philologie 28)
(Germany 22, p. 203, 101)
Reviews :
Delcourt, J. : ESt 41, 1910, 103 - 105

Dyboski, R. : Allg.Litbl. 17, 1908, col. 82

Grossmann, H. : ASNS 119, 1907, 227 - 230

'1099 PUSCH, L. F.   : *Die Substantivierung von Verben mit Satzkomplementen im Englischen und Deutschen*, Diss. Mainz, 1971/1972.

1100 RENSKY, M.   : *Nominal Tendencies in English*, PhP 7, 1964, pp. 135 - 150.
(to have a look ...)

'1101 ROGOVSKAJA, B. I.: *Analitičeskaja konstrukcija tipa to give a laugh v sovremennom anglijskom jazyke* (The analytical construction of the to give a laugh type in contemporary English), 1 - L Ped I, 1947, 159 p..

'1102 ROTOMSKIENE, T.   : *Substantivacija prilagatel'nych v sovremennom anglijskom jazyke* (The substantivation of the adjective in present-day English), Diss. Moscow, 1960.

'1103   - : *K probleme substantivacii prilagatel'nych v sovremennom anglijskom jazyke* (On the problem of the substantivation of adjectives in present-day English), Vilnians Pedagoginio Instituto Mokslo darbai 9, 1960, pp. 133 - 175.

' 408 SACHOVA, N. I.   : *Smyslovoe razvitie imeni suščestvitel'nogo work i glagola to work i obrazovannych ot ich osnovproizvodnych i složnych slov v anglijskom jazyke* (The semantic development of the substantive work and the verb to work and the derivatives and compounds from their stems).

'1104 SCHLAUCH, M.   : *English Creates New Nouns of its Own*, Word Study 23, 4, 1948, pp. 4 - 5.

'1105 SCHLOTHAUER, G.   : *Der reine Verbalstamm als Substantiv bei Shakespeare* Diss. Jena 4.12.1951, Jena, 1951, 357 lvs.n..
(Germany 67, p. 339)

1106 SCHWAMBORN, H.   : *Nominale Elemente des Englischen*, NS, N. F., 6, 1957, pp. 117 - 121.

'1107 SIL'NICKAJA, G. V.   : *Transformacionnyj analiz i ego rol' v semantičeskoj klassifikacii slov.* (*Na materiale suščestvitel'nych i glagolov, svjazannych drug s drugom po konversii)* (Transformational analysis and its role in the semantic classification of words. On the material of the substantives and verbs related through conversion), UZ Bašk U 1964, vyp. 21, SFilN No. 9, pp. 217 - 221.

'1108 SINIČKINA, L. N.   : *O nekotorych tipach frazeologičeskich glagol'nych sočetanij v anglijskom jazyke* (Concerning some types of phraseological verbal collocations in English), Rostovskij-na-dony pedagogičeskij Institut. UZ kafedr anglijskogo, nemeckogo i francuzskogo jazykov, vyp. 2, 30, 1958, pp. 33 - 55. (to have care, to have a smoke ...)

1109 SMITH, C.   : *On Causative Verbs and Derived Nominals in English*, Ling I 3, 1, 1972, pp. 136 - 138.

1110 THIELE, O.   : *Die konsonantischen Suffixe der Abstrakta des Altenglischen*, Diss. Strassburg 1901, Darmstadt : G. Otto, 1902, xii, 136 p.. (Germany 17, p. 328, 71) Reviews : Eckhardt, E.   : ESt 33, 1904, 102 - 105 Heuser, W.   : Anglia B 14, 1903, 213

'1111 TRNKA, B.   : *Analyse a synthese v nověangličtine* , MNHMA, Sbornik zu batého, Prague, 1926, pp. 380 - 389.

1112   - : *Analysis and Synthesis in English*, ES 10, 1928, pp. 138 - 144.

1113 VACHEK, J.   : *Some Less Familiar Aspects of the Analytical Trend
                         in English*, BSE 3, 1961, pp. 9 - 71.
                         (... to have a look)

'1114 VINOKUROVA, L. P. : *O substantivacij v anglijskom jazyke* (On substan-
                          tivation in English), L Ped I, UZ, tom. 253/45, 1959
                          pp. 21 - 34.

1115 WÄCHTLER, K.   : *Zur substantivischen Wortbildung mittels Lehnsuffix
                          im amerikanischen Englisch*, in Wortbildung, Syntax
                          und Morphologie, Festschrift zum 60. Geburtstag von
                          Hans Marchand am 1. Oktober 1967, ed. by Herbert E.
                          Brekle and Leonhard Lipka, The Hague - Paris : Mou-
                          ton, 1968, pp. 230 - 241.

'1116 WARNKE, K.   : *On the Formation of English Words by Means of Ab-
                          laut*, Diss. Halle, Halle : M. Niemeyer, 1878, 54 p.
                          Reviews :
                          Asher, D. : ESt 3, 1880, 357 - 359

'1117 ZAGORNIKO, A. J. : *O tak nazyvaenoi nepolnoi ili česastičnoi konversii
                          v sovremennom anglijskom jazyke* (On the so-called
                          incomplete or partial conversion in present-day En-
                          glish), Rostovskij-na-dony pedagogičeskij Institut.
                          UZ kafedr anglijskogo, nemeckogo i francuzskogo ja-
                          zykov, vyp. 2, 30, 1958, pp. 15 - 32.

Addenda :

1065 a FEY, I.   : *Konversionssubstantive und Konversionsverben in Fach-
                         sprachen und Schichten des Englischen*, Diss. Würz-
                         burg 9.7.1971, Würzburg, 1971, iii, (1), 224 p., vit.
                         (DNB C 1972, 9 ; p. 10, 107)

1065 b   - : *Konversionssubstantive und Konversionsverben in Fach-
                         sprachen und Schichten des Englischen (Conversion-
                         Nouns and Conversion-Verbs in Technical Terminology*

and in the Colloquial, Slang and Cant Strata of the English Language) , Diss. Würzburg, 1971, 224 p., in English and American Studies in German, Summaries of Theses and Monographs. A Supplement to Anglia 1971, Tübingen : Max Niemeyer,ix, (1), 190 p., pp. 19 - 21.

-ACY / -ASY :

*1118 ALLEN, H. B. : *Will Democracy Kill -asy* ? Word Study 32, May 1957, pp. 1 - 3.

-AGE :

1119 GADDE, F. : *On the History and Use of the Suffixes -ERY (-RY), -AGE and -MENT in English*, Diss. Lund, Svea English Treatises, Lund : Gleerupska Univ. Bokh.; Cambridge : W. Heffer & Sons Ltd., 1910, viii, 143 p..
Reviews :
Borst, E. : ESt 45, 1912, 75 - 77
Draat, P. F. v. : Museum 20, 1913, col. 55 - 56
Gadde, F. : GRM 3, 1911, 508 - 509
Paues, A. C. : MLR 9, 1914, 410 - 412

1120 HETZER, R. : *Das Suffix -age*, Diss. Prague, 1944, 199 p..
(Germany 60, p. 748)

1121 MALMBERG, G. : *Tvenne studier över suffixer* , Örebro, 23 p..
(2. Some remarks on the suffix -age in English)

1122 SEBASTIAN, H. : *Teacherage*, AS 11, 1936, p. 271.
(A new word)

-AL₁ :

1123 MALKIEL, Y.   : *Three Old French Sources of the English arriv-al,*
                               withdraw-al Type, JEGP 43, 1944, pp. 80 - 87.

1124 STRACHAN, L. R. M.: *" Al ", Noun-Suffix : " Disallowal", " Disallowance"*
                               N & Q , s.11, 7, 1913, p. 414.
                               (refers to No. 1125)

1125 V., Q.   : *" -al", Noun-Suffix : " Disallowal", " Disallowance"*
                               N & Q , s. 11, 7, 1913, p. 267.

-ATE₁ :

1126 ANON.   : *Etymological Notes : ' Advisorate',* AS 22, 1947, p.
                               232.

-ATION :

1127 P., L.   : *" Workation",* AS 24, 1949, p. 285.
                               (cf. vacation)

-BURGER :

1128 ANON.   : *More Progeny of ' Hamburger ',* AS 15, 1940, p. 452.

1129 MEREDITH, M. J.   : *Still More ' -burgers ' and ' bar-b-cues',* AS 17,
                               1942, p. 132.

1130   - : *' Gazelleburgers' in Persian Palaces,* AS 19, 1944,
                               pp. 308 - 309.

1131 ODELL, R.   : *More and More '-burgers ',* AS 25, 1950, pp. 315 -
                               316.

1132 PRESCOTT, J.   : *More ' -burgers ',* AS 23, 1948, pp. 73 - 74.

1133 SOUDEK, L.   : *The Development and Use of the Morpheme burger in American English*, Linguistics 68, 1971, pp. 61 - 89.
(With an index of burger-formations)

1134 WILLIAMS, A.   : *Hamburger Progeny*, AS 14, 1939, p. 154.

-CADE :

1135 G., R. S.   : *Motorcade*, AS 5, 1930, pp. 495 - 496.

1136 HENCH, A. L.   : *Autocade*, AS 6, 1930/1931, pp. 463 - 464.

1137 WERNER, W. L.   : *" Motorcade " and " to Demagogue "*, AS 6, 1930/1931, p. 155.

1138   - : *The Earliest Motorcade*, AS 7, 1931/1932, p. 388.

1139 WITHINGTON, R.   : *Motorcade*, AS 6, 1930/1931, p. 313.

-CILLIN :

1140 MEREDITH, M. J.   : *Irradiation of the Suffix -cillin*, AS 23, 1948, p. 222.

-DOM :

1141 WENTWORTH, H.   : *The Allegedly Dead Suffix -dom in Modern English*, PMLA 56, 1941, pp. 280 - 306.

-EL$_1$:

1142 OLSSON, Y.   : *Implications and Complications of the Stressed Suffix -el*, ES 45, Supplement, 1964, pp. 40 - 43.

-ERIA / -TERIA :

'1143 ANON.   : *Bookateria*, N & Q , Vol. 8, No. 9, December 1949.

1144 A., E.   : *Furnitureteria*, AS 6, 1931, p. 304.

1145 BARRY, Ph.   : *Cafeteria*, AS 3, 1928, pp. 35 - 37.

'1146 BEL'SKAJA, M. A.   : *Funcionirovanie v sovremennom anglijskom jazyke mor-
                           fem -(i)ana, -rama, -scape, -teria* (The function of
                           the modern English morphemes -(i)ana, -rama, -scape,
                           -teria), Filologičeskij sbornik. (Red. P. I. Iva-
                           nova & A. V. Rusakova), Leningrad : Izd. Leningrads·
                           kogo Universitet, 1969, 164 p., pp. 50 - 57.

1147 DAVIS, Ph.   : *Barberia*, AS 3, 1938, p. 477.

1148 EDGERTON, C. C.   : *Cafeteria*, AS 2, 1926/1927, pp. 214 - 215.

1149   - : *Cafeteria - a Correction*, AS 2, 1926/1927, p. 331.

1150 F., L. I.   : *A Few Notes*, AS 8, 1933, pp. 79 - 80.
                           (honeyteria)

1151 KAUFFMAN, B.   : *Booketeria*, AS 22, 1947, p. 306.

1152 MEREDITH, M. J.   : *More " Cafeteria" Progeny*, AS 3, 1928, p. 37.

1153   - : *More " Cafeteria " Progeny*, AS 3, 1928, p. 161.
                           (Casketeria, drugeteria, pastreria, radioteria)

1154 ODELL, R.   : *' Cattleteria'*, AS 26, 1951, p. 121.

1155 R., A.   : *Cafeteria Again*, AS 2, 1926/1927, p. 215.

1156 ROBERTS, W.   : *Cafeteria Again*, AS 3, 1928, p. 344.

1157 STEADMAN, J. M. jr.: *Basketeria and the Meaning of the Suffix -terid*,
                           AS 5, 1930, pp. 417 - 418.

-ERY (-RY) :

1119 GADDE, F.   : *On the History and Use of the Suffixes -ERY (-RY), -AGE and -MENT in English.*

1158 P., C. J.   : *Salonery*, AS 24, 1949, p. 316.

-ESE :

1159 THIELKE, K.   : *Das ne. Suffix -ese im Dienste der Stilcharakterisierung*, NS, N. F., 2, 1953, pp. 504 - 506.

-EX :

1160 MYERS, W. E.   : *Trade-Name Suffixes*, AS 2, 1926/1927, p. 448.

-FEST :

1161 POUND, L.   : *Odd Formations.*
                          a) Domestication of the Suffix -fest, Dialect Notes 4, 5, 1916, pp. 353 - 354.

-FUL₁ :

1012 KOSTOMAROV, V. G.   : *Zametki po anglijskomu slovoobrazovaniju : suffiksy suščestvitel'nych ee i ful* (Notes on English word-formation : the substantival suffixes ee and ful).

-FURTER :

1162 WILLIAMS, F. C.   : *Gangway for the -furter*, AS 27, 1952, pp. 153 - 154.

-IANA :

1146 BEL'SKAJA, M. A.   : *Funcionirovanie v sovremennom anglijskom jazyke morfem -(i)ana, -rama, -scape, -teria .*

1163 JONES, J.   : *On the Suffix -ana*, AS 8, 1933, p. 71.

-IN :

1164 BALD, W.   : *Neologismen mit in im Englischen und Deutschen*, Lebende Sprachen 13, 1968, pp. 65 - 68.

1165 PREUSS, F.   : *Das Wortfeld sit-in* , NS, N. F., 11, 1962, pp. 327 - 329.

1166 SCHMITZ, A.   : *Laugh-in* ..., Idioma 6, 1969, pp. 6 - 7. (In-formations)

-ING :

1167 ALEXANDER, H. : *The Particle -ing in Place-Names*, Essays and Studies by Members of the English Association 2, 19` pp. 158 - 182.

1168 ANDREWS, Ch. M. : *The -ing Suffix in English Place-Names*, The Nation (N. Y.) 69, 1899, p. 427. (refers to Kemble, No. 1203)

1169 ARMSTRONG, J. L. : *The Gerund in Nineteenth-Century English*, PMLA 7, 1892, pp. 200 - 211.

1170 BOULT, J.   : *On the Syllable " -ing " in Names of Places in the British Isles* , The Antiquarian Magazine & Bibliographer 1, 1882, pp. 295 - 298.

'1171 BLUME, J. R.   : *Über den Ursprung und die Entwicklung des Gerundiums im Englischen*, Bremen, 1880, 63 p..

'1172 BRADHERING, H. : *Das englische Gerundium* (Published with) Programm der städtischen höheren Mädchenschule in Emden, Ostern 1895, Emden : Gerhard, 1895, pp. 3 - 17.

1173 CALLAWAY, M. jr. : *Concerning the Origin of the Gerund in English*, in Studies in English Philology. A Miscellany in

Honor of Frederick Klaeber, ed. by K. Malone and M. B. Ruud, Minneapolis : The University of Minnesota Press, 1929, x, 486 p., pp. 32 - 49.

1174 CARR, R.   : *On the Present Participle in the Northumbrian Dialect and on the Verbal Nouns, or Nouns of Action, Terminating in -ing*, History of the Berwickshire Naturalists' Club 1856 - 1862, pp. 356 - 365.

1175 CHRISTY, A.   : *The ' INGS ' and ' GINGS ' of the Domesday Survey, Especially Fryerning*, Transactions of the Essex Archaeological Society Vol 12, n.s., Colchester, 1913, pp. 94 - 100.

1176 CURME, G. O.   : *History of the English Gerund*, ESt 45, 1912, pp. 349 - 380.

1177   - : *The Gerund in Old English and German*, Anglia 38, 1914, pp. 491 - 498.

1178   - : *The Old English Gerund Again*, ESt 49, 1915/1916, p. 323.

1179 DAL, I.   : *Zur Entstehung des englischen Participiums Praesentis auf -ing*, NTS 16, 1952, pp. 5 - 116.
                Reviews :
                Keller, R. : ES 37, 1956, 75 - 78
                Preusler, W. : IF 61, 1954, 325 - 326

1180 DODGSON, J. M. : *The Significance of the Distribution of the English Place-Names in -ingas, -inga in South-East England*, Medieval Archeology Vol. 10, 1966 (1967), pp. 1 - 29.

1181   - : *The -ing in English Place-Names Like Birmingham and Altrincham*, BNF N. F. 2, 1967, pp. 221 - 245.

1182   - : *Various Forms of Old English -ing in English Place-Names*, BNF N. F. 2, 1967, pp. 325 - 396.

1183 : *Various English Place-Name Formations Containing Old English -ing*, BNF N. F. 3, 1968, pp. 141 - 189.

'1184 DUŠKOVÁ, L. : *Some Remarks on the Syntax of the -ing Form in Presnet-Day English*, PhP 12, 1969, pp. 94 - 99.

'1185 EIJKMAN, L. P. H. : *De uitgang -ing*, De Drie Talen 6, 1890, pp. 33 - 40, 65 - 74, 97 - 103.

1186 EINENKEL, E. : *Zur Geschichte des englischen Gerundiums*, Anglia 37, 1913, pp. 382 - 392.

1187 - : *Die Entwicklung des englischen Gerundiums*, Anglia 38, 1914, pp. 1 - 76.

1188 - : *Nachträge zum Gerundium*, Anglia 38, 1914, p. 212.

1189 - : *Zur Herkunft des englischen Gerundiums*, Anglia 38, 1914, pp. 499 - 504.

1190 EKWALL, E. : *English Place-Names in -ing*, Lund : C. W. K. Gleerup 1923, xix, 190 p. (= Skrifter utgivna av kungl. Humanistika Vetenskaps samfundet i Lund 6).
Reviews :
Anon.   : Nph 9, 1924, 237
'Anon.   : TLS 13, 1923
Binz, G.   : Anglia B 37, 1926, 14 -22
Brandl, A. : ASNS 147, 1924, 143
Mansion, J.: ES 8, 1926, 117 - 119
Mawer, A. : The English Historical Review 39, 1924, 456 - 457
Meer, H. J. v. : Museum 32, 1925, col. 207 - 208
Mosse, F. : Revue Germanique 16, 1925, 208 - 210
'Tolkien, J. R. R. : The Year's Work in English Studies 4, 1923, 30 - 32
Zachrisson, R. E. : ESt 62, 1927, 82 - 87

- 2nd edition, Lund : C. W. K. Gleerup, 1962, xix, 243 p..

Reviews :

Kolb, E.   : Anglia 86, 1968, 182
Lehnert, M. : DLZ 84, 1963, col. 450 - 451
Liljegren, S. B. : NS, N. F., 12, 1963, 483
S(ahl)g(re)n, J. : NoB 50, 1962, 219
Smith, E. S. : Names 10, 1962, 291 - 292
Vermeer, P. M. : ES 44, 1963, 130 - 131

1191 ELLINGER, J.   : *Das Partizip Präsens in gerundialer Verwendung*, ESt 36, 1906, pp. 244 - 247.
(refers to Willert, No. 1224)

1192 ERDMANN, A.   : *Essay on the History and Modern Use of the Verbal Forms in -ING in the English Language*. Part I : *Old Anglo-Saxon Period*, Stockholm : P. A. Nyman, 1871, 44 p..

1193 FAUBERT, E. A.   : *Les formes en ' ING '*, Cetadol Rech. Trad. Automatique 6, 1967, pp. 75 - 84.

1194 FEW, W. P.   : *Verbal Nouns in -inde in Middle English and the Participial -ing Suffix*, Harvard Studies and Notes in Philology and Literature 5, 1896, pp. 269 - 276.
(This chapter is extracted from an unpublished thesis *On the -ing Suffix in Middle English with Special Reference to Participles and -ing Verbals*, Harvard University, 1896)

1195 FRIDMAN, Ch. Ch.: *O differencacii omonimov of glagol'nogo suščestvitel'nogo na -ing i gerundija v sovremennom anglijskom jazyke* (On the differenciation between the homonymic forms of the verbal noun in -ing and the gerund in present-day English), UZ Chab P I, 8, 1962, pp. 39 - 73.

594 GERIKE, F.   : *Das Partizipium Präsentis bei Chaucer*.

1196 GOVE, Ph. B.   : *" Gerund/ Noun " and " Participle/ Adjective "*, AS 40, 1965, pp. 40 - 46.

1197 GRADY, M.   : *On the Essential Nominalizing Function of English -ing*, Linguistics 34, 1967, pp. 5 - 11.

'1198 GUTKINA, M. A.   : *Ot glagol'noe suščestvitel'noe i vozniknovenie*
gerundija v sredneanglijskij period (XII – XV
vv) (The deverbative nouns and the origin of
the gerund in the ME. period (XIIth – XVth centuries), Leningrad : im. F. Engel'sa, kafedra
inostrannych jazykov, 1962, 24 p..

'1199 HARTJE, Th.   : *Das Partizip des Präsens im Frühmittelenglischen*,
Diss. Kiel 13.11.1922, Kiel, 1922, 47 p..
(Summary Kiel 1922, 2 p.)
(Germany 38, p. 510)

'1200 IRWIN, B. J.   : *The Development of the –ing Ending of the Verbal*
Noun and the Present Participle from c. 700 to
c. 1400, Ph.D. Diss. The University of Wisconsin,
1967, 210 p..
(DAb 28, 2, 1967, 653 – A – 654-A) ·

1201 KARLSTRÖM, S.   : *Old English Compound Place-Names in –ing*, Diss.
Uppsala, Uppsala Universitets Årsskrift, Filosofi
Språkvetenskap och historiska Vetenskaper 2, Upp-
sala : A.-B. Lundequistska Bokhandeln, 1927, xxii
194 p., (2).
Reviews :
Karlström, S. : Indogerm. Jahrbuch 14, 1930, 248
Wallenberg, J. K. : Zeitschrift für Ortsnamenfor-
schung 4, 1928, 283 – 292

'1202 KELLNER, L.   : *Zur Sprache Christopher Marlowes*,(Published with
Sechsunddreissigster Jahresbericht über die k.k.
Staats-Oberrealschule und die Gewerbliche Fortbil-
dungsschule im III. Bezirke (Landstrasse) in
Wien für das Schuljahr 1886/1887, Vienna : Verlag
der k.k. Staats-Oberrealschule, 1887, pp. 3 – 26.
(Verbal adjectives in -ing)

1203 KEMBLE, M.   : *On a Peculiar Use of the Anglo-Saxon Patronymical*
Termination –ing, Proceedings of the Philological

Society for 1848 - 1849 and 1849 - 1850, Vol. 4, London, 1850, pp. 1 - 10.

'1204 KRÁMSKÝ, J. : *Poznámka k anglické vazbě na ing* (A note on the English -ing form), Methodické rozhledy z cizích jazyků, November - December 1956, pp. 37 - 40.

1205 KRUISINGA, E. : *Contribution to English Syntax. XIX : The Verbal -ing in Living English*, ES 12, 1930, pp. 24 - 31, 58 - 66.

'1206 - : *De weekwoordvorm op -ing*, Levende Talen 74, 1933.

1207 LANGENHOVE, G. Ch. van : *On the Origin of the Gerund in English*, Phonology. Université de Gand, Recueil de Travaux publiés par la faculté de Philosophie et Lettres, 56e fascicule, Gand : van Rysselberghe & Rombaut; Paris : E. Champion, 1925, xxviii, 132 p..

Reviews :

B., C. : MLR 21, 1926, 345

Bryan, W. F. : MLN 43, 1928, 478 - 481

Callaway, M. : PhQ 7, 1928, 203 - 204

'Carnoy, A. : Leuvensche Bijdragen, Bijblad, nos. 3-4, 1925, xvii, 97 - 98

Malone, K. : JEGP 27, 1928, 398 - 400

'Pons, E. : RBPh 5, 1926, 1042 - 1043

Serjeantson, M. S. : ES 14, 1932, 235 - 236

Western, A. : Anglia B 37, 1926, 25 - 27

*1208 McLIN, V. E. : *Uses of -ING Forms in Present-Day Syntax*, Ph. D. Diss. Howard University, 1970, 169 p..

1209 MOERKERKEN, P. H. van : *Over den uitgang " ing "*, Taalstudie 2, 1880, pp. 37 - 42.

*1210 ÖDMAN, N. P. : *Remarks on the Origin ans Syntax of the Verbal Forms in -ing in Modern English*, in Theses in English, French and German, Gothenburg, 1870, pp. 39 - 54.

1211 ONIONS, C. T. : *The History of the English Gerund*, ESt 48, 1914/1915, pp. 169 - 171.
(cf. ESt 45, 1912, p. 351 ff)

214

'1212 OREMBOVSKAJA, M. N. : *Ing-forma v sovremennom anglijskom jazyke* (The -ing-form in present-day English), Tbilisskij Universitet, 1955, 169 p..

1213 PIERCE, J. E. : *A Look at the So-Called -ing-Forms of English Verbs*, Linguistics 50, 1969, pp. 59 - 69.

'1214 RANDOLPH, E. E. : *The -ing Words in English, with Special Referenc to the Present Participle*, Ph. D. Diss. University of North Carolina, 1907.

1215 RANTAVAARA, I. : *Ing-Forms in the Service of Rhythm and Style in Virginia Woolf's ' The Waves '*, NphM 61, 1960, pp. 79 - 97.

1216 REANEY, P. H. : *Essex Place-Names in " -ing "*, MLR 19, 1924, pp. 466 - 469.

1217 ROOTH, E. : *Zur Geschichte der englischen Partizip-Präsens Form auf -ing*, SNPh 14, 1941/1942, pp. 71 - 85.

1218 ROUND, J. H. : *The Terminal " -ING " in Place-Names*, The Antiquarian Magazine & Bibliographer 2, 1882, pp. 104 - 105. (cf. vol. 1, p. 295)

1219 SMITH, A. C. : *Analogical Development of -ing and the Interpretation of Patrington*, Leeds Studies in English and Kindred Languages 5, 1936, pp. 71 - 73.

'1220 SMITH, R. : *Participle and Infinitive in -ing*, Bulletin of the University of South Carolina No. 27, October 1911, 43 p..

1221 WATTS, Th. : *On the Anglo-Saxon Termination ING*, Proceedings of the Philological Society for 1848-1849 and 1849-1850, vol. 4, 1850, pp. 83 - 86.

'1222 WEGENER, W. : *Abhandlung über die englische Verbalform auf -ing*, Königsberg, 1872 (= Programm der städtischen Realschule zu Königsberg, 1872).

1223 WEYHE, H.   : *Zu den altenglischen Verbalabstrakten auf -nes und
-ing, -ung,* Habilitationsschrift Leipzig 18.11. 1910,
Borna-Leipzig : R. Noske, 1910, 49 p..
(Germany 26, p. 562)
Reviews :
Weyhe, H.   : GRM 3, 1911, 509

1224 WILLERT, H.   : *Vom Gerundium,* ESt 35, 1905, pp. 372 - 382.

1225   - : *Vom substantivischen Infinitiv,* ESt 48, 1914/1915,
pp. 246 - 250.

1226 WONDER, J. P.   : *Ambiguity and the English Gerund,* Lingua 25, 1970,
pp. 254 - 267.

1227 ZACHRISSON, R. E.: *English Place-Names in -ing of Scandinavian Origin,*
Uppsala : Almqvist & Wiksells, 1924, 130 p..
Reviews :
Binz, G.   : Anglia B 37, 1926, 22 - 25
Förster, M.: ZONF 3, 1927/1928, 66 - 68
Gordon, E. V. : MLR 21, 1926, 76 - 77

1228   - : *Studies on the -ing in Old English. Place-Names with
Some Etymological Notes,* SNPh 9, 1936/1937, pp. 66 -
119.

-IS :

1229 BARKER, H. F.   : *Surnames in -is,* AS 2, 1926/1927, pp. 316 - 318.

-ISM :

'1230 ANON.   : *Humorous Definitions of Certain ' isms ',* New York
Times, April 30, 1950, III, p. 3.

'1231 DODGE, M. : *Know Your isms*, New York : Farrar, 1950, 74 p..

'1232 GERHARD, E. S. : *A Few isms*, Word Study 13, 4, February 1938, pp. 5 - 6.

1233 MACKENZIE, F. : *Les emprunts de l'Angleterre à la France. Quelques termes à désinence -isme*, Mélanges de linguistique française offerts à M. Charles Bruneau (= Société de publications romanes et françaises sous la direction de Mario Roques, 45), Genève : E. Droz, 1954, x, 2u5, (2); pp. 117 - 120.

'1234 WALTON, M. et al. : *Isms : A Dictionary of Words Ending in -ism, -ology, and -phobia, with Some Similar Terms Arranged in Subject Order*, 2nd ed., rev. by Phyllis E. Charlesworth Sheffield : Sheffield City Libraries, 1968, 100 p.. (Previous ed. 1964)

'1235 WASSERMAN, L. : *Handbook of Political ' isms '*, New York : Association Press, 1941, 147 p..

1236 WERNER, W. L. : *' Nazi-ism ' and ' Nazism '*, AS 14, 1939, p. 318.

1237 WHITE, W. : *" McCarthyism " in Korea*, AS 40, 1965, pp. 301 - 302.

-MANSHIP :

'1238 RUSSELL, I. W. : *The Suffix -manship*, South Atlantic Bulletin 31, 1966, p. 3. (Abstract of a paper)

-MENT :

1239 ANON. : *Advisement et al.*, AS 21, 1946, p. 78. (advisement, disillusionment, surprisement, recruitement, groupment ...)

1119 GADDE, F.   : *On the History and Use of the Suffixes -ERY (-RY),*
-AGE and -MENT in English.

'1240 PAREIGYTÈ, E.   : *Priesagos -ment anglų kalboje atsiradimo klausimu*
(On the origin of the suffix -ment in English),
Kalbotyra 2, 1960, pp. 157 - 166, tab..
(Russian summary)

'1241 ROEDIGER, M.   : *Die Bedeutung des Suffixes ment,* Diss. Berlin 14.5.
1904, Berlin : Mayer & Müller, 1904, vi, 127 p..
(Germany 19, p. 22, 193)

-MOBILE :

1242 ALDRICH, R. I.   : *-mobile ,* AS 39, 1964, pp. 77 - 79.

1243 KAUFFMAN, B.   : *Types of Mobiles,* AS 25, 1950, p. 311.

1244 LUMIANSKY, R. M.   : ' *Freezemobile* ', AS 23, 1948, p. 158.

1245 O., R.   : *Progeny of ' automobile* ', AS 23, 1948, p. 209.

1246 PREUSS, F.   : *-mobile,* NS, N. F., 8, 1959, pp. 480 - 482.

-NESS :

'1247 ANON.   : *The Nesselrode to Ruin,* Time 79, May 11, 1962, p. 70.
(On the proliferation of the suffix -ness)

'1248 KING, H. R.   : *E pluribus togetherness,* Harper's , August 1957, pp.
51 - 53.

1249 OTA, F.   : *The Pronunciation of -ed, -edly, and -edness,* in
English and American Literature in Commemoration of
Professor Takejiro Nakayama's 61rst Birthday, Tokyo :
Shohakusha, 1961, pp. 281 - 293.

1250 WALDO, G. S.   : *Crooked, Crookedly, Crookedness,* ELT 12, 1957/1958,
pp. 51 - 59.

1223 WEYHE, H.   : *Zu den altenglischen Verbalabstrakten auf -nes und -ing, -ung.*

1251 WILLIAMS, Th.   : *On the -ness Peril*, AS 40, 1965, pp. 279 - 286.

-NIK :

1252 ACKERMAN, L. M.   : *Facetious Variations of ' Sputnik '*, AS 33, 1958, pp. 154 - 156.

1253 CĂPLESCU, R.   : *Sputnicii lunicii şi limba engleză*, RFRG 4, 1960, pp. 349 - 353.

'1254 DAVIS, O. L. jr.   : *The Sputnik Joke : Where is it ?* Tennessee Folklore Society Bulletin 24, 1958, pp. 1 - 2.

1255 FENZL, R.   : *Is the Suffix -nik Growing Fashionable?* Idioma 2, 6, 1965, pp. 260 - 261.

1256 HANSEN, K.   : *Sputniks, Spätniks und Spottniks*, Sprachpflege 10, 1960, p. 200.

1257 HARDER, K. B.   : *1. More Instances of -nik*, AS 41, 1966, pp. 150 - 154.

'1258 KIPARSKY, V.   : *Les aventures d'un suffixe*, RESL 40, 1964, pp. 114 - 118.

1259 MINTON, A.   : *Sputnik and Some of its Offshootniks*, Names 6, 195? pp. 112 - 117.

'1260 POČEPŎV, G. G.   : *Sputnik v anglijskom jazyke* (Sputnik in English), IJaS 1959, 6, pp. 83 - 89.

'1261 PREUSS, F.   : *Ableger des Sputnik* , Sprachforum 3, 1959/1960, pp 318 - 320.

1262 RUDNYCKYJ, J. B.   : *" Sputnik " and Its Derivatives in North American English,* in Proceedings of the Linguistic Circle

of Manitoba and North Dakota, Vol. 1, No. 1, 1959,
(Winnipeg, May 1959), pp. 27 - 28.

1263   - : *Sputnik and -nik Derivatives in the Present Language
of North America*, Etudes Slaves et Est-Européennes
(Slavic and East-European Studies), 4, Automne-Hiver
1959/1960, Parts 3-4, pp. 142 - 150.

'1264 SMALSTOCKI, R.   : *The Impact of the " Sputnik " on the English Language
of the U. S. A.*, in Papers of the Shevchenko Scienti-
fic Society, Inc., No. 3, Chicago, 1958, pp. 1 - 12.

1265 WHITE, W.   : *Sputnik and Its Satellites*, AS 33, 1958, pp. 153 -
154.

-OID :

1266 BOYS, Th.   : *Pronunciation of Words Ending in " -oid "*, N & Q,n.s.
2, 7, 1859, p. 507.
(refers to Fitz-Henry, No. 1268, and Buckton, No.
1267)

1267 BUCKTON, T. J.   : *Pronunciation of Words Ending in " -oid "*, N & Q,
n.s. 2, 7, 1859, p. 468.

1268 FITZ-HENRY, F.   : *Pronunciation of Words Ending in " -oid "*, N & Q,
n.s. 2, 7, 1859, p. 394.

-OLA :

1269 HARDER, K. B.   : *Nayola*, AS 36, 1961, p. 306.

1270 MOST, M.   : *An Instance of ' Linguola '*, AS 35, 1960, pp. 301 -
302.

1271 RANDLE, W.   : *Payola*, AS 36, 1961, pp. 104 - 116.

1272   - : *Foreign Usage of ' Payola '*, AS 36, 1961, pp. 275 -
277.

-OLOGY :

'1273 HARRY, J. E.   : *Ology*, Words 4, 1938, p. 120.

1274 POSTON, L. III   : *2. " Bugology "*, AS 39, 1964, p. 298.

'1234 WALTON, M. et al. : *Isms : A Dictionary of Words Ending in −ism, −ology, and −phobia, with Some Similar Terms Arranged in Subject Order.*

' 860 WHEELER, G. C.   : *A Blast for Formicology (Comments and Communications).*

-OMA :

'1275 KEIL, H.   : *The Historical Relationship Between the Concept of Tumor and the Ending −oma,* Bulletin of the History of Medicine, July - August 1950.

-ON, -LON :

1276 ALDRICH, R.   : *' −on ', ' −lon '*, AS 33, 1958, pp. 147 - 148.

-PHOBIA :

'1234 WALTON, M. et al. : *Isms : A Dictionary of Words Ending in −ism, −ology, and −phobia, with Some Similar Terms Arranged in Subject Order.*

-RĀD :

1277 BRADY, C.   : *The Old English Nominal Compounds in −rād,* PMLA 67, 1952, pp. 538 - 571.

-RAMA :

1278 BALD, W. : *Neologismen der englischen Werbesprache mit dem Suffix -rama*, Lebende Sprachen 14, 1969, pp. 6 - 9.

'1146 BEL'SKAJA, M. A. : *Funcionirovanie v sovremennom anglijskom jazyke morfem -(i)ana, -rama, -scape, -teria.*

'1279 CURTIS, O. : *Trigere shows ' dinneramas ' for Evening*, Austin (Texas), Statesman,October 28, 1955, p. 9.
(Dress designer Pauline Trigere coins this name for elegant pajamas worn at dinner)

'1280 DOPPAGNE, A. : *Parlez en rama* ..., Vie et Langage 92, October 1959, pp. 517 - 524; November 1959, 568 - 575.
(A collection of words ending in -rama from several languages)

1281 LANGE-KOWAL : *Panorama - Crédirama*, Lebende Sprachen 10, 1965, pp. 70 - 71.

'1282 LESNER, S. : *' Ramas ' of All Kinds Hold Spotlight Here*, Chicago : Daily News, September 9, 1955, p. 26.

1283 LOTZ, J. : *The Suffix -rama*, AS 29, 1954, pp. 156 - 158.

'1284 MORSEBERGER, R. E.: *Speaking of Books*, New York Times Book Review, February 26, 1961, p. 2.
(On words coined with the suffixes -rama and -thon)

1285 MOSSÉ, F. : *Honoré de Balzac and the Suffix ' -rama '*, AS 30, 1955, pp. 77 - 79.

'1286 PHILLIPSON, J. S. : *Wordarama*, Word Study 38, December 1962, pp. 6 - 7.
(On nouns formed with the suffix -ama)

1287 RYAN, W. M. : *A Plethorama*, AS 36, 1961, pp. 230 - 233.

-s$_2$:

'1288 MOLHOVA, J.   : *A New Substantival Suffix -s in Contemporary English*, GSUF 60, 1966, pp. 14 - 22.

'1289 VORONCOVA, G. I. : *Ob imennom formante s v sovremennom anglijskom jazyke* (The nominal suffix s in present-day English), IJaŠ 1948, 3, pp. 31 - 37; 4, pp. 6 - 18.

-SCAPE :

1290 ALDRICH, R. I.   : *The Development of " -scape "*, AS 41, 1966, pp. 155-157.

'1146 BEL'SKAJA, M. A. : *Funcionirovanie v sovremennom anglijskom jazyke morfem -(i)ana, -rama, -scape, -teria.*

-SION, -TION :

1291 TRAGER, F. H.   : *English -sion, -tion Nouns*, CJL 7, 1961, pp. 86 - 94.

-THON :

1292 NOLTE, E.   : *The ' -thon ' Suffix*, AS 29, 1954, p. 229.

'1284 MORSEBERGER, R. E.: *Speaking of Books.*

-TORIUM / -ORIUM :

1293 COSGRAVE, P. J.   : *' Corsetorium '*, AS 23, 1948, p. 75.

1294 READ, A. W.   : *' Odditorium ' - Believe it or Not*, AS 15, 1940, pp. 442.

1295 WILLIAMS, F. C.   : *Gymtorium*, AS 27, 1952, p. 153.

-TRON :

'1296 BAREŠ, K. : *Významova nosnost přípony -tron v angličtine* (Semantic capacity of the suffix -tron in English), Československý terminologický Časopis 3, 1, Bratislava, 1964, pp. 11 - 29.

-UNG :

1223 WEYHE, H. : *Zu den altenglischen Verbalabstrakten auf -nes und -ing, -ung.*

-VILLE :

1297 BAUERLE, R. F. : *The Highly Productive Suffix ' -ville '*, AS 35, 1960, pp. 312 - 314.

224

2) DERIVATION OF ADJECTIVES

(General studies ...)

'1298 ALOVA, N. P. : *Otnositel'nye prilagatel'nye veščestnogo značenija i ich sinonimy.* (*Na materiale sovremennom anglijskom jazyke*) (Relational adjectives with the meaning ' material ' and their synonyms in present-day English), Diss. Kiev, 1965 (ANUKr - L).

'1299 BOROVIK, M. A. : *Transformacionnyj analiz nekotorych proizvodnych prilagatel'nych sovremennogo anglijskogo jazyka* (Transformational analysis of some derived adjectives in modern English), UZ LP I, 272, 1965, pp. 41 - 58, tab..

1300 BRUGGENCATE, K. ten : *Some Remarks on the Use and Derivation of Adjectives*, Taalstudie 7, 1886, pp. 224 - 232.

1301 CARR, E. B. : *Notes Concerning Language Names*, AS 28, 1953, pp. 62 - 64.
(-ish, -ic, -an, -ian, -ite, -ese)

1302 CHAPMAN, R. W. : *Adjectives from Proper Names*, S. P. E. Tract No. 52 Oxford : Clarendon Press, 1939, pp. 47 - 90.

1303 COATES, J. : *Denominal Adjectives : a Study in Syntactic Relationships Between Modifier and Head*, Lingua 27, 1971, pp. 160 - 169.
(The article is derived from her M. A. thesis, London, 1968)

1304 FARSI, A. A. : *Classification of Adjectives*, LL 18, 1968, pp. 45 - 60.

1305 FUNK, W.-P. : *Adjectives with Negative Affixes in Modern English and the Problem of Synonymy*, ZAA 19, 1971, pp. 364 - 386.

'1306 KARASČUK, P. M.　: *Nekotorye voprosy affiksal'nogo slovoproizvodstva* (*na materiale prilagatel'nych sovremennogo anglijskogo jazyka)* (Some problems of affixation : English adjectives), UZ Dal U 5, 1962, pp. 107 - 125, tab..

1307 KÖNIG, E.　: *Transitive Adjektive*, LBer 14, 1971, pp. 42 - 50.

'1308 KOČETOV, V. P.　: *Parallel'nye suffiksal'nye obrazovanija anglijskich prilagatel'nych s odinakovoj osnovoj* (Parallel suffixal adjective formations from simple bases in English), Fil. sbornik LGU , pp. 58 - 64.

'1309 KOLIN, N.　: *The Adjectival Suffixes in English*, Sofija : Nauka i izkustvo, 1968, 108 p..

1310 LJUNG, M.　: *English Denominal Adjectives. A Generative Study of the Semantics of a Group of High-Frequency Denominal Adjectives in English*, Lund, 1970, 249 p..
(= Gothenburg Studies in English 21, Acta Universitatis Gothoburgensis)

1311 LORD, J. B.　: *Sequence in Clusters of Prenominal Adjectives and Adjectivals in English*, JEL 4, 1970, pp. 57 - 69.

1312 MARCHAND, H.　: *On Attributive and Predicative Derived Adjectives and Some Problems Related to the Distinction*, Anglia 84, 1966, pp. 131 - 149.

1312 a MEROŠNIČENKO, G. V. : *Opredelitel'nye narečija v sovremennom anglijskom jazyke* (Attributive adverbs in English), AK Diss. Moscow, 1955 (1 - M Ped I).

1313 PETERSON, T. H.　: *A Transformational Analysis of Some Derived Verbs and Adjectives in English*, PEGS Paper No. 7, November 1, 1967, Washington, D.C., Center for Applied Linguistics.

1314 SCHNEIDER, I.　: *Das englische Zugehörigkeitsadjektiv in seiner historischen Entwicklung*, Diss. Mainz 26.2.1949; 1949, 122 lvs.n..
(Germany 65, p. 332)

1315 SCOTT, R. I.   : " *Qualm* " *as a Verb,* " *Lunch* " *as an Adjective,* AS 38
                      1963, p. 159.

'1316 SLUCHOVSKAJA, T. A. : *Die aus Substantiven gebildeten Adjektiva im Sy-*
                      stem der englischen Sprache der Gegenwart, Diss. Lo-
                      monossow University, 1951.
                      (Russian dissertation quoted in German, cf. ZAA 1,
                      1953, p. 248)
                      Reviews :
                      'Anon.   : IJaš 3, 1952, 125

1317 SMITH, G. C. MOORE :*Superlative Adjectives Formed from Substantives,*
                      RES 5, 1929, p. 203.
                      (beautiest, childest, harlottyest, hazardest, ma-
                      jestiest, rubbishest, savourest, sugarest)

1318 TOURBIER, R.   : *Das Adverb als attributives Adjektiv im Neuenglischer*
                      Diss. Berlin 22.5.1928, Leipzig : Akademische Verlags
                      gesellschaft, 1928, 80 p..
                      (Germany 44, p. 56)

1319 VALESIO, P.   : *Suffissi aggettivali fra l'inglese e l'italiano,*
                      Le St 2, 1967, pp. 357 - 368.
                      (English and Russian summaries)

1320 W.   : *On English Adjectives,* The Philological Museum 1,
                      1832, pp. 359 - 372.

'1321 WALKER, J. A. : *Adjective Suffixes in Old English,* Ph. D. Diss. Cam-
                      bridge, Mass., 1948.

1322   - : *The Rank-Number Relationship of Adjectival Suffixes*
                      in Old English, Ph Q 27, 1948, pp. 264 - 272.

-ABLE :

1323 ABRAHAM, W.   : *Passiv und Verbalableitung auf e. -able, dt. -bar,*
                          FoL 4, 1970, pp. 38 - 52.

1324 AUGHTRY, Ch.   : *Who Uses ' Knowledgeable ' ?* AS 34, 1959, pp. 71 -
                          72.

1009 DANIELSSON, B.   : *Studies on the Accentuation of Polysyllabic Latin,*
                          Greek, and Romance Loan-Words in English with Spe-
                          cial Reference to those Ending in -able, -ate, -ator,
                          -ible, -ic, -ical and -ize.

'1325 GALL, F.   : *On English Adjectives in -able,* London, 1877.

1326 HALL, F.   : *On English Adjectives in -ABLE with Special Refe-*
                          rence to RELIABLE, London : Trübner & Co., 1877, vii,
                          238 p..
                          Reviews :
                          Anon.   : The Saturday Review of Literature 43,
                                     1877, 680 - 681
                          Anon.   : The Nation 26, 1878, 138 - 139
                          'Beljame, A. : Revue Critique n.s. 12, 1, 12 - 14
                          Lindner, F. : ESt 1, 1877, 503 - 505

1327 KING, A.   : *' Jeep ' and ' Peep ', ' Pipable ' and ' Jeepable ',*
                          AS 37, 1962, pp. 77 - 78.

1328 POLDAUF, I.   : *Die Bildung der englischen Adjektiva auf -ble. Ein*
                          Beitrag zur Theorie des synchronen Wortbildungsleh-
                          re, ZAA 7, 1959, pp. 229 - 245.

'1329 TERZJAN, R. V.   : *Otglagol'nye prilagatel'nye s suffiksom -able v*
                          sovremennom anglijskom jazyke (Deverbative adjec-
                          tives in -able in modern English), UZ Erev U 79,
                          1962, No. 2, pp. 15 - 22.

1330 WILLIAMSON, F.   : *" Tentable ", Adjective,* N & Q 152, 1927, p. 207.

-AL₂ :

1331 HALL, R. A. jr.   : *' Dialectal', 'Dialectic', 'Dialectical'*, AS 17, 1942, pp. 282 - 283.

1332 HENCH, A. L.   : *' Contractural' versus 'Contractual'*, AS 24, 1949, p. 307.

'1333 ISITT, D.   : *A Synchronic Investigation into the Principles Governing the Use of the Suffixes -al, -ic, -ly, -y in English*, Fil. lic. Thesis, University of Göteborg, 1967. (unpublished)

1334 PRESCOTT, J.   : *'Candidatorial' and 'Candidatorially'*, AS 20, 1945, p. 305.

-ATE₂ :

'1335 BELOZEROVA, E. P.   : *Ob assimiljacii latinskich prilagatel'nych na -ate v anglijskom jazyke v XVI - XVII vekach* (On the assimilation of Latin adjectives in -ate in 16th and 17th centuries English), UZ M Ped I, 1961, No. 166, KLFAJa, pp. 221 - 234.

'1336   - : *K voprosu ob obrazovanii prilagatel'nych ot pričastij (Obrazovanie v anglijskom jazyke e prilagatel'nych ot Latinskich pričastij Participium Perfecti Passivi glagolov na -are)* (On the adjectivization of Latin participles in English), UZ IMO 11, 1963, pp. 15 - 28.

1009 DANIELSSON, B.   : *Studies on the Accentuation of Polysyllabic Latin, Greek, and Romance Loan-Words in English with Special Reference to those Ending in -able, -ate, -ate -ible, -ic, -ical, and -ize.*

1337 DETER, H.   : *Alte Partizipia auf -en, -ed und -ate, die im modernen Englisch zu Adjektiven geworden sind*, Diss.

Berlin 17.10.1934, Saalfeld / Ostpr.: Günther, (1934),
ii, 99 p., vita.
(Germany 50, p. 571)
Reviews :
Marcus, H. : ASNS 167, 1935, 139

-ATIVE :

1338 LINDELÖF, U. : *Some Observations on the English Adjective-Formations*
in -ative and -atory, Helsingfors, 1943, 20 p..
(= Societas Scientiarum Fennica Commentationes Humanarum Litterarum 13, 4)

-ATORY :

1338 LINDELÖF, U. : *Some Observations on the English Adjective-Formations*
in -ative and -atory.

-ED :

1339 COX, J. H. : *Partyed*, AS 7, 1931/1932, p. 392.

1337 DETER, H. : *Alte Partizipia auf -en, -ed und -ate, die im modernen*
Englisch zu Adjektiven geworden sind.

1340 GERRING, H. : *The Pronunciation of Adjectives and Attributive Past*
Participles in -ed, SMSpr 13, 1937, pp. 145 - 186.

1341 HIRTLE, W. H. : *-ed Adjectives Like ' Verandahed' and 'blue-eyed'*, JL
6, 1970, pp. 19 - 36.

1342 KATAYAMA, N. : *-edly no hatsuon ni tsuite* (On the pronunciation of
the English suffix *-edly*), HNR 19, 1964, pp. 1 - 13.

1249 OTA, F. : *The Pronunciation of -ed, -edly and -edness.*

608 ROCHOWANSKA, I. : *Anglická adjektivní kompozita končící na -ing a -ed*
(The English compound adjectives in -ing and -ed).

1343 SHOCKLEY, M. S. : *' Campaniled'*, AS 29, 1954, p. 238.

1250 WALDO, G. S. : *Crooked, Crookedly, Crookedness.*

-EL$_2$ / -IEL :

1344 LANGE-KOWAL : *Wortbildungen mit den Suffixen -el und -iel*, Lebende Sprachen 13, 1968, p. 71.

-EN$_1$:

'1345 VOLDEBA, R. : *Adjectives Derived from Nouns by Means of the Ending -en*, De Drie Talen 30, 1914, pp. 113 - 115, 129 - 133.

-FUL$_2$:

1346 BROWN, A. F. : *The Derivation of English Adjectives Ending in -ful*, Ph. D. Diss. University of Pennsylvania, 1958, 55 p..
(DAb 19, 4, 1958, 803 - 804)

-IC / -ICAL :

'1347 CLARKE, E. J. : *A Study of English Orthography, with Special Reference to the Spelling of the Suffix (ik)*, M. A. Liverpool, 1966/1967.
(England 17, p. 14; 302)

1009 DANIELSSON, B. : *Studies on the Accentuation of Polysyllabic Latin, Greek, and Romance Loan-Words in English with Special Reference to those Ending in -able, -ate, -ate -ible, -ic, -ical, and -ize.*

'1348 EIJKMAN, L. P. H. : *De uitgangen -ic en -ical*, De Drie Talen 40, 1924, pp. 65 - 68.

231

1331 HALL, R. A. jr.　: *'Dialectal', 'Dialectic', 'Dialectical'.*

'1333 ISITT, D.　: *A Synchronic Investigation into the Principles Governing the Use of the Suffixes -al, -ic, -ly, -y in English.*

-ISH :

'1349 MAŠKOVSKAJA, V. I.　: *Anglijskie proizvodnye prilagatel'nye na -y i -ish i ich ispol'zovanie poeme Bajrona " Don Žuan " (* Derived English adjectives in -y and -ish and their use in Byron' Don Juan), Ak. Diss. Moscow, 1956, (1 - M Ped I).

824 NEUHAUS, H. J.　: *Beschränkungen in der Grammatik der Wortableitungen im Englischen.*

825　- : *Beschränkungen in der Grammatik der Wortableitungen im Englischen (Constraints in the Grammar of Word-Derivations in English).*

-LESS :

876 HAYAKAWA, H.　: *Negation in William Faulkner.*

-LEWE :

1350 POGATSCHER, A.　: *Das mittelenglische Suffix -lewe,* Anglia B 13, 1902, pp. 235 - 236.

-LY / -LIE :

1351 BROWN, H.　: *The Modern Development of Middle English -ly, -lie in Rhyme,* Harvard Studies and Notes in Philology and Literature Vol. 18, 1935, pp. 43 - 45.

'1333 ISITT, D.　: *A Synchronic Investigation into the Principles Governing the Use of the Suffixes -al, -ic, -ly, -y in English.*

1352 PILTZ, O.   : *Zur englischen Wortbildungslehre.*
      3. Ueber like und die Bildungssilbe ly , ASNS 10,
      1852, pp. 361 - 380; 11, 1852, pp. 192 - 208.

1353   - : *Zur englischen Wortbildungslehre.*
      3. Ueber lic und die Bildungssilbe ly, ASNS 11,
      1852, pp. 365 - 382; 12, 1853, pp. 295 - 312; 13,
      1853, pp. 293 - 309; 14, 1853, pp. 342 - 378.

1354 SHOOK, L. K.   : *A Technical Construction in Old English. Translatior*
      Loans in -lic, Medieval Studies, Pontefical Institu-
      te of Medieval Studies, Toronto, 2, 1940, pp. 253 -
      257.

1355 SLATER, J.   : *A Renewed Meaning for the Suffix -ly,* AS 38, 1963,
      pp. 301.
      (Type : hourly)

1355 a UHLER, K.   : *Die Bedeutungsgleichheit der altenglischen Adjektiv*
      und Adverbia mit und ohne -lic (-lice), Heidelberg:
      Carl Winter, 1926, ix, 68 p..
      (= Anglistische Forschungen 62)
      Reviews :
      Callaway, M. jr. : MLN 43, 1928, 203 - 204
      Malone, K.   : JEGP 25, 1926, 586 - 588
      W., S. L. P.   : MLR 21, 1926, 344

$-Y_2$:

'1333 ISITT, D.   : *A Synchronic Investigation into the Principles Go-*
      verning the Use of the Suffixes -al, -ic, -ly, -y
      in English.

'1349 MAŠKOVSKAJA, V. I.   : *Anglijskie proizvodnye prilagatel'nye na -y i -ish*
      i ich ispol'zovanie v poeme Bajrona " Don Žuan"
      (Derived English adjectives in -y and -ish and the
      use in Byron's Don Juan).

'1356 OBA, K.   : *The Adjective Suffix -y in Present-Day English,*
      Kanaz Jk 1, 1963, pp. 57 - 77.

3) DERIVATION OF VERBS

(General studies ...)

' 900 ANON.   : ' *Debunk' out of 'Delouse'.*

'1357 ARAKIN, V. D.   : *Vozniknovenie kornevogo ili bessuffiksal'nogo sposoba slovoobrazovanija v anglijskom jazyke*, in Sbornik statej po jazykoznaniju. Pamjati zaslužennogo dejatelja nauki Professora Maksima Vladimiroviča Sergievskogo, Moscow, 1961, pp. 43 - 50.
(On book ⟶ to book in English)

1358 BLADIN, V.   : *Studies on Denominative Verbs in English*, Diss. Uppsala, Uppsala : Almqvist & Wiksells, 1911, viii, 184 p..
Reviews :
Anon.   : N & Q , s. 11, 5, 1912, 19
Krummacher, M. : NS 22, 1915, 197 - 198
M(acawley), G. C.: MLR 8, 1913, 274 - 275

1359 BÖHNKE, M.   : *Die Flexion des Verbums in Laʒamons Brut*, Diss. Berlin 11.8.1906, Berlin : Mayer & Müller, 1906, vi, (2), 89 p., vita.
(Germany 21, p. 16, 89)

1360 BOWES, A.   : *Verbalized Surnames*, N & Q , s. 12, 9, 1921, p. 433.
(to Pelmanize, to grangerize, to bowdlerize, to galvanize, to kyanize, to devil...)

1361 BRILIOTH, B.   : *Intensiva och iterativa verb, bildade genom affix i Engelskan*, Nordisk Tidsskrift for Filologi s. 3, 20, 1911, pp. 97 - 166.

1362 CASTRO, J. P. de   : *Verbalized Surnames*, N & Q, s. 12, 9, 1921, p. 432.

1363 CHANG, P.   : *Lun Ying-yü ming-tz'n Chuan-ch'eng tung-tz'n chi ch'i tso-yung* (On the conversion of English nouns into verbs), HFYW 2, 1958, pp. 150 - 157.

1364 COARD, R. L.   : *The Verb Managerie*, Georgia Review 19, Spring 1965, pp. 77 - 80.
(On verbs derived from animal names; refers to the chapter ' Words from the Names of Animals' in Greenough - Kittredge, No. 100)

1365 CUNNINGHAM, W.   : *'Dessert' as a Verb*, AS 33, 1958, p. 229.

1065 a FEY, I.   : *Konversionssubstantive und Konversionsverben in Fach sprachen und Schichten des Englischen.*

1065 b   - : *Konversionssubstantive und Konversionsverben in Fach sprachen und Schichten des Englischen (Conversion-Nouns and Conversion-Verbs in Technical Terminology and in the Colloquial, Slang and Cant Strata of the English Language).*

'1366 FÜLLER, L.   : *Das Verbum in der Ancrene Riwle*, Diss. Jena 11.3. 1938; (1937), 99 lvs.n..
(Parts of it published : Jena : Neuenhahn, 1937, 38 p.)
(Germany 54, p. 368)

795 GUILLEMARD, F. H. H.: *Verbalized Surnames.*

'1367 HALE, C. P.   : *Tailoring Terms : ' to White-Horse', 'to Dead-Horse* N & Q , January 20, 166, p. 41.

798 HARRISON, H. G.   : *Verbalized Surnames.*

902 HENCH, A. L.   : *Two More ' De-' Verbs.*

1368 HOWREN, R.   : *The Generation of Old English Weak Verbs*, Lg 43, 1967, pp. 674 - 685.

'1369 JANUS   : *A Spectator's Note Book*, London, Spectator, August 9, 1940, p. 137; August 16, 1940, p. 161.
(' to embus' is a new formation on the analogy of 'embark')

1370 KULAK, M.   : *Die semantischen Kategorien der mit Nullmorphem ab-*
                          geleiteten desubstantivischen Verben des heutigen En-
                          glischen und Deutschen, Diss. Tübingen 21.2.1964, Tü-
                          bingen, 1964, iii, 253 p., vita.
                          (Germany 80, p. 995)
                          Reviews :
                          Goergens, F. J. : ZMaF 34, 1967, 325 - 329

1371 LANGE, H.   : *Das Zeitwort in den beiden Handschriften von Laʒamons*
                          Brut, Diss. Strassburg 1905, Strassburg : Elsass-Lo-
                          thringische Druckerei und Lithographie-Anstalt, 1906,
                          130 p., vita.
                          (Derivation of weak verbs)

815 M., G. M.   : *Verbalized Surnames.*

787 McGOVERN, J. B.   : *Verbalized Surnames.*

1371 a MACKIN, R.   : *Exercises in English Patterns and Usages : 3, the*
                          Verb, Tenses, Patterns and Idioms; 4, Forms of Words,
                          Inflection; 5, Forms of Words, Derivation, Oxford
                          University Press, 1962, iv, 60 p.; 1966, iv, 68 p.;
                          1966, iv, 59 p..

1372 McMILLAN, J. B.   : *' Charivari' as a Verb*, AS 22, 1947, p. 74.

639 MARCHAND, H.   : *Compound and Pseudo-Compound Verbs in Present-Day*
                          English.

1373   - : *Die Ableitung desubstantivischer Verben mit Nullmor-*
                      phem im Französischen und die entsprechenden Verhält-
                      nisse im Englischen und Deutschen, ZFSL 73, 1963, pp.
                      164 - 179.

1374   - : *Die Ableitung desubstantivischer Verben mit Nullmor-*
                      phem im Englischen, Französischen und Deutschen, NS,
                      N. F., 13, 1964, pp. 105 - 118.

1375   - : *Die Ableitung deadjektivischer Verben im Deutschen,*
                      Englischen, Französischen, IF 74, 1969, pp. 155 -
                      173.

903 : *Die deadjektivischen reversativen Verben im Deutsche Englischen und Französischen : entmilitarisieren, demilitarize, démilitariser.*

'1313 PETERSON, T. H. : *A Transformational Analysis of Some Derived Verbs and Adjectives in English.*

1376 PRENNER, M. : *The Current Tendency Toward Denominative Verbs*, AS 13, 1938, pp. 193 - 196.

1377 RAITH, J. : *Die englischen Nasalverben*, Diss. München 9.3.1931, Leipzig : B. Tauchnitz, 1931, 128 p..
(= Beiträge zur englischen Philologie, 17)
(Germany 47, p. 558)
Reviews :
Dehmer, H. : NS 41, 1933, 465 - 466
Holthausen, F. : Anglia B 43, 1932, 88 - 89

1378 REUTER, O. : *On the Development of English Verbs from Latin and French Past Participles*, Societas Scientiarum Fennica, Commentationes Humanarum Litterarum 6, 6, Helsingfors : Akademiska Bokhandeln, 1934, (vi), 170 p..
Reviews :
B., A. O. : MLR 30, 1935, 267 - 268
Flom, G. T.: JEGP 34, 1935, 250 - 253
Serjeantson, M. S. : ES 20, 1938, 42 - 43

839 ROCKINGHAM : *Verbalized Surnames.*

1379 SCHRACK, D. : *Ne. 'to spotlight' und 'to stagemanage'. Studien zu Entwicklung und Struktur der verbalen Pseudokomposita im Englischen mit Berücksichtigung anderer ger manischer Sprachen. Ein Beitrag zum Problem von ' Sprache' und ' Sprechen'*, Diss. Tübingen 1.4.1966 Tübingen, 1966, xvi, 237 p., vita.
(Germany 82, p. vii, 56)

1380 SCHULDT, C. : *Die Bildung der schwachen Verba im Altenglischen*,
Diss. Kiel 27.5.1905, Kiel : Lüdtke & Martens, 1905,
30 p., (1), vita.
(= Kieler Studien zur englischen Philologie, N. F.
1)
(Germany 20, p. 301, 83)
Reviews :
Barnouw, A. J. : ASNS 119, 1907, 448 - 449
Jordan, R. : Anglia B 18, 1907, 33 - 36
Kock, E. A. : ESt 44, 1911/1912, 387 - 388

1381 SCHWARZ, W. : *Studien über die aus dem Lateinischen entlehnten Zeit-
wörter der englischen Sprache*, Diss. Strassburg 19o2,
Strassburg : Hertzer, Hubert & Fritsch, 1903, viii,
62 p., vita, (1 p. errata).

1382 SCHWERDTFEGER, G. : *Das schwache Verbum in Aelfrics Homilien*, Diss. Marburg, Marburg : O. Ehrhardt, 1893, 59 p., vita.

1315 SCOTT, R. I. : *" Qualm" as a Verb, "Lunch" as an Adjective*, AS 38,
1963, p. 159.

725 SHUMAN, R. B. : *To 'Daughter out' and 'to Sheriff-out', Two New Coinages*.

1107 SIL'NICKAJA, G. V. : *Transformacionnyj analiz i ego rol' v semantičeskoj
klassifikacii slov. (Na materiale suščestvitel'nych
i glagolov, svjazannych drug s drugom po konversii)*
(Transformational analysis and its role in the semantic
classification of words. On the material of the substantives and verbs related through conversion).

1383 SOGA, M. : *Similarities Between Japanese and English Verb Derivations*, Lingua 25, 1970, pp. 268 - 290.

1384 SOSAL'SKAJA, E. G. : *The Stylistic Use of Denominal Verbs in Present-Day
English* (Quoted in German, reference taken from ZAA
1, 1953, p. 248), Paper, Moscow Pedagogical State
Institute of Foreign Languages, 21 lvs., polycopied.

847 SPARKE, A.   : *Verbalized Surnames.*

1385 STRONG, M. E.   : *New Verbs,* AS 1, 1925/1926, p. 292.
(to rather, ...)

'1386 SWEET, M.   : *The Third Class of Weak Verbs of Primitive Teutonic with Special Reference to its Development in Anglo-Saxon,* Diss. Bryn Mawr, 1892.

1387 THÜNS, B.   : *Das Verbum bei Orm. Ein Beitrag zur ae. Grammatik,* Diss. Leipzig 21.2.1909, Weida i. Th. : Thomas & Hubert, 1909, 77 p., vita.
(Germany 24, p. 508)
(esp. pp. 36 - 59)

1137 WERNER, W. L.   : *"Motorcâde" and "to Demagogue".*

1388   - : *" Referee" as a Verb,* AS 8, 1933, p. 81.

861 WHITEBROOK, M.   : *Verbalized Surnames.*

863 WOOD, F. L.   : *Verbalized Surnames.*

-ATE$_3$:

1009 DANIELSSON, B.   : *Studies on the Accentuation of Polysyllabic Latin, Greek, and Romance Loan-Words in English with Special Reference to those Ending in -able, -ate, -ator -ible, -ic, -ical, and -ize.*

-EN$_2$:

1389 H., L. S.   : *Safen,* AS 6, 1930/1931, p. 305.

1390 JESPERSEN, O.   : *The History of a Suffix,* AL 1,1, 1939, pp. 48 - 56.

1390 a PALMGREN, C.   : *De N.E. en-verben i historik belysning,* Nordisk Tidsskift for Filologi, 3rd series, 19, 1910/1911, pp. 27 - 51.

-ETTAN :

1391 MARCKWARDT, A.   : *The Verbal Suffix -ettan in Old English,* Lg 18, 1942, pp. 275 - 281.

-IFY :

1392 DAVIS, T. W.   : *Alkalize, Alkalinize, and Alkalify,* Science 85, January 15, 1937, pp. 75 - 76.

1393 ERICSON, E. E.   : *' Happify' - its Status,* AS 33, 1958, p. 295.

1394 MAHN, L.   : *Zur Morphologie und Semantik englischer Verben auf -IFY mit Berücksichtigung französischer und deutscher Entsprechungen,* Diss. Tübingen 1971, Tübingen : Tübinger Beiträge zur Linguistik 27, 1971, viii, 247 p..

1395   - : *Zur Morphologie und Semantik englischer Verben auf -IFY mit Berücksichtigung französischer und deutscher Entsprechungen (On the Morphology and Semantics of English Verbs Ending in -IFY with Consideration of Relative Verbs in French and German),* Diss. Tübingen, Tübinger Beiträge zur Linguistik 27, Tübingen, 1971, 247 p.,in English and American Studies in German, Summaries of Theses and Monographs. A Supplement to Anglia, 1971, Tübingen : M. Niemeyer, ix, (1), 190 p.; pp. 19 - 21.

-IZE :

1392 DAVIS, T. W.   : *Alkalize, Alkalinize, and Alkalify.*

1009 DANIELSSON, B.   : *Studies on the Accentuation of Polysyllabic Latin, Greek, and Romance Loan-Words in English with Special Reference to those Ending in -able, -ate, -ator,*

-ible, -ic, -ical and -ize.

1396 EMENEAU, M. B.   : *Some Neologisms in "-ize"* , AS 22, 1947, pp. 71 - 72.
(to personalize, to comfortize, to winterize)

1397 GREENE, Ch. P.   : *Forumize*, AS 3, 1928, pp. 432 - 433.

1398 HARDER, K. B.   : *Is 'finalise (-ize) ' an Australian Coinage?* AS 36, 1961, pp. 239 - 240.

1399 HERMANN, W.   : *Verbalendung -ize oder -ise?* NS, N. F., 3, 1954, pp. 552 - 554.

1400 IRWIN, R. L.   : *On Dropping the '-ize'*, CE 12, 1950, p. 345.
(also in English Journal 40, 1951, p. 164)

'1401 LERCH, E.   : *Deutsch -isieren, französisch -iser, englisch -ize (ise)*, Sprachkunde 2, 1938, pp. 4 - 9.

903 MARCHAND, H.   : *Die deadjektivischen reversativen Verben im Deutschen, Englischen und Französischen : entmilitarisieren, demilitarize, démilitariser.*

'1402 MILLER, W. L.   : *The IZE Have it*, The Reporter, December 29, 1955, p. 19.
(The overuse of -ize as a verb suffix)

'1403 PALZER, A.   : *Zur Geschichte von englisch -ize. Gebrauch und Vorkommen der Endung im englischen Schrifttum von der Renaissance bis zum 18.Jahrhundert*, Diss. Mainz 26.: 1954, (1954), xxxvi, 223 lvs.n..
(Germany 70, p. 508)

1404 PERKINS, A. E.   : *New Verbs in -IZE*, AS 3, 1928, p. 434.
(to machinize, to routinize, to rapturize)

'1405 STEPHENS, G. D.   : *Wise, ize, bar, and bug*, CEA Critic, January, 1958, p. 1.
(A listing of coined terms)

1406 TRACY, K.   : *" Finalize" : a Case History*, AS 40, 1965, pp. 302 - 304.

-JAN :

1407 BAMMESBERGER, A.   : *Deverbative jan Verba des Altenglischen*, Diss. München 11.6.1965, München : Mikrokopie G.m.b.H., 1965, x, 146 p., vita.
(Germany 81, p. 927)

-L :

1408 FLOM, G. T.   : *A List of English Dialect Verbs with the Suffix -l*, Dialect Notes 2, 1900 - 1904, pp. 404 - 415.

-SIAN :

1409 FAISS, K.   : *Old English Verbs in -sian. Bemerkungen zu Lars-G. Hallanders Studie*, LaS 2, 1969, pp. 233 - 243.

1410 HALLANDER, L.-G.   : *Old English Verbs in -SIAN. A Semantic and Derivational Study*, Stockholm : Almqvist & Wiksell, 1966, 619 p..
(= Acta Universitatis Stockholmiensis, Stockholm Studies in English 15)
Reviews :
Ball, C. J. E.   : RES 21, 1970, 187 - 189
Koziol, H.   : ASNS 207, 1971, 119 - 121
Lindberg, C.   : SNPh 38, 1966, 402 - 405
Potter, S.   : MLR 65, 1970, 861 - 862
Schentke, M.   : ZAA 16, 1968, 79 - 80

242

4) DERIVATION OF ADVERBS

(General studies ...)

1411 BORST, E.　　　: *Die Gradadverbien im Englischen*, Heidelberg : Carl
　　　　　　　　　　Winters Universitätsbuchhandlung, 1902, vii, 170 p..
　　　　　　　　　　(= Anglistische Forschungen 10)
　　　　　　　　　　Reviews :
　　　　　　　　　　Stoffel　　　　: ESt 35,1905,383 - 395

1412 BRUGGENCATE, K. ten : *Contributions to English Grammar*, Taalstudie 11,
　　　　　　　　　　1890, pp. 109 - 115 (of the English part).
　　　　　　　　　　(esp. pp. 114 - 115)

1413 CAMPBELL, A.　　: *Old English Grammar*, Oxford : Clarendon Press, 1959,
　　　　　　　　　　xiv, 423 p..
　　　　　　　　　　(pp. 275 - 277 : formation of adverbs)

1414 DONGEN, W. A. van : *Adverbs Formed From Monosyllabic Words in -y*,
　　　　　　　　　　ES 1, 1919, pp. 75 - 77.

1415 FETTIG, A.　　　: *Die Gradadverbien im Mittelenglischen*, Diss. Heidel-
　　　　　　　　　　berg 22.1.1935, Heidelberg : Carl Winters Universi-
　　　　　　　　　　tätsbuchhandlung, 1934, 222 p..
　　　　　　　　　　(= Anglistische Forschungen 79)
　　　　　　　　　　(Germany 51, p. 180)

'1416 FRÖHLICH, A.　　: *Englisches Adjektiv-Adverb*, Praxis 3, 1956, pp.
　　　　　　　　　　6 - 8.

1417 GROSS, E.　　　: *Bildung des Adverbs bei Chaucer*, Diss. Berlin 21.5.
　　　　　　　　　　1921, Weimar : Uschmann, 1921, 48 p..
　　　　　　　　　　(Germany 37, p. 1102)

1418 HAAS, H.　　　　: *Studien zur Adverbfunktion von Adjektivformen in
　　　　　　　　　　frühneuenglischer Zeit. (Die Stufen der gradadver-
　　　　　　　　　　biellen Funktion von Adjektiven zur Modifizierung
　　　　　　　　　　von Adjektiven, untersucht an ausgewählten Texten
　　　　　　　　　　und dargestellt an ausgewählten Beispielen)*, Diss.
　　　　　　　　　　Köln 22.12.1958, (1958), 301 p..
　　　　　　　　　　(Germany 74, p. 420)

1419 JESSEN, Th.   : *Ueber die Bildung des Adverbs im Mittelenglischen*,
                          Diss. Kiel 25.7.1922, Kiel, 1921, 99 lvs..
                          (Abstract : Kiel : Schmidt & Klaunig, 2 lvs.)
                          (Germany 38, p. 511)

1420 JONSON, G.   : *Adverbs of Degree in the Observer*, MSpråk 61, 1967,
                          pp. 337 - 353.

1421 KIRCHNER, G.   : *Gradadverbien. Restriktiva und Verwandtes im heu-
                          tigen Englisch (britisch und amerikanisch)*, Halle:
                          VEB M. Niemeyer Verlag, 1955, 126 p..
                          Reviews :
                          Heuer, H.   : ASNS 194, 1958, 72 - 73
                          Thurber, R. M. : JEGP 57, 1958, 530
                          (see also Poldauf, No. 1427)

1422 KNOWLES, D. R. J. : *De-adjectival Adverbials in Transformational Gram-
                          mar*, Ph. D. London, 1970, 339 lvs..

1423 KÜHNER, G.   : *Die Intensiv-Adverbien des Frühneuenglischen*, Diss.
                          Heidelberg 27.7.1934, Ludwigshafen : König & Lieb,
                          1934, viii, 108 p., vita.
                          (Germany 50, p. 428)

1424 NICOLAI, O.   : *Die Bildung des Adverbs im Altenglischen*, Diss.
                          Kiel 10.1.1907, Kiel : H. Fiencke, 1907, 58 p., vita.
                          (Germany 22, p. 345, 79)

1425 NILSEN, D.L. F.   : *English Adverbials*, The Hague : Mouton, 1972.
                          (= Janua linguarum, series practica 125)

1426 POČEPCOV, G. G.   : *Ot prilagatel'nye narečija v anglijskom jazyke
                          (v sopostavlenii s sootvetstvujuščimi narecijami
                          v russkom jazyke)* (Adverbs formed from adjectives
                          in English (in comparison with similar adverbs in
                          Russian) 1 - M Ped I, 1953, 374 p..

1427 POLDAUF, I.   : *Further Comments on Gustav Kirchners Gradadverbien*,
                          PhP 2, 1959, pp. 1 - 6.

'1428 SPECTOR, R. D.   : *Adverbial Adjectives*, Word Study 33, December 1957
    pp. 7 - 8.

'1429 SPITZBARDT, H.   : *Die modernen Gradadverbien. Ein Beitrag zum engli-
schen Sprachgebrauch des 20. Jahrhunderts*, Diss.
Jena 22.9.1954, Jena, 1954, xv, 289 lvs.n..
(Germany 70, p. 392)

1430   - : *English Adverbs of Degree and Their Semantic Fiel*
PhP 8, 1965, pp. 349 - 359 .

' 616 WOODWARD, E. H.   : *Adverbial Adjectives.*

$-LY_2/ -LIE_2$:

1351 BROWN, H.   : *The Modern Development of Middle English -ly, -lie
in Rhyme.*

1431 BUDDE, E. H.   : *Die Frage -ly- oder nicht? beim englischen Adverb*
Praxis 2, 1955, pp. 55 - 57.

'1333 ISITT, D.   : *A Synchronic Investigation into the Principles Governing the Use of the Suffixes -al, -ic, -ly, -y
in English.*

'1432 KALABINA, S. I.   : *Semantičeskie svojstva obrazovanij s suffiksom -l*
v sostave strukturno-semantičeskoj modeli s glago
nym " jadrom" (Les caractéristiques sémantiques
formes au suffixe -ly étudiées à l'aide de la for
mule VAly. Analyse " trnasformationelle" du conte
de -ly en anglais moderne), VMU 17, 1962, No. 4,
pp. 39 - 47.

' 1342 KATAYAMA, N.   : *-edly no hatsuon ni tsuite* (On the pronunciation
of the suffix -edly).

'1249 OTA, F.   : *The Pronunciation of -ed, -edly and -edness.*

245

1352 PILTZ, O.   : *Zur englischen Wortbildungslehre.*
                        3. Ueber like und die Bildungssilbe ly.

1353   - : *Zur englischen Wortbildungslehre.*
                        3. Ueber lic und die Bildungssilbe ly.

1334 PRESCOTT, J.   : *' Candidatorial' and 'Candidatorially'.*

1433 PULGRAM, E.   : *A Socio-Linguistic View of Innovation : -ly and -wise,* Word 24, 2, pp. 380 - 391.

1355 SLATER, J.   : *A Renewed Meaning for the Suffix "-ly".*

1355 a UHLER, K.   : *Die Bedeutungsgleichheit der altenglischen Adjektiva und Adverbia mit und ohne -lic (-lice).*

1250 WALDO, G. S.   : *Crooked, Crookedly, Crookedness.*

-WISE :

1434 ANON.   : *Vogue of '-wise',* AS 28, 1953, p. 65.

1435 ANTRIM, H. T.   : *An Instance of a '-wise' Adverb from 1920,* AS 37, 1962, p. 159.
                        (Seneca-wise)

'1436 FINK, J. E.   : *A Caveat for Journalists,* Word Study 39, December, 1963, p. 7.
                        (An example of a -wise compound from Walden)

1433 PULGRAM, E.   : *A Socio-Linguistic View of Innovation : -ly and -wise.*

1437 RAHN, W.   : *Das Suffix -wise im heutigen amerikanischen und britischen Englisch,* in Literatur und Sprache der Vereinigten Staaten, Aufsätze zu Ehren von Hans Galinsky, ed. by Hans Helmcke, Klaus Lubbers and Renate Schmidt-v.-Bardeleben, Heidelberg : Carl Winter Universitätsverlag, 1969, 247 p.; pp. 228 - 241.
                        (cf. Schönfelder, K.-H. : ZAA 19, 1971, 325 - 327)

'1405 STEPHENS, G. D.　　: *Wise, ize, bar, and bug.*

'1438 WELLS, R. W.　　　: *Wordwise I am Fed –Wise up*, Harper's, August, 1956
　　　　　　　　　　　　p. 39.
　　　　　　　　　　　　(Overuse of -wise as a suffix)

247

C) DERIVATION WITHOUT A FORMAL MORPHEME, DERIVATION BY MEANS OF A ZERO-MOR-
PHEME, CONVERSION (General studies ....)

'1357 ARAKIN, V. D.   : *Vozniknovenie kornevogo, ili bessuffiksal'nogo spo-*
          soba slovoobrazovanija v anglijskom jazyke.
          (On book ⟶ to book in English)

'1439 BELYJ, V. V.   : *K voprosu o konversii* (On conversion. Concerning
          an article of Ju. A. Žluktenko), UZ Mor U 20,
          1962, pp. 94 - 112, fig..

1059 BERGENER, C.   : *A Contribution to the Study of the Conversion of*
          Adjectives into Nouns in English.

1440 BIESE, Y. M.   : *Origin and Development of Conversions in English,*
          Annales Academiae Scientiarum Fennicae, B, XLV, 2,
          Helsinki : Suomalaisen Kirjallisunden Seuran Kir-
          japainon O. Y., 1941, vi, 495 p., 33 diagrams.
          Reviews :
          Horn, W. : ASNS 185, 1948, 145 - 146
          Mosse, F. : BSL 46 (133), 1950, 152

'1363 CHANG, P.   : *Lun Ying-yü ming-tz'n chuan-ch'eng tung-tz'n chi*
          ch'i tso-yung (On the conversion of English nouns
          into verbs).

1063 CLARK, J. W.   : *The Gawain-Poet and the Substantival Adjective.*

1441 COARD, R. L.   : *Collisional Shift,* AS 36, 1961, pp. 137 - 139.
          (refers to Lee)

'1442   - : *Shifting Parts of Speech,* Word Study 37, February
          1962, pp. 5 - 6.

1364   - : *The Verb Managerie.*

1365 CUNNINGHAM, W.   : *' Dessert' as a Verb.*

248

'1443 ČUNTONOVA, A. A. : *Adverbial'noe upotreblenie imeni suščestvitel'nogo v anglijskom jazyke* (The adverbial use of the noun in English), UZ Bašk U 1963, vyp. 13, SFil N No. 5 (9), pp. 117 - 120.

'1444 - : *Ob-ektno-adverbial'noe upotreblenie suščestvitel'- nogo v sovremennom anglijskom jazyke* (The noun use as an adverbial object in modern English), UZ Bašk U 1964, vyp. 15, SFil N No. 6, pp. 111 - 117.

'1445 - : *Upotreblenie substantivnych sočetanij v adverbial'- noj funkcii* (The use of substantival combinations in adverbial function), UZ Bašk U 1964, vyp. 21, SFil N No. 9, pp. 121 - 126.

1065 a FEY, I. : *Konversionssubstantive und Konversionsverben in Fachsprachen und Schichten des Englischen.*

1065 b - : *Konversionssubstantive und Konversionsverben in Fachsprachen und Schichten des Englischen (Con- version-Nouns and Conversion-Verbs in Technical Ter minology and in the Colloquial, Slang and Cant Stra ta of the English Language).*

'1446 FIEBACH, R.-M. : *Der stilistische Wert der Funktionsverschiebung bei Thomas Nashe*, Diss. Berlin 26.7.1957, (1957), vi, 259 lvs.n.. (Germany 73, p. 71)

' 1416 FRÖHLICH, A. : *Englisches Adjektiv-Adverb.*

' 494 - : *Adjektivisch-attributive Substantiva und Ketten- wörter im Englischen.*

1071 GERBER, E. : *Die Substantivierung des Adjektivs im XV. und XVI. Jahrhundert mit besonderer Berücksichtigung des zu Adjektiven hinzutretenden one.*

1418 HAAS, H. : *Studien zur Adverbsfunktion von Adjektivformen in frühneuenglischer Zeit. (Die Stufen der gradadver*

biellen Funktion von Adjektiven zur Modifizierung von
Adjektiven untersucht an ausgewählten Texten und dar-
gestellt an ausgesuchten Beispielen.

'1367 HALE, C. P.   : *Tailoring Terms : ' to White-Horse', ' to Dead-Horse'.*

798 HARRISON, H. G.   : *Verbalized Surnames.*

' 127 HOFFMANN, A.   : *Nominale Ausdrucksweise im modernen Englisch.*

1074   - : *Zur nominalen Ausdrucksweise im Englischen (Methodo-*
logische Überlegungen und Versuch einer Analyse).

1075   - : *Die verbo-nominale Konstruktion - eine spezifische*
Form der nominalen Ausdrucksweise im modernen Englisch.

1077 IRMER, R.   : *Die mit Nullmorphem abgeleiteten deverbalen Substan-*
tive des heutigen Englisch.

'1447 JAROVICI, E.   : *Conversirnea în engleza medie*, RFRG 7, 1963, pp. 305
- 314.
(Russian and English summaries)

805 JOPP, G.   : *Die Modifikation des Verbalbegriffs bei Galsworthy.*

'1448 KARAŠČUK, P. M.   : *Konversija kak sposob slovoobrazovanija v sovremen-*
nom anglijskom jazyke (Word-formation by conversion
in present-day English), UZ Dal U 4, 1962, pp. 3 - 18.

1078 KASTOVSKY, D.   : *Old English Deverbal Substantives Derived by Means of*
a Zero Morpheme.

148   - : *Wortbildung und Nullmorphem.*

1449 KELLER, R.   : *Die Ellipse in der neuenglischen Sprache als syntak-*
tisch-semantisches Problem, Diss. Zürich, Winterthur
- Töss : Gehring & Co., 1944, 164 p., vita.

'1079 KENNEDY, A. G.   : *On the Substantivation of Adjectives in Chaucer.*

'1450 KIENDLER, G.   : *Konvertierte Formen in den Dramen Otways und Lees.*
Ein Vergleich mit der Sprache Shakespeares, Diss.

Graz 1951, v, 202 lvs..

(Graz 1, 2705)

1451 KONKOL, (geb. MAYER), E. : *Die Konversion im Frühneuenglischen in der Zeit von etwa 1580 bis 1600. Ein Beitrag zur Erforschung der sprachlichen Neuprägungen bei Kyd, Marlowe, Peele, Greene, Spenser und Nashe,* Diss. Köln 14.6.1960, München : Fotodruck Mikrokopie, 1960, (ii), 274 p., vi ta.
(Germany 76, p. 459)

1370 KULAK, M. : *Die semantischen Kategorien der mit Nullmorphem abgeleiteten desubstantivischen Verben des heutigen Englischen und Deutschen.*

1452 LEE, D. W. : *Functional Change in Early English,* Columbia University Diss.,Menasha, Wisc. : George Banta Publishing Company, 1948, ix, (1), 128 p., vita.
Reviews :
Einarsson, S. : MLN 64, 1949, 498 - 500
Eliason, N. E. : Lg 25, 1949, 68 - 69
Fisher, J. H. : Word 6, 1950, 190 - 192
Hill, A. A. : AS 24, 1949, 59 - 61
Price, H. T. : JEGP 48, 1949, 151 - 152
Prins, A. A. : ES 32, 1951, 31 - 32
(see also Coard, R. L. No. 1441)

'1453 - : *Functional Change,* Word Study 25, 5, 1950, pp. 1 - 4.

'1454 LICHOSERST, N. : *O produktivnosti konversii v sovremennom anglijskom jazyke* (On the produductivity of conversion in modern English), NZ Kiev P II n 5, 1962, pp. 43 - 50.

1455 LINDHEIM, B. v. : *Syntaktische Funktionsverschiebung als Mittel des barocken Stils bei Shakespeare,* Shakespeare-Jahrbuch 90, 1954, pp. 229 - 251.

1372 McMILLAN, J. B. : *' Charivari' as a Verb.*

1373 MARCHAND, H. : *Die Ableitung desubstantivischer Verben mit Null-morphem im Französischen und die entsprechenden Verhältnisse im Englischen und Deutschen.*

1456   - : *On a Question of Contrary Analysis with Derivation-ally Connected but Morphologically Uncharacterized Words*, ES 44, 1963, pp. 176 - 187.

1374   - : *Die Ableitung desubstantivischer Verben mit Null-morphem im Englischen, Französischen und Deutschen.*

1457   - : *A Set of Criteria for the Establishing of Derivation-al Relationship Between Words Unmarked by Derivational Morphemes*, IF 69, 1964/1965, pp. 10 - 19.

* 1085 MATHESIUS, V. : *O nominálních tendencích v slovesné predikaci no-voanglicke:*
(On ' to have a look ' etc.)

* 1458 MILLER, J. C. : *Conversion and Fusion in Modern English : A Con-cise History of the Scholarly Recognition of these Linguistic Processes*, Ph.D. Diss. Stanford University, 1939.
(Abstract in Stanford University Abstracts of Dissertations 14, 1938/1939, pp. 45 - 51)

1090 NICKEL, G. : *Complex Verbal Structures in English.*

1091 OLSSON, Y. : *On the Syntax of the English Verb with Special Reference to have a look and Similar Complex Structures.*

1459 PASSEK, V. V. : *Nekotorye voprosy konversii*, VJa 1957, No. 1, pp. 144 - 148.
(On conversion and alternation of sounds in present-day English)

1460 PENNANEN, E. : *Conversion and Zero-Derivation in English*, Acta Universitatis Tamperensis, Ser. A, vol. 40, 1971, 76 p..

1094 PHOENIX, W.   : *Die Substantivierung des Adjektivs, Partizips und Zahlwortes im Angelsächsischen.*

1095 POSTON, L. III   : *'Happy', 'Merry' and 'Jolly' as Nouns.*

1461 PREUSS, F.   : *Konversion oder Zero-Derivation,* Lebende Sprachen
         7, 4-5, 1962, pp. 97 - 105
         8, 1 , 1963, pp. 1 - 3
         8, 2 , 1963, pp. 33 - 35
         8, 4-5, 1963, pp. 109 - 112
         8, 6 , 1963, pp. 164 - 166.

1098 PRIESS, M.   : *Die Bedeutungen des abstrakten substantivierten Adjektivs und des entsprechenden abstrakten Substantiv bei Shakespeare.*

1462 RENSKY, M.   : *English Verbo-Nominal Phrases,* TLP 1, Prague, 1964, pp. 289 - 299.

1100   - : *Nominal Tendencies in English.*

1463   - : *The Noun-Verb Quotient in English and Czech. A Tentative Statistic Analysis,* PhP 8, 1965, pp. 289 - 302.

' 838 REVARD, C.   : *Affixal Derivation, Zero Derivation, and " Semantic Transformations" .*

'1101 ROGOVSKAJA, B. I.   : *Analitičeskaja konstrukcija tipa to give a laugh v sovremennom anglijskom jazyke* (The analytical construction of the to give a laugh type in contemporary English).

'1102 ROTOMSKIENE, T.   : *Substantivacija prilagatel'nych v sovremennom anglijskom jazyke* (The substantivation of the adjective in present-day English).

'1103   - : *K probleme substantivacii prilagatel'nych v sovremennom anglijskom jazyke* (On the substantivation of the adjective in present-day English).

408 ŠACHOVA, N. I. : *Smyslovoe razvitie imeni suščestvitel'nogo work i glagola to work i obrazovannych ot ich osnov proizvodnych i složnych slov v anglijskom jazyke* (The semantic development of the substantive work and the verb to work and the derivatives and compounds from their stems).

104 SCHLAUCH, M. : *English Creates New Nouns of Its Own.*

105 SCHLOTHAUER, G. : *Der reine Verbalstamm als Substantiv bei Shakespeare.*

464 SCHMITZ, H. : *Wesen des Funktionswechsels und seine Stellung innerhalb der Gesamtentwicklung des Neuenglischen,* Diss. Vienna, 1946, 55 lvs..
(Vienna 1945 - 1949, p. 55, 1171)

315 SCOTT, R. I. : *" Qualm" as a Verb, "Lunch" as an Adjective.*

725 SHUMAN, R. B. : *To ' Daughter-out' and to 'Sheriff-out', Two New Coinages.*

107 SIL'NICKAJA, G. V. : *Transformacionnyj analiz i ego rol' v semantičeskoj klassifikacii slov. (Na materiale suščestvitel'nych i glagolov, svjazannych drug s drugom po konversii)* (Transformational analysis and its role in the semantic classification of words. On the material of substantives and verbs related through conversion).

108 SINICKINA, L. N. : *O nekotorych tipach frazeologičeskich glagol'nych sočetanij v anglijskom jazyke* (Concerning some types of phraseological verbal collocations in English).

465 SMIRNICKIJ, A. I. : *Tak nazyvaemaja konversija i čeredovanie zvukov v anglijskom jazyke* (The so-called conversion and sound change in English), IJaŠ 1953, No. 5, pp. 22-31.

'1466   - : *Po povodu konversiji v anglijskom jazyke* (On the origin of conversion in English), DSi Ja 1954, No. 3, pp. 12 - 124.

1317 SMITH, G. C. M.   : *Superlative Adjectives Formed from Substantives.*

'1467 SOBOLEVA, P. A.   : *Ob osnovnom i proizvodnom slove pri slovoobrazo-vatel'nych otnošenijach po konversii* (On the relations between the main word and the derivative in the process of conversion), VJa 2, 1959, pp. 91 - 95.

'1468 SOUDEK, L.   : *Conversions in British and American Substandard English*, RLB 2, 1968, pp. 64 - 72.

'1428 SPECTOR, R. D.   : *Adverbial Adjectives.*

1318 TOURBIER, R.   : *Das Adverb als attributives Adjektiv im Neuenglischen.*

'1111 TRNKA, B.   : *Analyse a synthese v novĕanglictine.*

1112   - : *Analysis and Synthesis in English.*

'1469 TROICKAJA, G. P.   : *Konversija kak sposob slovoobrazovanija v sovremennom anglijskom jazyke* (Word-formation by conversion in modern English), UZ LP I, 226, 1962, pp. 383 - 402.

1355 a UHLER, K.   : *Die Bedeutungsgleichheit der altenglischen Adjektiva und Adverbia mit und ohne -lic (-lice).*

1113 VACHEK, J.   : *Some Less Familiar Aspects of the Analytical Trend in English.*

'1470 VEUHOFF, K. F.   : *Shakespeares Funktionsverschiebungen. Ein Beitrag zur Erforschung der sprachlichen Neuprägungen Shakespeares*, Diss. Münster 9.1.1954, (1954), 118 1v n..

                         (Germany 70, p. 652)

'1114 VINOKUROVA, L. P.   : *O substantivacij v anglijskom jazyke* (On substantivation in English).

1137 .WERNER, W. L.   : *" Motorcade" and "to Demagogue"*.

1388   - : *" Referee" as a Verb*.

' 616 WOODWARD, E. H.   : *Adverbial Adjectives*.

'1117 ZAGORNIKO, A. J.   : *O tak nazyvaenoi nepolnoi ili česastičnoi konversii v sovremennom anglijskom jazyke* (On the so-called incomplete or partial conversion in present-day English).

'1471 ŽLUKTENKO, Ju. A.   : *Konversija v sovremennom anglijskom jazyke kak morfologo-sintaksičeskij sposob slovoobrazovanija* (Conversion in present-day English as a morphological-syntactical means of word-formation), VJa 1958, No. 5, pp. 53 - 64.

1) BAHUVRĪHI-COMPOUNDS

1472 HATCHER, A. G.   : *Bahuvrihi in Sears Roebuck*, MLN 59, 1944, pp. 515 - 526.

'1473 LAST, W.   : *Das Bahuvrihi-Compositum im Englischen*, Diss. Greifswald 26.1.1921.
(Germany 48, p. 1932)
published under the title :
Das Bahuvrihi-Compositum im Altenglischen, Mittelenglischen und Neuenglischen, mit einem Geleitwort von Heinrich Spies, Greifswald : H. Adler, 1925, 124 p..
Reviews :
Franz, W. : ESt 61, 1926/1927, 283 - 284
Preusler, W. : Zeitschrift für frz. und engl. Unterricht 25, 1926, 377

1473 a TENGSTRAND, E.   : *Three Middle English Bahuvrīhi Adjectives*, SMSpr
17, 1949, pp. 210 - 226.
(nesshe-wombe, harde-wombe, clere-syghte)
Reviews :
Behre, F.   : MSpråk 44, 1950, 215 -216
'Wilson, R. M. : YW 30, 1949, 26

2) ' IMPERATIVE COMPOUNDS'
(Type : follow-me-lad, pickpocket ...)

1474 ANDRESEN, K. G.   : *Imperativnamen*, ASNS 43, 1868, pp. 395 - 404.
(English examples on p. 404)
(refers to Schulze, G. No. 1480)

'1475 FORSSNER, T.   : *Deutsche und englische Imperativnamen*, Skolprogr.
Östersunds Lärov. 1921/1922, pp. 1 - 19.

1476 HORN, W.   : *Wahlspruchwörter und Imperativbildungen* , ASNS
179, 1942, pp. 28 - 30.

1477   - : *Der Name Shakespeare*, ASNS 185, 1948, pp. 26 - 35.

1478 KOZIOL, H.   : *Imperativbildungen und Wahlspruchwörter*, GRM 27,
1939, pp. 148 - 150.

1479 SCHNEIDER, P.   : ' *Turnarounds*', *on Land, on Sea, and in the Air*,
AS 27, 1952, pp. 141 - 143.

1480 SCHULZE, G.   : *Imperativisch gebildete Substantiva*, ASNS 43, 1868,
pp. 13 - 40.
(English examples on p. 40)

1481 UHRSTRÖM, W.   : *Pickpocket, Turnkey, Wraprascal, and Similar Formations in English*, Stockholm : Magn. Bergvall,
1918, 80 p..
Reviews :

Anon.   : N & Q s.12, 7, 1920, 20
'Bøgholm, N. : NTF 4, Raekke 9, 1920, 138
Fischer, W. : Anglia B 31, 1920, 48
'Hoops, J.   : Wissenschaftliche Forschungsberichte
                9, 1923, 103

D) DERIVATION FROM SPECIFIC WORDS

AEÞELE   :

1482 BÄHR, D.   : *Ae. aeþele und freo, ihre Ableitungen und Synonyma*
                        im Alt- und Mittelenglischen. Wortgeschichtliche Stu-
                        dien zum Wandel des englischen Freiheitsbegriffes im
                        Mittelenglischen, Diss. Berlin F.U. 28.1.1959, Berlin,
                        1959, 135 p..
                        (Germany 75, p. 59)

FREO   :

1482 BÄHR, D.   : *Ae aeþele und freo, ihre Ableitungen und Synonyma*
                        im Alt- und Mittelenglischen. Wortgeschichtliche Stu-
                        dien zum Wandel des englischen Freiheitsbegriffes im
                        Mittelenglischen.

RŪN / RUNE :

1483 GOETZ, H.-G.   : *Geschichte des Wortes rūn (rune) und seiner Ableitun-*
                        gen im Englischen, Diss. Göttingen 30.6.1964, Göttin-
                        gen, 1964, 121 p..
                        (Germany 80, p. 431)

SENTIMENTAL   :

1484 ALLEN, B. S.   : *The Dates of 'Sentimental' and Its Derivatives,* PMLA
                        48,1933 , pp. 303 - 307.

IV. BACKFORMATION

1485 CHRISTENSEN, E. G.   : ' Destruct' as a Verb, AS 36, 1961, p. 234.

'1486 COFFIN, H. C.   : Back-Formations, Words 1, No. 6, September 15,
                              1935, pp. 7 - 8.

1487 GERBERT, M.   : Verbale Rückbildungen in der technischen Fachspra-
                              che des Englischen, WZTUD 16, 1967, pp. 803 - 809.

1488 HALL, R. A.   : How We Noun-Incorporate in English, AS 31, 1956,
                              pp. 83 - 88.

'1489 JESPERSEN, O.   : Om Substraktionsdannelser, saerligt på dansk og
                              engelsk, in Festskrift til Vilhelm Thomson, Copen-
                              hague, 1894.

1490   - : A Few Back-Formations, ESt 70, 1935/1936, pp. 117
                              - 122.

1491 JOHNSON, F.   : A Note on 'Television' and 'Televue', AS 25, 1950,
                              pp. 157 - 158.

639 MARCHAND, H.   : Compound and Pseudo-Compound Verbs in Present-Day
                              English.

1492   - : On Content as a Criterion of Derivational Relation-
                              ship with Backderived Words, IF 68, 1963, pp. 170
                              - 175.

'1493 MYACHINA, A. V.   : K voprosu o suščnosti reversii v anglijskom jazyke
                              (The principal features of back-formations in En-
                              glish), Filol. Nauki 6, 1968, pp. 34 - 39.

1494 PENNANEN, E.   : Contributions to the Study of BackFormation in En-
                              glish, Acta Academiae Socialis A IV, Tampere, 1966,
                              172 p..

1495 PREUSS, F.   : Backformation oder Noun-Incorporation, Lebende
                              Sprachen 5, 4-5, 1960, pp. 110 - 112.
                              - II, 5, 6 , 1960, pp. 165 - 167

-III, Lebende Sprachen 6, 1, 1961, pp. 6 - 7

-IV, Lebende Sprachen 6, 2, 1961, p. 39.

1496   - : *Noch einmal : Backformations*, Lebende Sprachen 7, 2, 1962, p. 37.

1379 SCHRACK, D.   : *Ne. 'to Spotlight' und 'to Stagemanage'. Studien zur Entwicklung und Struktur der verbalen Pseudokomposita im Englischen mit Berücksichtigung anderer germanischer Sprachen. Ein Beitrag zum Problem von ' Sprache' und 'Sprechen'.*

1497 WITTMANN, E.   : *Clipped Words : A Study of Back-Formations and Curtailments in Present-Day English*, Dialect Notes 4, 2, 1914, pp. 115 - 145.

V. BLENDS, CLIPPINGS, PORTMANTEAU - WORDS, ACRONYMS

1498 ANON. : *Improvised Words*, The Atlantic Monthly 102, 1908, pp. 714 - 716.

1499 ANON. : *' Brunch' Again*, AS 14, 1939, p. 238.

1500 ANON. : *'Artyping'*, AS 22, 1947, p. 232.

'1501 ANON. : *Acronyms Dictionary*, Gale Research Company, Detroit 1960.

'1502 ANON. : *The Acronymous Society*, Time 78, July 28, 1961. (On the widespread use of acronyms in American English)

'1503 ANON. : *The Slurb*, Time 79, January 26, 1962, p. 54. (Slurb coined to denote 'sloppy, sleazy, slovenly, slipshod ' suburban development)

1504 ACKERMAN, L. M. : *' Combo'*, AS 37, 1962, pp. 78 - 79. (= combination)

1505 ADAMS, V. J. : *A Study of the Process of Word-Blending and an Examination of the Types Found, in Present-Day Written English*, M. A. London 1966, 235 lvs..

1506 BAUER, F. : *Wort- und Konstruktionsmischungen im Englischen*, Diss. Tübingen 30.11.1926,Tübingen, 1926, iv, (1), 171 lvs., vita. (Germany 43, p. 462)

1507 BAUM, S. V. : *From 'Awol' to 'Veep' : The Growth and Specialization of the Acronym*, AS 30, 1955, pp. 103 - 110.

1508 - : *Feminine Characteristics of the Acronym*, AS 31, 1956, pp. 224 - 225.

1509 - : *Formal Dress for Initial Words*, AS 32, 1957, pp. 73 - 75.

1510   - : *The Acronym, Pure and Impure*, AS 37, 1962, pp.
                                   48 - 50.

1511 BEHR, U.   : *Wortkontaminationen in der neuenglischen Schrift-
                             sprache*, Diss. Berlin 6.5.1936, Würzburg : R. Mayr,
                             1935, 154 p., (1), vita.
                             (Germany 52, p. 38)
                             Reviews :
                             L., G.   : ASNS 170, 1936, 290

1512 BERGDAL, E.   : *Auent " Sappodil"*, AS 4, 1929, p. 133.

1513   - : *Sappodil and Sapidillo*, AS 6, 1930/1931, pp. 16 -
                             18.

1514 BERGER, M. D.   : *More on " Combo"*, AS 38, 1963, p. 156.

1515 BERGSTRÖM, G. A.   : *On Blendings of Synonymous or Cognate Expressions
                             in English. A Contribution to the Study of Conta-
                             mination*, Diss. Lund, Lund : H. Ohlsson, 1906,
                             xv, (1), 211 p..

'1516 BERLIZON, S. B.   : *Sokraščenie v sovremennom anglijskom jazyke*
                             (Shortenings in modern English), IJaŠ 1963, pp.
                             93 - 100.

'1517 BERMAN, J. M.   : *O "vstavočnom" tipe slovoobrazovanija* (Word-
                             formation by blending in present-day English),
                             VJa 1959, No. 2, pp. 104 - 107.

'1518   - : *K voprosu o vstavočnom slovoobrazovanii*, IJaŠ 4,
                             1960, pp. 106 - 112.
                             (On the problem of blending)

1519   - : *Contribution on Blending*, ZAA 9, 1961, pp. 278 -
                             281.

1520 BERREY, L. V.   : *Newly-Wedded Words*, AS 14, 1939, pp. 3 - 10.

1521 BOLINGER, D. L.   : *Verbal Evocation*, Lingua 10, 1961, pp. 113 - 127.
(also in *Forms of English. Accent, Morpheme, Order*
ed. by Isamu Abe and Tetsuya Kanekiyo, Cambridge,
Mass. : Harvard University Press, 1965, pp. 253 -
265)

1522 BYINGTON, S. T.   : *Blends*, AS 3, 1928, p. 13.
(sonorant, Amerindian, Amerind)

1523 COLLITZ, K. HECHTENBERG : *Another Addition to the American Vocabulary*,
AS 4, 1929, p. 21.

1524   - : *" Sappodil" and " Sappodilla"*, AS 4, 1929, pp. 375
- 376.
(sap + daffodil)

1525 DARLING, M.   : *Here Comes ' Brunch'*, AS 9, 1934, p. 151.

'1526 DIERICKX, J.   : *Les " mots-valises" de l'anglais et du français*,
RLaV 32, 5, 1966, pp. 451 - 459.

'1527 DOTY, R. C.   : *Parlez-vous NATO ?*, New York Times Magazine, October 18, 1959, p. 20, 22.
(Acronyms and agglomerations in NATO officialese

1528 EHRENTREICH, A.   : *Abkürzungen im Amerikanischen*, Die lebenden Fremdsprachen 1, 1949, pp. 219 - 221.

1529   - : *Sprachliche Spielereien im Amerikanischen*, NS, N.
3, 1954, pp. 362 - 363.

'1530 ERICSON, E. E.   : *Our American Blend-Habit*, Words 7, March 1941, pp.
12 - 14.

1531 FENZL, R.   : *Blends Selected from TIME Magazine*, Idioma 3, 4,
1966, pp. 164 - 168.

'1532 FRAZIER, G.   : *Double Talk* , Life, July 5, 1943, pp. 74, 77 - 78.
(A descriptive article on the blend of sense and
non-sense and portmanteau-words by serious-faced
jokers from Lewis Carroll to contemporary masters

of 'double talk', supplemented (July 26) by two
letters from readers)

'1533 GOLDSTEIN, M. : *Dictionary of Modern Acronyms & Abbreviations*, India-
napolis : Howard W. Sams & Co., 1963, 158 p..

1534 HANSEN, K. : *Das Spiel mit der Abkürzung im Englischen. Ein Beitrag zur Frage der sprachlichen Triebkräfte*, WZUB 9,
1959/1960, pp. 379 - 389.

1535 - : *Haplologische Wortverschmelzungen*, Sprachpflege 1960,
12, pp. 244 - 245.

1536 - : *Makkaronische Sprachformen - Hybride Wortbildungen*,
ZAA 9, 1961, pp. 49 - 64.

'1537 - : *Formen des Sprachspiels im Neuenglischen*, Diss. Berlin H. U. 23.5.1962, Berlin, 1962, 360 lvs.n..
(Germany 78, p. 18)

1538 - : *Wortverschmelzungen*, ZAA 11, 1963, pp. 117 - 142.

1539 HARDER, K. B. : *" Vidiot"*, AS 32, 1957, p. 158.
(Video + idiot)

1540 HARGREAVES, H. : *English Abbreviations in Speech*, NS, N. F., 6, 1957,
pp. 177 - 181.

1541 HENCH, A. L. : *The Coining of " Stanine"*, AS 26, 1951, pp. 72 - 74.
(Standard nine-point scale)

1542 HOLTHAUSEN, F. : *Wortmischungen*, GRM 6, 1914, p. 117.

1543 - : *Wortmischungen*, Anglia B 54, 1943/1944, p. 177.
(refers to Bergström, No. 1515)

1544 - : *Wortmischungen*, ASNS 187, 1950, p. 75.

1545 HORN, W. : *Die Wort- und Konstruktionsmischungen im Englischen*,
GRM 9, 1921, pp. 342 - 358.

143 JESPERSEN, O. : *Nature and Art in Language.*

1546 JONES, J. J. : *Two Clipped Words*, AS 6, 1930/1931, p. 227.
(tarpaulin, cots)

158 KOHL, N. : *Das Wortspiel in der Shakespearischen Komödie. Studien zur Interdependenz von verbalem und aktionalem Spiel in den frühen Komödien und den späten Stücken.*

1547 KOZIOL, H. : *Blends*, NS, N. F., 3, 1954, p. 25.

'1548 — : *Kontaminationen lautähnlicher Wörter und Verwandtes im Englischen*, in Mnemes Charin, Gedenkschrift für Paul Kretschmer, Vienna, 1956, Vol. 1, pp. 181 - 188.

' 168 KREUTZER, E. : *Sprache und Spiel im " Ulysses" von James Joyce.*

' 186 LANDAU, E. : *Wortspiele bei Beaumont und Fletcher.*

1549 LEVY, R. : *Haplologic Blends in French and in English*, Symposium 4, 1950, pp. 53 - 69.

1550 McATEE, W. L. : *More Amalgams*, AS 20, 1945, pp. 76 - 77.
(execucasting, humanagement, histomap, musicalamity mail-o-mat)

1551 McCAIN, J. W. jr. : *Friding; a New Word in American English*, AS 8, 1933, pp. 80 - 81.

1552 MANN, G. : *Kurzformen im militärischen Englisch*, ASNS 184, 1944, pp. 53 - 54.

'1553 MATTHEWS, C. C. : *A Dictionary of Abbreviations*, London, 1947.

818 MAUTNER, F. H. : *Word Formation by Shortening and Affixation : The ' Sudetens' and the 'Yougos'.*

1554 MEREDITH, M. J. : : *' Videot' - a Television Addict*, AS 33, 1958, p. 151.

'1555 MOSER, R. C.   : *Space-Age Acronyms; Abbreviated Designations*, New York : Plenum, 1964, 427 p..

'1556 MÜLLER, L.   : *Neuenglische Kurzformbildungen*, Diss. Giessen 2.3. 1923, Giessen : Verlag des Engl. Seminars, 1923, 44 p..
(Germany 39, p. 326)
Also published in: Giessener Beiträge zur Erforschung der Sprache und Kultur Englands und Nordamerikas I, 2, 1923, pp. 33 - 76.

1557 MÜLLER-SCHOTTE, H. : *Das blending und sein Ergebnis, das portmanteau-word*, NS, N. F., 2, 1953, pp. 449 - 454.

1558   - : *Zur Theorie und Praxis der englischen Abkürzungen*, Lebende Sprachen 13, 4-5, 1968, pp. 105 - 112.

1559 MUNROE, H. C.   : " *Profitunity*, AS 6, 1930/1931, p. 394.
(profit + opportunity)

241 NELLE, P.   : *Das Wortspiel im englischen Drama des 16.Jahrhunderts vor Shakspere*.

1560 P., L.   : ' *Callithumpians*, AS 17, 1942, pp. 231 - 214.
(callithump ⊂ calliope + thump)

'1561 PARTRIDGE, E.   : *A Dictionary of Abbreviations*, London, 1942.

'1562 PEARCE, T. M.   : *Acronym Talk, or ' Tomorrow's' English*, Word Study, May 1947, pp. 6 - 8.

265 POUND, L.   : *Indefinite Composites and Word-Coinage*.

1563   - : *Blends. Their Relation to English Word-Formation*, Heidelberg : Carl Winters Universitätsbuchhandlung, 1914, 58 p..
(= Anglistische Forschungen 42)
Reviews :
'Glöde, O. : Literaturblatt 36, 271 - 272
Wood, F. A.: JEGP 14, 1915, 585 - 588
(Pound, L.: GRM 7, 1915/1919, 560 self-advertisem.)

1564   - : *Odd Formations.*
                         c) Some Haplologic Shortenings, Dialect Notes
                         4, 5, 1916, pp. 354 - 355.

'1565 ROBBINS, R. H.   ° : *Acronyms and Abbreviations from Aviation*, AS 26,
                         1951, pp. 67 - 70.

'1566 ROHDE, E.   : *Abkürzungen durch Anfangsbuchstaben*, MSprȧk 1,
                         1907, pp. 53 - 59.

1567 SCHULTZ, W. E.   : *College Abbreviations*, AS 5, 1930, pp. 240 - 244.

'1568 SCHWARTZ, R. J.   : *The Complete Dictionary of Abbreviations*, London,
                         1955.

1569 SCHWARZ, U.   : *Die Struktur der englischen Portemanteau-Wörter*,
                         LBer 7, 1970, pp. 40 - 44.

'1570 SHANKLE, G. E.   : *Current Abbreviations*, New York, 1945.

'1571 SHELDON, E. K.   : *What' a Capade ?* Word Study 37, April 1962, p. 6.
                         (A case of suffix clipping)

1572 SHULMAN, D.   : *Blend Words and Place-Names*, AS 14, 1939, pp. 233
                         234.

1573 SLETTENGREN, E.   : *Contributions to the Study of Aphaeretic Words
                         in English*, Diss. Lund, Lund : Berlingska Bok-
                         tryckeriet, 1912, xi, 181 p..
                         Reviews :
                         Franz, W.   : ESt 47, 1913/1914, 231 - 235

'1574 STEPHENSON, H. J.   : *Abbreviations*, New York, 1943.

'1575 STUPIN, L. P.   : *Abbreviatury i problema ich vključenija v tolkovye
                         slovari (Na materiale Bol'šogo tolkovogo slovarj*
                         Webstera 1961 g) (Abbreviations and the problem
                         of their enlistment in etymological dictionaries.
                         (On the material of Webster's New Etymological
                         Dictionary (1961))), Voprosy teorii i istorii ja-
                         zyka, Leningrad, 1963, pp. 290 - 298.

1576 SUNDEN, K. (F.) : *Contributions to the Study of Elliptical Words in Modern English*, Diss. Uppsala, Uppsala : Almqvist & Wiksells Boktryckeri A.-B., 1904, 233 p..

331 SUTHERLAND, R. D. : *Language and Lewis Carroll.*

' 335 TAYLOR, A. M. : *The Language of World War II. Abbreviations, Captions, Quotations, Slogans, Titles, and Other Terms and Phrases.*

1577 WELLS, R. S. : *Acronymy*, in For Roman Jakobson. Essays on the Occasion of His Sixtieth Birthday, The Hague : Mouton, 1956, pp. 662 - 667.

1578 WENTWORTH, H. : *Twenty-Nine Synonyms for ' Portmanteau-Word'*, AS 8, 1933, pp. 78 - 79.

'1579 - : *Blend-Words in English*, Ph.D. Diss. Cornell University, Ithaca, New York, 1934.

1580 - : *" Sandwich" Words and Rime-Caused Nonce Words*, West Virginia University Bulletin Series 40, No. 3 - I, September 1939, Philological Studies Vol. III, pp. 65 - 71.

1581 WITHINGTON, R. : *A Portmanteau Word of 1761 : TOMAX*, MLN 37, 1922, pp. 377 - 379.

1582 - : *Other"Portmanteau" Words*, MLN 40, 1925, pp. 188 - 189.

1583 - : *" Portmanteau" Words Again*, N & Q 150, 1926, pp. 328 - 329.

1584 - : *" Portmanteau" and " Pseudo-Portmanteau" Words*, N & Q 157, 1929, pp. 77 - 78.

1585 - : *Some New " Portmanteau" Words*, PhQ 9, 1930, pp. 158 - 164.

1586 - : *More " Portmanteau" Coinages*, AS 7, 1931/1932, pp. 200 - 203.

1587   - : *Dickensian and Other Blends*, AS 8, 1933, pp. 73
                              - 75.

1497 WITTMANN, E.   : *Clipped Words : A Study of Back-Formations and
                              Curtailments in Present-Day English.*

1588 WOOD, F. A.   : *Iterative, Blends, and " Streckformen"*, MPh 9,
                              1911/1912, pp. 157 - 194.

1589   - : *Some English Blends*, MLN 27, 1912, p. 179.

1590   - : *Language and Nonce-Words*, Dialect Notes 4, 1,
                              1913, pp. 42 - 44.

VI. PHONETIC SYMBOLISM

'1591 BERGER, E.   : *Lautnachahmung in den Werken Rudyard Kiplings*, Diss. Vienna, 1960, iii, 190 lvs.. (Vienna 1958 - 1963, p. 47, 851)

1592 BLOOMFIELD, L.   : *Final Root-Forming Morphemes*, AS 28, 1953, pp. 158 - 164.

1593 BOLINGER, D. L.   : *Word Affinities*, AS 15, 1940, pp. 62 - 73. (also in *Forms of English. Accent, Morpheme, Order*, ed. by Isamu Abe and Tetsuya Kanekiyo, Cambridge, Mass. Harvard University Press, 1965, pp. 191 - 202)

1594 BUDDE, E. H.   : *Lautsymbolik und Wortmalereien im heutigen Englisch*, NphZ 3, 1951, pp. 248 - 253.

1595 DIKE, E. B.   : *The N.E.D. : Words of Divination and Onomatopoetic Terms*, MLN 48, 1933, pp. 521 - 525.

1596 FRÖHLICH, A.   : *Zusammenhang zwischen Lautform und Bedeutung bei englischen Wörtern*, NS 33, 1925, pp. 27 - 42,127 - 141.

96 GONDA, J.   : *Some Remarks on Onomatopoeia, Sound-Symbolism and Word-Formation à Propos of the Theories of C. N. Maxwell.*

1597 HILMER, H.   : *Schallnachahmung, Wortschöpfung und Bedeutungswandel auf Grundlage der Wahrnehmungen von Schlag, Fall und Bruch und derartigen Vorgängen dargestellt an einigen Lautwurzeln der deutschen und der englischen Sprache*, Halle : Max Niemeyer, 1914, xvii, 356 p..

1598 HOUTZAGER, M. E.   : *Unconscious Sound- and Sense-Assimilations*, Diss. Amsterdam, Amsterdam : H. J. Paris, 1935, vi, 194 p..

1599 JESPERSEN, O.   : *Symbolic Value of the Vowel I*, in Linguistica, Selected Papers in English, French and German, Copenhague : Levin & Munksgaard, 1933, pp. 283 - 303. (cf. ASNS 144, 1922, 136 - 137) (First published in Philologica, Vol. I, London and Prague, 1922)

1600 KOZIOL, H.   : *Schalldeutungen und Schalldeutungswörter*, Orbis 6, 1957, pp. 185 - 191.

214 MARCHAND, H.   : *Phonetic Symbolism in English Word-Formation.*

1601 MARCUS, H.   : *Lautmalereien im englischen Schrifttum der Gegenwart*, ESt 75, 1942/1943, pp. 175 - 192.

1602 REINIUS, J.   : *Onomatopoetische Bezeichnungen für menschliche Wesen besonders im Deutschen und Englischen*, SMSpr 4, 1908 pp. 189 - 204.

'1603 SENNEWALD, geb. KÖCKERITZ, Ch.:*Die Namengebung bei Dickens, eine Studie über Lautsymbolik*, Diss. Berlin 6.5.1936, Berlin : Segnitz, 1936, 122 p..
(also Palaestra 203, Leipzig : Mayer & Müller, 1936 121 p.)
(Germany 52, p. 55)

1604 SPIES, H.   : *Alliteration und Reimklang im modern-englischen Kulturleben*, ESt 54, 1920, pp. 149 - 158.

1605 WEDGWOOD, H.   : *On Onomatopoeia*, Proceedings of the Philological Society 2, 1844-1846, pp. 109 - 118.

VII. WORD - FORMATION BY MEANS OF REDUPLICATION

1606 ANON. : *Reduplicate Forms in English*, Knickerbocker 20, 1842, pp. 452 - 455.

1607 BIESE, Y. M. : *Neuenglisch tick-tack und Verwandtes*, NphM 40, 1939, pp. 146 - 205.

1608 BRYSON, A. B. : *Reduplications*, Word Study 28, 4, 1953, p. 7. (see also editor's note)

1609 CHOMJAKOV, V. A. : *Rol povtora i ritmy v obrazovanii slengizmov* (The role of reduplication and rhythm in the formation of slang expressions), Mežvuzovskaja konferencija po itogam naučno-issledovatel'skoj raboty za 1963 god (Volog Ped I, Čerepov Ped I) Programma i TD Vologda 1964, pp. 169 - 170.

1610 DRAAT, P. F. van : *Reduplicatory Emphasis*, ESt 74, 1940/1941, pp. 156 - 167. (refers to Eckhardt, No. 56 and Koziol, No. 1622)

1611 DUCKERT, A. R. : *A Boo-boo*, AS 33, 1958, pp. 230 - 231. (see also editor's note)

56 ECKHARDT, E. : *Reim und Stabreim im Dienste der neuenglischen Wortbildung*, ESt 72, 1937/1938, pp. 161 - 191.

1612 - : *Entgegnung*, ESt 73, 1938/1939, pp. 317 - 318. (refers to Koziol, No. 1622)

1613 FRIEDERICH, W. : *More Reduplicative Words*, Idioma 3, 1966, pp. 12 - 13.

1614 HANSEN, K. : *Reim- und Ablautverdoppelungen*, ZAA 12, 1964, pp. 5 - 31.

1615 - : *Rhyming Slang und Reimformen im Slang*, ZAA 14, 1966, pp. 341 - 366.

1616 HARDER, K. B.   : *On Matters Iterative*, AS 40, 1965, pp. 134 - 135.
                            (refers to Thun, No. 1643)

'1617 HETHERINGTON, J. N. : *On Repetition and Reduplication in Language*, Pro-
                            ceedings of the Literary and Philosophical Society
                            of Liverpool 30, 1876, pp. 129 - 152.

1618 KIRCHNER, G.   : *Silbenverdopplung ohne Vokaländerung*, Anglia 65,
                            1941, pp. 328 - 340.

1619   - : *Still Another Note on ' Hubba-hubba'*, AS 32, 1957,
                            p. 80.

1620   - : *Der Reimklang im Englischen*, ZAA 4, 1956, pp. 389
                            - 447; 7, 1959, pp. 281 - 287.

'1621 KOCH, F.   : *Linguistische Allotria. Laut-, Ablaut- und Reim-
                            bildungen der englischen Sprache*,Eisenach : J. Bac-
                            meister, 1874, iv, 94 p..
                            (2nd ed. 1880)
                            Reviews :
                            Anon.   : Taalstudie 1, 1879, 296 - 298
                            Asher, D. : ASNS 53, 1874, 109 - 110

1622 KOZIOL, H.   : *Zu den Reim- und Ablautbildungen im Englischen*,
                            ESt 73, 1938/1939, pp. 158 - 159.
                            (refers to Eckhardt, No.56)

1623   - : *Die Silbenverdopplung im Englischen*, ESt 75, 1942/1
                            pp. 67 - 73.

1624   - : *Rhyming Slang*, Sprache 2, 1950 - 1952, pp. 77 - 84.

1625   - : *Zur literarischen Verwendung des Rhyming Slang*,
                            ASNS 202, 1966, pp. 105 - 108.

1626 LANGENFELT, G.   : *Hurly-burly, Hallaloo, Hullabaloo*, NphM 51, 1950,
                            pp. 1 - 18.

1627   - : *Additions to Hurly-burly, Hallaloo, Hullabaloo*,
                            NphM 52, 1951, pp. 247 - 248.

1628 LEHNERT, M. : *Die Sprache der englischen Kinderstube*, in Festschrift für Walter Fischer, Heidelberg : Carl Winter- Universitätsverlag, 1959, viii, 332 p.; pp. 270 - 301.

1629 McATEE, W. L. : *Double-Barreled Words*, AS 34, 1959, pp. 73 - 75.

'1630 MARCHAND, H. : *Derivation by Means of Rime*, Studies by Members of the English Department 4, Istanbul, 1953, pp. 1 - 13.

1631 - : *Motivation by Linguistic Form*, SNPh 29, 1957, pp. 54 - 66.

1632 MOE, A. F. : *'Hubba-hubba' : A Denial of Its Derivation from Chinese*, AS 36, 1961, pp. 188 - 194.

1633 MÜLLER, M. : *Die Reim- und Ablautkomposita des Englischen*, Diss. Strassburg 30.1.1909, Strassburg : M. DuMont Schauberg, 1909, vi, 105 p., vita.
(Germany 24, p. 638)

1634 PERRIN, P. G. : *' Hubba-Hubba' Scholium VI*, AS 32, 1957, pp. 237 - 238.

1635 PICKEREL, S. M. : *Cockney Rhyming Slang*, Lebende Sprachen 17, 1, 1972, p. 8.

1636 PYLES, Th. : *More on "Hubba-hubba"*, AS 30, 1955, pp. 157 - 158.

1637 - : *Still More on "Hubba-hubba"*, AS 30, 1955, pp. 305 - 306.

1638 ROBACK, A. A. : *Another Possible Source of "Hubba-hubba"*, AS 30, 1955, pp. 306 - 307.

1639 ROGERS, P. B. : *Reduplications*, Word Study 29, 3, 1954, pp. 6 - 7.

1640 SCHMIDT, F. : *Curiosities of Word Formation : The Reduplicative Compound*, Idioma 2, 1965, pp. 261 - 263.

'1641 SOUDEK, L. : *Types of Rhyming Slang in British and American English*, SFFUK 17, 1965 (1967), pp. 179 - 187. (Slov. summary)

1642 STANZEL, F. : *Zur Herkunft des Rhyming Slang*, Sprache 3, 1957, pp. 193 - 202.

1643 THUN, N. : *Reduplicative Words in English. A Study of Formations of the Types Tick-tick, Hurly-burly and Shill shally*, Diss. Uppsala, Lund : Carl Bloms Boktrycker A.-B., 1963, xii, 347 p..
Reviews :

'Fente, R.	:	Filologia Moderna 17/18, 1965, 119 - 120
Hansen, K.	:	ZAA 13, 1965, 412 - 415
Harder, K. B.	:	AS 40, 1965, 134 - 135
Kirchner, G.	:	DLZ 88, 1967, 130 - 133
Koziol, H.	:	ASNS 201, 1965, 369 - 371
Korponay, B.		ALH 17, 1967, 209 - 210
Lipka, L.	:	IF 69, 1964/1965, 295 - 296
Pohl, J.	:	RBPh 44, 1966, 273 - 276
'Samarin, W. J.	:	JAfrL 5, 1966, 160 - 163
Standop, E.	:	Erasmus 17, 1965, 482 - 484
Stubelius, S.	:	SNPh 35, 1963, 318 - 322
Tellier, A. R.	:	BSL 62, 1967, 2, 72 - 75
Viereck, W.	:	ZMaF 35, 1968, 182 - 185

1644 TRACHTMANN, L. E. : *A Note on "Hubba Hubba "*, AS 29, 1954, pp. 237 - 238.

1645 WATT, W. C. : *English Reduplication*, JEL 2, 1968, pp. 96 - 129.

1646 WEINBERGER, A. D. : *Some Data and Conjectures on the History of "Hubba Hubba"*, AS 22, 1947, pp. 34 - 39.

1647 WHEATLEY, H. B. : *A Dictionary of Reduplicated Words in the English Language*, TPS 1865, Appendix (1866), 104 p..

1648 WILLERT, H.　　　: *Reimende Ausdrücke im Neuenglischen*, in Festschrift
　　　　　　　　　　　　Adolf Tobler zum siebzigsten Geburtstage, darge-
　　　　　　　　　　　　bracht von der Berliner Gesellschaft für das Studium
　　　　　　　　　　　　der neueren Sprachen, Braunschweig : G. Westermann,
　　　　　　　　　　　　1905, vi, 477 p.; pp. 437 - 458.
　　　　　　　　　　　　Reviews :
　　　　　　　　　　　　'Andrae, A. : Neue Phil. Rundschau 1906, 182 - 184

1588 WOOD, F. A.　　　 : *Iterative, Blends, and "Streckformen"*.

1649 YOST, G. jr.　　　 : *" Hubba-hubba" and 'Gismo'*, AS 34, 1959, pp. 149 -
　　　　　　　　　　　　150.

VIII. NEOLOGISMS

| 1650 ANON. | *Coinage*, AS 15, 1940, pp. 216 - 217. |

1651 ANON.   : *Columnist's English*, AS 16, 1941, p. 158.

1652 ANON.   : *Daily Coinage of Words*, AS 1, 1925/1926, pp. 685 - 686.

'1653 ANON.   : *Deliberately Invented Words*, Word Study , November 1, p. 1.

1654 ANON.   : *Filmese*, AS 16, 1941, pp. 156 - 157.

1655 ANON.   : *Filmese*, AS 17, 1942, p. 131.

1656 ANON.   : *Filmese*, AS 19, 1944, p. 76.

1657 ANON.   : *Free Wheeling*, AS 16, 1941, pp. 158 - 159.

'1658 ANON.   : *HARRY ALLEN Dies; Taxi Pioneer*, New York Times 88, June 27, 1965, p. 64.
(Coined and copyrighted the word taxicab in 1907)

1659 ANON.   : *Jottings*, AS 13, 1938, pp. 157 - 158.

1660 ANON.   : *Jottings*, AS 19, 1944, pp. 150 - 151.

1661 ANON.   : *Jottings*, AS 21, 1946, p. 44.

1662 ANON.   : *Jottings*, AS 22, 1947, pp. 237 - 238.

1663 ANON.   : *Motor Notes*, AS 25, 1950, p. 78.

1664 ANON.   : *Neologisms*, AS 14, 1939, p. 316.

1665 ANON.   : *Some Neologisms*, AS 12, 1937, p. 243.

1666 ANON.   : *Trade Coinages*, AS 11, 1936, pp. 374 - 375.

1667 ANON.   : *Trade-Name Novelties*, AS 19, 1944, pp. 232 - 233.

1668 ANON.   : *Verbal Novelties*, AS 10, 1935, pp. 154 - 155.

1669 ANON.   : *Verbal Novelties*, AS 11, 1936, pp. 373 - 374.
                      (to peopleize, snackerie, cowswainette ...)

1670 ANON.   : *Verbal Novelties*, AS 12, 1937, pp. 235 - 237.

1671 ANON.   : *Verbal Novelties*, AS 13, 1938, p. 240.

1672 ANON.   : *Verbal Novelties*, AS 19, 1944, pp. 77 - 78.

1673 ANON.   : *Verbal Novelties*, AS 21, 1946, pp. 156 - 157.

1674 ANON.   : *Words, Words, Words*, AS 17, 1942, pp. 283 - 284.

1675 ANON.   : *Words, Words, Words*, AS 18, 1943, p. 237.

1676 ANON.   : *Words, Words, Words*, AS 19, 1944, pp. 148 - 150.

1677 ACKERMAN, L. M. : *More Words*, AS 33, 1958, pp. 157 - 158.
                      (agribusiness, skinjuries ...)

'1678 AUER, B. M.   : *A Letter from the Publisher*, Time 81, May 24, 1963,
                      p. 13.
                      (A selection of "new words and phrases" from that week's
                      issue)

'1679 BABCOCK, C. M. : *Scrabledegook - a National Verbomania*, Inside the ALD,
                      April 1959, pp. 1, 3.
                      (Modern American word coinages)

1680 BEATH, P. R.   : *Neologisms of the Film Industry*, AS 8, 1933, pp. 73 -
                      74.

1681 BERG, P. C.   : *A Dictionary of New Words in English*, London : G.
                      Allen & Unwin Ltd., 1953, 176 p..
                      Reviews :
                      Osselton, N. E. : ES 34, 1953, 93 - 95

' 22 BINDMANN, W. : *Wortschatz und Syntax bei Benjamin Disraeli (Lord Bea-
                      consfield), unter besonderer Berücksichtigung der Neo-*

logismen und moderner syntaktischer Erscheinungen.

'1682 BOLINGER, D. L.   : *The Living Language*, Words 4, February, March, May 1938, pp. 29 - 32, 43 - 46, 67 - 70.

1683   - : *Neologisms*, AS 16, 1941, pp. 64 - 67.

1684   - : *Among the New Words*, AS 16, 1941, pp. 144 - 148. (-worthy, -er, -ize)

1685   - : *Among the New Words*, AS 16, 1941, pp. 306 - 309. (-ee, -teria, -aroo, -ette ...)

1686   - : *Among the New Words*, AS 17, 1942, pp. 120 - 123. (-er, -eer, -at, -ism, -ite ...)

1687   - : *Among the New Words*, AS 17, 1942, pp. 202 - 206.

1688   - : *Among the New Words*, AS 17, 1942, pp. 269 - 273. (-ette, -aroo, -ana ...)

1689   - : *Among the New Words*, AS 18, 1943, pp. 62 - 65. (-oriat, -buster, -eer, -legger ...)

1690   - : *Among the New Words*, AS 18, 1943, pp. 146 - 151. (-master, -cast, -burger ...)

1691   - : *Among the New Words*, AS 18, 1943, pp. 301 - 305.

1692   - : *Among the New Words*, AS 19, 1944, pp. 60 - 64. (Sb + happy)

'1693   - : *New Words and Meanings*, Britannica Yearbook 1944.

1694 BOOTT, F.   : *On Certain Neologisms*, The Andover Review 3, 1885, pp. 135 - 149.

'1695 BORGES, J. L.   : *Joyce y los neologismos*, SUR 62, 1939, pp. 59 - 61.

'1696 BRAUBURGER, H. : *Studien zu den amerikanischen.Neologismen des 17. und 18. Jahrhunderts. Unter besonderer Berücksich-*

tigung des englischen Sprachmaterials, Diss. Köln
20.10.1954, (1954), xii, 273 lvs.n..
(Germany 70, p. 457)

'1697 BREWER, F. P.   : *Register of New Words*, TAPA 1888, Vol. 19.

'1698 BRIGGS, T. H.   : *Needed Words*, Word Study 10, 5, 1935, pp. 2 - 3.

1699 BYINGTON, S. T.   : *From Mr. Byington's Brief Case*, AS 17, 1942, pp. 66
                         - 67.

1700   - : *Mr. Byington's Brief Case (II)*, AS 19, 1944, pp.
                         118 - 128.
                         (burdensome, southwide, to berate ...)

1701 C., P. J.   : *Random Jottings*, AS 23, 1948, pp. 75 - 76.

1702   - : *Random Notes*, AS 23, 1948, p. 256.

1703   - : *Verbal Novelties*, AS 24, 1949, pp. 233 - 234.

'1704 CARLIN, M. H.   : *Words, Words, Words*, Catholic World, November 1957,
                         pp. 132 - 137.

'1705 CARSON, C. B.   : *New Words for Our Time*, Colorado Quarterly 10, Sum-
                         mer 1961, pp. 57 - 69.

1706 COLLINSON, W. E.   : *Recent Neologisms in English. With Some German Equi-
                         valents*, MSpråk 50, 1956, pp. 268 - 281.

'1707 COLODNY, I.   : *Word Smiths*, Words 4, September 1938, p. 83.

1708 CONLEY, J.   : *Scholastic Neologisms in Usk's " Testament of Love"*,
                         N & Q 209, June 1964, p. 209.

1709 COSGRAVE, P. J.   : *Jottings*, AS 23, 1948, pp. 306 - 307.

1710   - : *Jottings*, AS 24, 1949, pp. 315 - 316.

'1711 CRABB, A. L.   : *Words, Words, Words*, National Parent - Teacher Maga-
                         zine 54, June 1960, pp. 17 - 18.

'1712 CUNNINGHAM, J. V.   : *New Words and War Material*, Word Study 1949, p. 7.

' 44 DALY, B. A.   : *The Sources of New Words and New Meanings in English Since 1800.*

1713 DANTON, G. H.   : *Jottings*, AS 13, 1938, p. 320.

1714 DAVIS, E. B.   : *Some New Words by War out of Wood*, AS 19, 1944, pp. 91 - 96.

999 DOBBIE, E. V. K.   : *Agent-Noun Neologisms.*

'1715 EVANS, B.   : *New World, New Words*, New York Times Magazine, April 9, 1961, pp. 62, 64, 66.

1150 F., L. I.   : *A Few Notes.*

'1716 FARBSTEIN, W. E.   : *Neologisms*, The New York Times Magazine, December 2, 1956, pp. 52 - 53.

1717 FRIEDERICH, W.   : *Englische Neuwörter und Nachträge*, Idioma 5, 1968, pp. 201 - 207.

1718   - : *Englische Neuwörter und Nachträge*, Idioma 6, 1969, pp. 8 - 12, 65 - 66, 167 - 170, 226 - 230.

1719   - : *Neuwörter im englischen naturwissenschaftlich - tec nischen Wortschatz*,Lebende Sprachen 17, 3, 1972, pp 65 - 73.
     '(cf. 3, p. 67; 4 - 5, p. 67; 6, p. 67; 1, p. 68)

1720 GLÄSER, R.   : *Neuwörter im politischen Englisch*, ZAA 9, 1963, pp. 229 - 247.

1721 GOWERS, E.   : *Some Thoughts on New Words*, Essays and Studies n.s. 10, 1957, pp. 1 - 15.

1722 HALL, R.   : *New Words and Antedatings from Cudworth's " Treatise of Freewill"*, N & Q 205, 1960, pp. 427 - 432.

1723   - : *Shaftesbury : Some Antedatings and New Words*, N & Q 206, 1961, pp. 251 - 253.

1724   - : *Some New Seventeenth-Century Words and Antedatings*, N & Q 208, 1963, pp. 59 - 61.

1725   - : *Cudworth : More New Words*, N & Q 208, June 1963, pp. 212 - 213.

1726 HARRISON, Th. P.   : *Some Folk Words*, AS 5, 1930, pp. 219 - 223.

1727 HENCH, A. L.   : *Some Lexical Notes*, AS 6, 1930/1931, pp. 253 - 256.
(radiocast, mindscape, cavalcade, motorcade, aerocade)

1728   - : *Some Word Notes*, AS 7, 1931/1932, pp. 319 - 320.
(infracaninophile, good-willish, the sooners, mobster)

1729   - : *Verbal Novelties*, AS 21, 1946, pp. 156 - 157.

1730 HIDDEMANN, H.   : *Neues englisches Wortgut*, Die lebenden Fremdsprachen 2, 1950, pp. 242 - 245 (to be continued)

'1731 HIETSCH, O.   : *Englische Neologismen*, MSpråk 50, 1956, pp. 281 - 301.

1732   - : *Englische und deutsche Neologismen : ein kleiner Beitrag zur modernen Lexikographie*, MSpråk 54, 1960, pp. 33 - 54.

1733 HILLS, E. C.   : *New Words in California*, MLN 38, 1923, pp. 187 - 188.
(esp. in -eria, -ery, -atorium)

1734   - : *More New Words*, AS 1, 1925/1926, p. 246.
(smoketeria)

1735 HOFFMAN, D. G.   : *New Words From the Music Circus*, AS 26, 1951, pp. 75 - 76.

282

1736 HORNSTEIN, L. H. : *Current Neologisms*, AS 27, 1952, pp. 71 - 73.

1737 - : *Some Recent Neologisms*, AS 30, 1955, pp. 231 - 233.

1738 HÜLSBERGEN, H. : *Studien zu den amerikanischen Neologismen des 19. Jahrhunderts*, Diss. Köln 28.2.1957, Köln : Fotokopie, 1956, xviii, (1), 451 p., (1), vita. (Germany 73, p. 512)

1739 JAGGARD, W. : *New Words, or Meanings, Noted Recently*, N & Q 169, 1935, p. 62. (signarlist, marginalizer)

1740 - : *New Words*, N & Q 168, 1935, p. 421. (cinemactress, railophone, guffer, beet-worker)

1741 - : *New Words*, N & Q 168, 1935, p. 297. (anthologician, boondoggle, ...)

1742 - : *New Words*, N & Q 168, 1935, pp. 313 - 314. (glassine, poshest, tight-rope-ist, unkinkable)

'1743 - : *New Words*, N & Q 168, 1935, p. 331.

'1744 - : *New Words*, N & Q 169, 1935, p. 9.

'1369 JANUS : *A Spectator's Notebook.*

1745 L., N. R. : *Notes*, AS 4, 1929, pp. 155 - 156. (nookery, bumperette)

'1746 LINSKIJ, S. S. : *Neologizmy v slovarnom sostave anglijskogo jazyka XVI veka. Sposoby ich vvedenija i populjarizacii pisateljami i leksikografami* (Neologisms in 16th century English vocabulary. Their introduction and popularization by authors and lexicographers), Dis Vladivostok, 1959.

'1747 - : *Sposoby vvedenija i populjarizacii neologizmov, upotrebljaemye anglijskimi pisateljami i leksiko-*

grafami XVI veka (Methods for introducing and popularizing neologisms used by 16th century authors and lexicographers), UZ Dal U 4, 1962, SFil, pp. 19 - 24.

'1004   - : *Neologizmy s obščim značeniem "dejstvujuščego lica"* (*nomina agentis) v slovarnom sostave anglijskogo jazyka XVI veka* (Agent noun neologisms in 16th century English vocabulary).

1748 LOCKARD, E. N.   : *Fertile Virgins and Fissle Breeders : Nuclear Neologisms*, AS 25, 1950, pp. 23 - 27.

'1749 LOVEMAN, A.   : *Words, Words, Words,* The Saturday Review of Literature December 21, 1946, p. 20.

'1750 McCONNELL, R. M.   : *War Words and Tired Symbols,* ETC 12, Winter 1955, pp. 103 - 108.

1751 MATTHEWS, B.   : *A Final Note on Recent Briticisms,* MLN 12, 1897, pp. 65 - 69.
(unwellness, stereo-plates, co-opt, liveable-in, propriteriat ...)

*1752   - : *The Latest Novelties in Language,* Harper's Magazine, June 1920, 141, pp. 82 - 87.

1753 MEREDITH, M. J.   : *Cinema-Coinages,* AS 3, 1928, p. 492.
(cinemactress, cinemaddicts, cinemagnification)

1754   - : *Verbal Novelties,* AS 9, 1934, pp. 317 - 318.

*1755 MOIR, W.   : *World of Words,* English Journal 42, 1953, pp. 153 - 155.

1756 ODELL, R.   : *Jottings,* AS 26, 1951, pp. 155 - 156.
(Russtralian, bookologist, flipmagilder, colbyize, snoborium, shop-o-phone, chairmandeer, unlaydownable)

'1757 OLEKSENKO, N. G.   : *Neologizmy v sovremennom anglijskom jazyke perioda 1939-1945 gg. (Na materiale gazety " Dejli Uorker" London* (Neologisms in modern English from 1939 - 1945. On the material of the paper " Daily Worker", London), Diss. Moscow, 1955 (1 - M Ped I).

'1758 ONIONS, C. T.   : *New English Words*, Living Age, September 1932, 343, p. 85.

'1759 OSENBURG, F. C.   : *More Neologisms*, Word Study 34, October 1960, pp. 4 - 5.

'1760 OTTEN, A. L.   : *Government Gibberish*, Wall Street Journal (Eastern ed.), May 4, 1967, p. 14.
(Includes new terms of jargon : to quantify, to re plicate, to annualize, attrite ... and such words as feed-back and add-on)

'1761 PARTRIDGE, E.   : *Words, Words, Words!*, London : Methuen, x, 230 p..

1762 PHILLIPSON, J. S.   : *Two New Words*, Word Study 39, December 1963, p. 6.
(to elevator, to moisturize)

1763 POUND, L.   : *Walt Whitman's Neologisms*, The American Mercury 4, 1925, pp. 199 - 201.

1764   - : *Some Word-Products of " Technocracy"*, AS 8, 1933, pp. 68 - 70.

1765 PRESCOTT, J.   : *A Miscellany of Neologisms*, AS 21, 1946, pp. 147 - 151.
(anti-Jacobite, to chain-smoke, childrened, to copy-read, to dewbathe, goldly ...)

1097 PREUSS, F.   : *Substantivische Neologismen aus Verb und Adverb.*

1766 PRICK v. WELY, F. P. H. : *War Words and Peace Pipings. (Material for a Study in Slang and Neologism)*, ES 4, 1922, pp. 10 - 19.

1006 PROCTOR, J. W.　　　: *New Agent Nouns Suggested.*

1767 REIFER, M.　　　　　: *Dictionary of New Words With an Introduction by*
　　　　　　　　　　　　　Eric Partridge, New York : Philosophical Library,
　　　　　　　　　　　　　1955, ix, 234 p., (2).
　　　　　　　　　　　　　Reviews :
　　　　　　　　　　　　　Martinet, A.　: Word 12, 1956, 493
　　　　　　　　　　　　　Russell, I. W.: MLN 72, 1957, 145 - 147

'1768 RUSSELL, I. W.　　　: *New Words and New Meanings*, Britannica Book of the
　　　　　　　　　　　　　Year 1945, p. 771.

1769　　　　　　　　　- : *Among the New Words*, AS 19, 1944, pp. 222 - 226,
　　　　　　　　　　　　　302 - 307.

1770　　　　　　　　　- : *Among the New Words*, AS 20, 1945, pp. 141 - 146,
　　　　　　　　　　　　　221 - 225, 229 - 303.

1771　　　　　　　　　- : *Among the New Words*, AS 21, 1946, pp. 137 - 145, 22
　　　　　　　　　　　　　220 - 226, 295 - 300.

1772　　　　　　　　　- : *Among the New Words*, AS 22, 1947, pp. 145 - 149,
　　　　　　　　　　　　　226 - 231.

1773　　　　　　　　　- : *Among the New Words*, AS 23, 1948, pp. 64 - 68,
　　　　　　　　　　　　　147 - 151, 285 - 295.

1774　　　　　　　　　- : *Among the New Words*, AS 24, 1949, pp. 72 - 76,
　　　　　　　　　　　　　143 - 147, 225 - 228, 30- - 307.

1775　　　　　　　　　- : *Among the New Words*, AS 25, 1950, pp. 64 - 66,
　　　　　　　　　　　　　143 - 147, 224 - 229.

1776　　　　　　　　　- : *Among the New Words*, AS 26, 1951, pp. 51 - 54,
　　　　　　　　　　　　　143 - 146, 291 - 295.

1777　　　　　　　　　- : *Among the New Words*, AS 27, 1952, pp. 49 - 53,
　　　　　　　　　　　　　204 - 208.

1778　　　　　　　　　- : *Among the New Words*, AS 28, 1953, pp. 47 - 51,
　　　　　　　　　　　　　208 - 212, 294 - 296.

1779   - : *Among the New Words*, AS 29, 1954, pp. 71 - 73, 214 - 217, 282 - 286.

1780   - : *Among the New Words*, AS 30, 1955, pp. 137 - 141, 283 - 288.

1781   - : *Among the New Words*, AS 31, 1956, pp. 61 - 64, 209 - 212, 284 - 288.

1782   - : *Among the New Words*, AS 32, 1957, pp. 136 - 139.

1783   - : *Among the New Words*, AS 33, 1958, pp. 125 - 129.

1784   - : *Among the New Words*, AS 34, 1959, pp. 46 - 48.

1785   - : *Among the New Words*, AS 35, 1960, pp. 56 - 59, 283 - 287.

1786   - : *Among the New Words*, AS 36, 1961, pp. 206 - 209, 281 - 284.

1787   - : *Among the New Words*, AS 37, 1962, pp. 145 - 147.

1788   - : *Among the New Words*, AS 38, 1963, pp. 228 - 230.

1789   - : *Among the New Words*, AS 39, 1964, pp. 144 - 146. 218 - 222.

1790   - : *Among the New Words*, AS 40, 1965, pp. 141 - 146, 208 - 215.

1791   with the assistance of McMillan, N. R. : *Among the New Words*, AS 41, 1966, pp. 137 - 141.

1792 RUSSELL, I. W. - BOYETT, W. W. : *Among the New Words*, AS 32, 1957, pp. 292 - 296.

1793   - : *Among the New Words*, AS 33, 1958, pp. 280 - 283.

1794   - : *Among the New Words*, AS 34, 1959, pp. 131 - 133.

1795 S., H. J.   : *Some of Mr. Bolinger's " New Words"*, AS 16, 1941, pp. 228 - 229.

'1796 SALEMSON, H. J.   : *James Joyce and the New Word*, Modern Quarterly 5, 1929, pp. 294 - 312.

'1797 SARGEAUNT, W.   : *Through the Interstellar Looking Glass*, Life, May 21, 1951, pp. 127 - 134.
(New words in science fiction)

' 287 SCHINDL, E.   : *Studien zum Wortschatz Sir Philip Sidneys. Neubildungen und Entlehnungen.*

1798 SCHULER, H. A.   : *A Hundred and Fifty Recent English Words*, Writer 7, 1894, pp. 21 - 23.

1799 SHAABER, M. A.   : *Miscellany*, AS 3, 1928, pp. 67 - 68.
(accomateria ...)

1800 SMITH, Ch.A.   : *New Words Self-Defined*, New York : Doubleday, Page & Co., 1919, viii, 215 p., (1).
Reviews :
Anon.   : The Nation (N. Y.), 110, 1920, 305 - 306

1801 SMITH, L. P.   : *Notes on New Words*, The Saturday Review of Literature, May 18, 1935, No.12, pp. 13 - 14.
(Jay-walker, diehard, viewpoint)

'1802 SOLOV'EVA, T. A.   : *O nekotorych neologizmach amerikanskoj političeskoj leksiki XX veka (Po rabotam V. Fostera)*
(On some neologisms of 20th century American political vocabulary. (On the material of the works of W. Foster)), Diss. Moscow, 1956 (M Gor Ped I).

'1405 STEPHENS, G. D.   : *Wise, ize, bar, and bug.*

1385 STRONG, M. E.   : *New Verbs.*

288

1803 TAYLOR, A.   : *A Curious List of Americanisms*, AS 30, 1955, pp. 151 - 152.

'1804 TOLCHIN, M.   : *About New Words*, New York Times Magazine, September 8, 1957, p. 68.

1805 V., W.   : *Neue englische Wörter*, NS 1, 1894, p. 436.

'1806 WEITZ, F.   : *Zum Aufsatz " Neues englisches Wortgut"*, Die lebenden Fremdsprachen 2, 1950, p. 378.

1807 WELBY, A.   : *New Words : Postrest (168, 313)*, N & Q 168, 1935, p. 358.

1808 WENTWORTH, H.   : *Verbal Novelties*, AS 9, 1934, pp. 75 - 76.
(bulkateer, orderette, Plutogogue, to holiday, walkathons, talkathons)

1809 WHITE, W.   : *Neologisms from Korea : " Fire-cide" and "Kelleris*
AS 39, 1964, pp. 308 - 309.

1810 WILLIAMS, F. C.   : *Jottings*, AS 27, 1952, pp. 152 - 153.

1811 WITHINGTON, R.   : *Some Neologisms from Recent Magazines*, AS 6, 1930/1931, pp. 277 - 289.

1812   - : *Neologisms and a Need*, AS 14, 1939, p. 70.

1813   - : *Verbal Pungencies*, AS 14, 1939, pp. 269 - 275.

1814   - : *Picturesque Speech*, AS 15, 1940, pp. 217 - 218.

1815   - : *Double-Edged Coinages*, AS 16, 1941, pp. 313 - 315.

II.

PARTICULAR ASPECTS THAT HAVE BEEN STUDIED IN ENGLISH WORD-FORMATION

IX. WORD - FORMATION AND GRAPHEMICS

(Spelling, hyphenation ...)

'1816 ALLEN, E. F.   : *To Hyphen or Not to Hyphen*, Better English 2, No. 4, October 1938, pp. 11 - 13.

' 413 AZARCH, N. A.   : *K voprosu ob otgraničenii složnych slov v slovo-sočetanij v sovremennom anglijskom jazyke* (On the segregation of compounds from word-combinations in contemporary English).

416 BALL, A. M.   : *The Compounding and Hyphenation of English Words.*

417 BARRETT, C. E.   : *A Graphemic Analysis of English Nominal Complexes.*

1817 BOLINGER, D. L.   : *Damned Hyphen*, AS 42, 1967, pp. 297 - 299.

423 BRINKMAN, E. A.   : *Attitudes and Practices in the Writing of Compound Words in Contemporary American English.*

'1347 CLARKE, E. J.   : *A Study of English Orthography, with Special Reference to the Spelling of the Suffix (ik).*

436 FENZL, R.   : *To Hyphen or Not to Hyphen ?*, Idioma 3, 1966, pp. 266 - 267.

789 FRIEDRICH, W.   : *Spelling Rules.*

956   - : *Orthographic Peculiarities of Certain Suffixes.*

438 HAMILTON, F. W.   : *Compound Words : A Study of the Principles of Compounding, the Components of Compounds, and the Use of the Hyphen.*

1399 HERMANN, W.   : *Verbalendung –ize oder –ise ?*

' 446 KENNEDY, A. G.   : *Hyphenation of Compound Nouns.*

'1023 McDAVID, R. I. jr.   : *Adviser and Advisor : Orthography and Semantic Differenciation.*

961 McMILLAN, J. B.　　　　　: *Doubling Consonants Before Suffixes.*

471 SCHMITZ, A.　　　　　　: *Bindestrich-Kombinationen im britischen Englisch.*

1818 SHIRLEY, H. H.　　　　　: *Hyphens and the Dictionary of American English,* AS 13, 1938, p. 59.

'1819 TEALL, E. N.　　　　　: *Punctuation with Chapters on Hyphenization and Capitalization,* New York, 1898.

'1820　　　　　　　　　　- : *Meet Mr. Hyphen and Put Him in His Place,* New York, 1937.

' 745 ZANDVOORT, R. W.　　　: *Varia Syntactica : III : On Hyphened Verb-Adverb Combinations.*

X. WORD - FORMATION AND PHONEMICS

1821 ARNOLD, G. F.   : *Stress in English Words*, Amsterdam : North-Holland Publishing Company, 1957, 96 p.. (Reprint from Lingua 6, 3 and 4, pp. 221 - 267, 397 - 441)

763 BLOOMFIELD, L.   : *The Structure of Learnèd Words*.

1822 BOLINGER, D. L.   : *Rime, Assonance, and Morpheme Analysis*, Word 6, 1950, pp. 117 - 136. (also in Bolinger, D. L. : *Forms of English Accent, Morpheme, Order*, ed. by Isamu Abe and Tetsuya Kanekiyo, Cambridge, Mass. : Harvard University Press, 1965, viii, 334 p.; pp. 203 - 226)

1823   - : *Stress and Information*, AS 33, 1958, pp. 5 - 20.

1824   - : *Ambiguities in Pitch Accent*, Word 17, 1961, pp. 309 - 317.

526 BOROWSKI, B.   : *Zum Nebenakzent beim altenglischen Nominalkompositum*.

1266 BOYS, Th.   : *Pronunciation of Words Ending in "-oid"*.

527 BRAND, F.   : *Die Betonung der Nominalkomposita im Neuenglischen*.

421 BRANTNER, G.   : *Prosaakzent und metrisches Schema in englischen Kompositen*.

1267 BUCKTON, T. J.   : *Pronunciation of Words Ending in "-oid"* .

564 BURANOV, D.   : *Osobennosti zvukovoj struktury slov, obrazovannych pri pomošči polusuffiksa -man v sovremennom anglijskom jazyke* (The characteristics of the phonological sound structure of words with the semi-suffix -man in modern English).

' 431 ČEKMAZOVA, N. A. : *Fonetičeskaja redukcija v anglijskom jazyke. (Na materiale oproščenija složnych slov i obrazovanija slabych form služebnych slov)* (Phonetic reduction in the English language. (Concerning weakened forr of compounds and the formation of weak-stressed forms of function words)).

' 432 — : *Fonetičeskaja redukcija v angliskom jazyke. (Na materiale oproščenija složnych slov i obrazovanija slabych form služebnych i vspomogatel'nych slov)* (Phonetic reduction in the English language. (Con- cerning weakened forms of compounds and the for- mation of weak-stressed forms of function and auxi- liary words).

1825 CHOMSKY, N. - HALLE, M. : *The Sound Pattern of English*, New York : Evan- ston; London : Harper & Row Publishers, 1968, xiv, 470 p.. (Studies in Language, N. Chomsky and Morris Halle editors)

870 COLLITZ, K. HECHTENBERG : *Accentuation of Prefixes in English.*

1826 CURME, G. O. : *The Development of Modern Group Stress in German and English.*

1009 DANIELSSON, B. : *Studies on the Accentuation of Polysyllabic Latin, Greek, and Romance Loan-Words in English with Spe- cial Reference to those Ending in -able, -ate, -ato; -ible, -ic, -ical and -ize.*

775 — : *Native, Classical, or Romance? Etymology and Ac- centuation in English.*

672 DIETRICH, G. : *Die Akzentverhältnisse im Englischen bei Adverb und Präposition in Verbindung mit einem Verb und Verwandtes.*

54 ECKHARDT, E.   : *Die neuenglische Verkürzung langer Tonsilbenvokale in abgeleiteten und zusammengesetzten Wörtern.*

55   - : *Nochmals zur neuenglischen Vokalverkürzung in Ableitungen und Zusammensetzungen.*

' 955 EDMONDS, J.   : *A Study of Some Very Confusing Suffixes; or, Phonetic Regularities in Some Words Derived from Romance Tongues.*

676 EITREM, H.   : *Stress in English Verb + Adverb Groups.*

' 677 ELLINGER, J.   : *Über die Betonung der aus Verb + Adverb bestehenden Wortgruppen.*

' 569 EYESTONE, M. A.   : *Tests and Treatment of Compound Substantives in Modern American English with Special Emphasis on Stress and Intonation Patterns.*

1268 FITZ-HENRY, F.   : *Pronunciation of Words Ending in "-oid".*

1340 GERRING, H.   : *The Pronunciation of Adjectives and Attributive Past Participles in -ed.*

' 532 GLIKINA, E. A.   : *Udarenie v složnych suščestvitel'nych i prilagatel'nych anglijskogo jazyka* (Stress in compound substantives and adjectives in English).

' 437   - : *Akcentnoe stroenie složnogo slova v sovremennom anglijskom jazyke* (The accentual structure of the compound in modern English).

' 534 GRAND, F.   : *Die Betonung der Nominalkomposita im Neuenglischen.*

904 HAGEN, S.   : *Note on the Pronunciation of EX in English.*

1827 HALLE, M. - KEYSER, S. J. : *English Stress. Its Form, Its Growth, and Its Role in Verse*, New York : Evanston; London : Harper & Row Publishers, 1971, xvii, 206 p..
(= Studies in Language, N. Chomsky and Morris Halle editors)

442 HEMPL, G.   : *The Stress of German and English Compounds in Geographical Names.*

799 HENISZ, B.   : *Derivation : Morphophonemic Alternation Patterns. Generative Formation Rules and System for Computer Processing.*

1828 HILL, A. A.   : *Stress in Recent English as a Distinguishing Mark Between Dissyllables Used as Noun or Verb,* AS 6, 1930/1931, pp. 443 - 448.

' 804 JONES, D.   : *The Use of Syllabic and Non-Syllabic l and n in Derivatives of English Words Ending in Syllabic l and n.*

'1342 KATAYAMA, N.   : *-edly no hatsuon ni tsuite* (On the pronunciation of the English suffix -edly).

' 451 KUKOLŠČIKOVA, L. E. : *Fonetičeskaja karakteristika složnych slov i atributivnych slovosočetanija v sovremennom anglijskom jazyke* (The phonetic character of compound words and predicative word groups in modern English).

202 LUICK, K.   : *Über Vokalverkürzung in abgeleiteten und zusammengesetzten Wörtern.*

' 457 LUTSTORF, H. Th.   : *The Stressing of Compounds in Modern English. A Study in Experimental Phonetics.*

961 McMILLAN, J. B.   : *Doubling Consonants Before Suffixes.*

' 459 MAKEY, H. O.   : *The Rhythm in Compounds ?*

212 MARCHAND, H.   : *Phonology, Morphophonology and Word-Formation.*

817   - : *Über zwei Prinzipien der Wortableitung in ihrer Anwendung auf das Französische und Englische.*

460   - : *Die Länge englischer Komposita und die entsprechenden Verhältnisse im Deutschen.*

819 METZGER, E.   : *Zur Betonung der lateinisch-romanischen Wörter*
                           im Neuenglischen mit besonderer Berücksichtigung
                           der Zeit von c. 1560 bis c.1660.

'1829 MIHATSCH, A.   : *Die Betonung der lateinischen Lehnwörter im En-*
                           glischen, Diss. Vienna, 1921.
                           (Vienna 2, p. 176; 2058)

821 MONROE, G. K.   : *Phonemic Transcription of Graphic Post-Base Af-*
                           fixes in English : A Computer Problem.

1830 NEWMAN, S. S.   : *On the Stress System of English*, Word 2, 1946,
                           pp. 171 - 187.

465 NYQUIST, A.   : *Stress, Intonation, Accent, Prominence in Dis-*
                           syllabic Double-Stress Compounds in Educated
                           Southern English.

'1249 OTA, F.   : *The Pronunciation of -ed, -edly and -edness.*

832 PILCH, H.   : *Nebenakzent und Wortableitung im Englischen.*

1831 SACK, F. L.   : *English Word Stress*, ELT 23, 1968 /1969, pp.
                           141 - 144.

282 SALOMON, H. I.   : *Wörter mit Doppelakzent im Neuenglischen.*

'1832 SARGEAUNT, J.   : *The Pronunciation of English Words Derived from*
                           the Latin, Preface and Notes by Henry Bradley,
                           S.P.E. Tract No. 4, 1920, pp. 1 - 31.

472 SCHUBIGER, M.   : *Zum sog. level Stress bei englischen Composita.*

'1833 SOKOLOVA, M. A.   : *Slovesnoe udarenie v sovremennoma anglijskom*
                           jazyke (Word stress in modern English), KDiss.
                           Moscow, 1955, (M Gor Ped I).

' 315   - : *O smyslorazličitel'noj funkcii vtorogo sil'nogo*
                           i vtorostepennogo udarenij v anglijskom jazyke
                           (On the distinctive function of the second main
                           stress and the secondary stress in the English

language).

'1834   - : *Eksperimental'no-fonetičeskoe issledovanie sloves-*
nogo udarenija v anglijskom jazyke (Experimental
phonetic study of word stress in English), UZ 1 -
MPed I, 1960, t. 20, pp. 373 - 395.

'477 SWOBODA, W.   : *Die englische und deutsche Betonung der Composita.*

'1835 TAMSON, G.   : *Über Wortbetonung im Englischen*, Diss. Göttingen
29.5.1897, Halle : E. Karras, 1897, vi, 32 p.,(1).
(Germany 12, p. 117; 100)
complete edition under the title :
Word-Stress in English : A Short Treatise on the Ac-
centuation of Words in ME as Compared with the Stress
in Old and Modern English, Halle : Max Niemeyer,
1898, xiii, 164 p..
(= Studien zur englischen Philologie 3)

1836 TOURBIER, R.   : *Experimentell-phonetische Studie über die Gruppe*
Adverb + Substantiv im Neuenglischen, ASNS 153, 1928
pp. 61 - 68.

737 TRAGER, E. C.   : *Superfix and Sememe. English Verbal Compounds.*

1837 VANVIK, A.   : *On Stress in Present-Day English. (Received Pro-*
nunciation), Acta Universitatis Bergensis. Series
Humaniorum Litterarum Arbok for Universitet Bergen
Humanistik Serie, 1960, No. 3, Bergen - Oslo :
Norwegian Universities Press, 1961, 108 p., 12
spectograms .
(esp. pp. 42 - 58, 64 - 68, 85 - 88)

' 341 VASIL'EV, V. A.   : *Rol' fonetičeskogo stroja v slovoobrazovanii i*
slovoizmenenii sovremennogo anglijskogo jazyka
(The role of phonetic structure in contemporary En
glish word-formation and word-change).

856 VOL'FSON, I. I. : *Vtorostepennoe udarenie v prostych i proizvodnych slovach anglijskogo jazyka* (Secondary stress in derived and underived words in English).

857 - : *Slovesnoe udarenie v anglijskom jazyke.* (*Zakonomernosti raspredelenija udarenija v mnogosložnych prostych i proizvodnych slovach)* (Word stress in English. (The regularities of the distribution of accent in polysyllabic underived and derived words).

1838 VOLFSONAS, J. : *Dangiaskiemenių žodziu kirčiavimas anglu kolboje* (Stress in polysyllabic English words), VPIMD 9, 1960, pp. 307 - 319. (English summary)

944 W., E. : *The Stress of the Uns.*

1250 WALDO, G. S. : *Crooked, Crookedly, Crookedness.*

1839 WEBER, G. : *Suffixvokal nach kurzer Tonsilbe vor r, n, m im Angelsächsischen*, Diss. Berlin 25.2.1927, Leipzig : Mayr & Müller, 1927, vii, 48 p..
complete edition : Leipzig : Mayer & Müller, 1927, xiv, 142 p..
(= Palaestra 156)
(Germany 43, p. 36)

XI. CONTRASTIVE STUDIES

ENGLISH - CZECH :

1463 RENSKÝ, M   : *The Noun-Verb Quotient in English and Czech.*

ENGLISH - FRENCH :

'1526 DIERICKX, J.   : *Les "mots-valises" de l'anglais et du français.*

1549 LEVY, R.   : *Haplologic Blends in French and English.*

817 MARCHAND, H.   : *Über zwei Prinzipien der Wortableitung in ihrer Anwendung auf das Französische und Englische.*

394 STEIN, G.   : *Primäre und sekundäre Adjektive im Französischen und Englischen.*

395   - : *Primäre und sekundäre Adjektive im Französischen und Englischen (Primary and Secondary Adjectives in French and English).*

ENGLISH - GEORGIAN :

' 684 GELAŠVILI, M. V. : *Sopostavitel'nyi analiz gruzinskich preverbov i anglijskich poslelegov* (A comparative analysis of English postverbs and Georgian preverbs).

' 685   - : *Sopostavitel'nyi analiz anglijskich postverbov : gruzinskich preverbov* (A comparative analysis of English postverbs and Georgian preverbs).

ENGLISH - GERMAN :

1323 ABRAHAM, W.   : *Passiv und Verbalableitung auf e. <u>-able</u>, dt. <u>-bar</u>.*

591 CARSTENSEN, B.   : *Weltweit und world-wide.*

1826 CURME, G. O.   : *The Development of Modern Group Stress in German and English.*

592 DONY, A.   : *Über einige volkstümliche Begriffsverstärkungen bei deutschen und englischen Adjektiven.*

1475 FORSSNER, T.   : *Deutsche und englische Imperativnamen.*

787 FRANCK, Th.   : *Wörter für Satzinhalte. Zur inhaltlichen Leistung abstrakter Wortstände im Deutschen und im Englischen.*

442 HEMPL, G.   : *The Stress of German and English Compounds in Geographical Names.*

1732 HIETSCH, O.   : *Englische und deutsche Neologismen : Ein kleiner Beitrag zur modernen Lexikographie.*

1597 HILMER, H.   : *Schallnachahmung, Wortschöpfung und Bedeutungswandel auf Grundlage der Wahrnehmungen von Schlag, Fall und Bruch und derartigen Vorgängen dargestellt an einigen Lautwurzeln der deutschen und der englischen Sprache.*

448 KOZIOL, H.   : *Shakespeares Komposita in deutschen Übersetzungen.*

1370 KULAK, M.   : *Die semantischen Kategorien der mit Nullmorphem abgeleiteten desubstantivischen Verben des heutigen Englischen und Deutschen.*

601 LIPKA, L.   : *Die Wortbildungstypen WATERPROOF und GRASS-GREEN und ihre Entsprechungen im Deutschen.*

708   - : *Ein Grenzgebiet zwischen Wortbildung und Wortsemantik : die Partikelverben im Englischen und Deutschen.*

201 LÜTJEN, H. P.   : *Kontrastive Grammatik des Deutschen und Englischen : Wortbildung.*

460 MARCHAND, H.   : *Die Länge englischer Komposita und die entsprechenden Verhältnisse im Deutschen.*

' 716 MEYER, H. J. : *Semantische Analyse der modernenglischen Verbal-partikel up im Vergleich zu verwandten englischen und deutschen Verbalpartikeln.*

'1099 PUSCH, L. F. : *Die Substantivierung von Verben mit Satzkomplementen im Englischen und Deutschen.*

1602 REINIUS, J. : *Onomatopoetische Bezeichnungen für menschliche Weser besonders im Deutschen und Englischen.*

468 RUFENER, J. : *Studies in the Motivation of English and German Compounds.*

610 SACHS, E. : *On steinalt, stock-still and Similar Formations.*

' 477 SWOBODA, W. : *Die englische und deutsche Betonung der Composita.*

' 738 VESELITSKIJ, V. V. : *Opyt sopostavitel'nogo izučenija slovosočetanij (Essai d'étude comparée de syntagmes. Examples : stand up - aufstehen).*

558 WANDRUSZKA, M. : *Englische und deutsche Nominalkomposition.*

ENGLISH - INDONESIAN :

' 840 ROSE, J. H. : *Relational Variation and Limited Productivity in Some Indonesian and English Verbal Derivatives.*

ENGLISH - ITALIAN :

' 488 CAMAIORA, L. L. : *A Description of Nominal Group Premodification in English and Italian, with a Brief Treatment of the Principal Structural Differences.*

1319 VALESIO, P. : *Suffissi aggettivali fra l'inglese e l'italiano.*

ENGLISH - JAPANESE :

1383 SOGA, M.   : *Similarities Between Japanese and English Verb Derivations.*

ENGLISH - LATIN :

698 HENDRICKSON, J. R.   : *Old English Prepositional Compounds in Relationship to Their Latin Originals.*

ENGLISH - LETTISH :

' 688 GRINBLATT, A. F.   : *Glagol'nye postpositivnye sočetanija v sovremennom anglijskom jazyke i ich ekvivalenty v latysskom jazyke.*

ENGLISH - NETHERLANDISH :

' 513 ROEY, J. van   : *Vergelijkende studie van de structuur der substantiefgroepen in het Engels en het Nederlands.*

ENGLISH - POLISH :

941 CYGAN, J.   : *On the Systems of Negation in English and Polish.*

549 MARTON, W.   : *English and Polish Nominal Compounds : A Transformational Contrastive Study.*

ENGLISH - RUSSIAN :

' 559 ACHMETOVA, S. G.   : *Sočetanie " prilagatel'noe + suščestvitel'noe " v anglijskom i russkom jazykach* (The combination " adjective + substantive" in the English and Russian languages).

' 245 OCHOTSKAJA, G. P.   : *Slovoslozenie i slovoproizvodstvo fiziceskich terminov i ich perevod na russkij jazyk* (Compounding and derivation of physical terminology and its translation into Russian).

'1426 POČEPCOV, G. G.   : *Otprilagatel'nye narečija v anglijskom jazyke (v sopostavlenii s sootvetstvujuščimi narečijami v russkom jazyke)* (Adverbs formed from adjectives in English (In comparison with similar adverbs in Russian).

ENGLISH - SPANISH   :

' 744 ZAMUDIO, M.   : *A Study of Spanish Equivalents of English Phrasal Verbs.*

ENGLISH - SWEDISH   :

' 410 ACHMANOVA, O. S.   : *K voprosu ob otličij složnych slov ot frazeologičeskich edinic. (Na materiale anglijskogo i švedskogo jazykov)* (On the difference between compounds and phraseological units. (On the material of English and Swedish).

ENGLISH - GERMANIC   :

948 HOHENSTEIN, C.   : *Das altenglische Präfix wiꝥ(er)- im Verlauf der englischen Sprachgeschichte mit Berücksichtigung der andern germanischen Dialekte.*

898 LENZE, J.   : *Das Präfix bi- in der altenglischen Nominal- und Verbalkomposition mit gelegentlicher Berücksichtigung der anderen germanischen Dialekte.*

895 MAISENHELDER, K.   : *Die altenglische Partikel " and" . (Mit Berücksichtigung anderer germanischer Sprachen).*

932 RÖHLING, M.   : *Das Präfix ofer- in der altenglischen Verbal- und Nominal-Komposition mit Berücksichtigung der übrigen germanischen Dialekte.*

1379 SCHRACK, D.	: *Ne. 'to spotlight' und 'to stagemanage' . Studien zur Entwicklung und Struktur der verbalen Pseudokomposita im Englischen mit Berücksichtigung anderer germanischer Sprachen.*

ENGLISH - FRENCH - GERMAN :

931 FENZL, R.	: *Der Minirock und die Folgen.*

'1401 LERCH, E.	: *Deutsch -isieren, französisch -iser, englisch -ize (-ise.).*

1394 MAHN, L.	: *Zur Morphologie und Semantik englischer Verben auf -IFY mit Berücksichtigung französischer und deutscher Entsprechungen.*

1395	- : *Zur Morphologie und Semantik englischer Verben auf -IFY mit Berücksichtigung französischer und deutscher Entsprechungen (On the Morphology and Semantics of English Verbs Ending in -IFY with Consideration of Relative Verbs in French and German).*

1373 MARCHAND, H.	: *Die Ableitung desubstantivischer Verben mit Nullmorphem im Französischen und die entsprechenden Verhältnisse im Englischen und Deutschen.*

1374	- : *Die Ableitung desubstantivischer Verben mit Nullmorphem im Englischen, Französischen und Deutschen.*

1375	- : *Die Ableitung deadjektivischer Verben im Deutschen, Englischen Französischen.*

903	- : *Die deadjektivischen reversativen Verben im Deutschen, Englischen und Französischen : entmilitarisieren, demilitarize, démilitariser.*

971 STEIN, G.	: *Zur Typologie der Suffixentstehung (Französisch, Englisch, Deutsch).*

ENGLISH - GERMAN - GREEK :

602 MASSEY, B. W. A.　　　: *The Compound Epithets of Shelley and Keats, Con-*
sidered from the Structural, the Historical, and
the Literary Standpoints, with Some Comparisons
from the Greek, the Old English and the German.

ENGLISH - FRENCH - GERMAN - ITALIAN :

535 HATCHER, A. G.　　　: *Modern English Word-Formation and Neo-Latin. A*
Study of the Origins of English (French, Italian
German) Copulative Compounds.

ENGLISH - FRENCH - GERMAN - ITALIAN - SPANISH - RUSSIAN :

852 TCHEKHOFF, C.　　　: *Les formations savantes grêco-latines en fran-*
çais, anglais, italien, espagnol, allemand et
russe. Norme et dêviations rêcentes.

XII. WORD - FORMATION IN SPECIFIC AUTHORS, IN SPECIFIC WORKS

AELFRIC (955 - 1020)

' 553 RUBKE, H. : *Die Nominalkomposita bei Aelfric. Eine Studie zum Wortschatz Aelfrics in seiner zeitlichen und dialektischen Gebundenheit.*

1382 SCHWERDTFEGER, G. : *Das schwache Verbum in Aelfrics Homilien.*

ALFRED THE GREAT (849 - 899)

' 896 BEEK, P. van : *The Prefix be- in King Alfred's Translation of Boethius ' De consolatione philosophiae'.*

909 BLOOMFIELD, L. : *Notes on the Preverb ge- in Alfredian English.*

' 912 GÖTZL, J. : *Die Aktionsarten des Verbums in König Alfreds Übersetzung des Orosius.*

' 800 HEROLD, C. P. : *The Morphology of King Alfred's Translation of the Orosius.*

916 LENZ, Ph. : *Der syntaktische Gebrauch der Partikel ge in den Werken Alfred des Grossen.*

378 SCHLEPPER, E. : *Die Neubildung von Substantiven in den Übersetzungen König Alfreds mit einem Ausblick auf Chaucer.*

AMIS, KINGSLEY (1922 -   )

' 497 KRAVCUK, N. V. : *Stilisticeskaja znacimost'mnogo clennych atributivnych imennych slovosocetanij. (Na materiale jazyka romanov C. Dikkensa i K. Emisa)* (On the stylistic effect of multicomponent attributive nominal collocations. (Using linguistic material from the novels of Ch. Dickens and K. Amis).

ARNOLD, MATTHEW (1822 - 1888)

633 LUDWIG, H. W. : *Die Self-Komposita bei Thomas Carlyle, Matthew Arnold und Gerard Manley Hopkins. Ein Beitrag zum Verhältnis von Sprache und Geist.*

634   - : *Die Self-Komposita bei Thomas Carlyle, Matthew Arnold und Gerard Manley Hopkins. Untersuchungen zum geistigen Gehalt einer sprachlichen Form.*

BALE, JOHN (1495 - 1563)

236 MOSER, O. : *Untersuchungen über die Sprache John Bale's.*

BALZAC, HONORE (1799 - 1850)

1285 MOSSE, F. : *Honoré de Balzac and the Suffix "-rama".*

BEAUMONT, FRANCIS (1534 - 1616)

' 91 GIELEN, R. : *Untersuchungen zur Namengebung bei Beaumont, Fletcher und Massinger.*

' 152 KIENDLER, H. : *Wortformen und Wortbildung in den Dramen F. Beaumonts und J. Fletchers. Ein Vergleich mit der Sprache Shakespeares sowie Middletons und Massingers.*

' 186 LANDAU, E. : *Wortspiele bei Beaumont und Fletcher.*

BENTHAM, JEREMY (1748 - 1832)

350 WALLAS, G. : *Notes on Jeremy Bentham's Attitude to Word-Creation and Other Notes on Needed Words.*

BRADSTREET, ANNE   (c.1612 - 1672)

607 PELTOLA, N.   : *The Compound Epithet and Its Use in American Poetry*
                           from Bradstreet through Whitman.

BRONTE, CHARLOTTE   (1816 - 1855) - BRONTE, EMILY   (1818 - 1848)

' 344 VÖGELE, H.   : *Aufbau und Sprache in Charlotte Brontës " Jane Eyre"*
                           und Emily Brontës " Wuthering Heights". Ein Vergleich.

BROWNING, ROBERT   (1812 - 1889)

' 604 MASSEY, B. W. A.   : *Browning's Vocabulary : Compound Epithets.*

BYRON, GEORGE GORDON   (1788 - 1824)

'1349 MAŠKOVSKAJA, V. I. : *Anglijskie proizvodnye prilagatel'nye na -y i -ish*
                           i ich ispol'zovanie v poeme Bajrona " Don Žuan"
                           (Derived English adjectives in -y and -ish and
                           their use in Byron's Don Juan).

CAEDMON   (FL, 670)

' 397 WIETELMANN, I.   : *Die Epitheta in den ' Caedmonischen Dichtungen'.*

CALDWELL, ERSKINE   (1903 -   )

' 95 GOLLE, G.   : *Sprache und Stil bei Erskine Caldwell.*

CARLYLE, THOMAS   (1795 - 1881)

74 FRANZ, W.   : *Zu Schmeding, Über Wortbildung bei Carlyle.*

178 KRUMMACHER, M.   : *Notizen über den Sprachgebrauch Carlyles.*

179   - : *Sprache und Stil in Carlyles " Friedrich".*

180   - : *Sprache und Stil in Carlyle's "Friedrich II".*

181   - : *Sprache und Stil in Carlyle's "Friedrich II".*

455 LINCKE, O.   : *Über die Wortzusammensetzung in Carlyles " Sartor Resartus".*

633 LUDWIG, H. W.   : *Die Self-Komposita bei Thomas Carlyle, Matthew Arnold und Gerard Manley Hopkins. Ein Beitrag zum Verhältnis von Sprache und Geist.*

634   - : *Die Self-Komposita bei Thomas Carlyle, Matthew Arnold und Gerard Manley Hopkins. Untersuchungen zum geistigen Gehalt einer sprachlichen Form.*

288 SCHMEDING, O.   : *Über Wortbildung bei Carlyle.*

CARROLL, LEWIS   (1832 - 1898)

'1532 FRAZIER, G.   : *Double Talk.*

331 SUTHERLAND, R. D.   : *Language and Lewis Carroll.*

CARSON, RACHEL   (1907 -   )

1070 GARNER, E. R.   : *The Derived Nominal in The Sea Around Us (Carson).*

CAXTON, WILLIAM   (1422 - 1491)

782 FALTENBACHER, H.   : *Die romanischen, speciell französischen und lateinischen (bezw. latinisierten) Lehnwörter bei Caxton (1422 ? - 1491).*

836 PRICE, H. T.   : *A History of Ablaut in Class 1 of the Strong Verbs from Caxton to the End of the Elizabethan Period.*

' 357 WIENCKE, H.   : *Die Sprache Caxtons.*

CHAUCER, GEOFFREY   (1340 ? - 1400)

' 381 AICHINGER, G.   : *Das Adjektiv in Chaucers Knightes Tale.*

593 EICHHORN, E.   : *Das Partizipium bei Gower im Vergleich mit Chaucer's Gebrauch.*

785 FISIAK, J.   : *Morphemic Structure of Chaucer's English.*

594 GERIKE, F.   : *Das Participium Präsentis bei Chaucer.*

1417 GROSS, E.   : *Bildung des Adverbs bei Chaucer.*

598 HOFFMANN, F.   : *Das Partizipium bei Spenser. Mit Berücksichtigung Chaucers und Shakespeares.*

599 HÜTTMANN, E.   : *Das Partizipium Präsentis bei Lydgate im Vergleich mit Chaucer's Gebrauch.*

'1079 KENNEDY, A. G.   : *On the Substantivation of Adjectives in Chaucer.*

276 REMUS, H.   : *Die kirchlichen und speciell wissenschaftlichen romanischen Lehnworte Chaucers.*

378 SCHLEPPER, E.   : *Die Neubildung von Substantiven in den Übersetzungen König Alfreds mit einem Ausblick auf Chaucer.*

CLARIODUS

196 LENZ, K.   : *Zur Lautlehre der französischen Elemente in den schottischen Dichtungen von 1500 - 1550 (G. Douglas; W. Dunbar; D. Lyndesay; Clariodus). Mit Bemerkungen zur Wortbildung und Wortbedeutung.*

COLERIDGE, SAMUEL TAYLOR (1772 - 1834)

' 422 BREITINGER, F.   : *Die Wortzusammensetzung in S. T. Coleridge's poetischen Werken.*

  434 COOPER, L.   : *Pleonastic Compounds in Coleridge.*

' 390 QUENTIN, E.   : *Die Form des Epithetons in den Gedichten Coleridges nach ihrem sprachlichen Ursprung und ihrem psychologisch-ästhetischen Wert betrachtet.*

' 351 WANETSCHEK, G.   : *Studien zum Wortschatz von Samuel Taylor Coleridge.*

CONGREVE, WILLIAM (1670 - 1729)

  294 SCHOPPER, G.   : *Aufbau und Sprache von Congreves Incognita.*

CUDWORTH, RALPH (1617 - 1688)

  1722 HALL, R.   : *New Words and Antedatings from Cudworth's " Treatise of Freewill".*

  1725   - : *Cudworth : More New Words.*

CYNEWULF (D. 785)

' 387 MAYR, K.   : *Das Adjektiv in Cynewulfs Elene.*

  303 SIMONS, R.   : *Worte und Wortverbindungen der echten Schriften Cynewulfs.*

' 398 WOLFF, H.   : *Die Epitheta in den "Cynewulfischen" Dichtungen.*

' 928 WUTH, A.   : *Aktionsarten der Verba bei Cynewulf.*

DAVENANT, SIR WILLIAM (1606 - 1668)

' 185 LAIG, F.   : *Englische und französische Elemente in Sir William*
                                    Davenants dramatischer Kunst.

DEFOE, DANIEL (1661 ? - 1731)

' 132 HORTEN, F.   : *Studien über die Sprache Defoes.*

DICKENS, CHARLES (1812 - 1870)

' 497 KRAVCUK, N. V.   : *Stilističeskaja značimost'mnogo člennych atribu-*
                                    tivnych imennych slovosočetanij. (*Na materiale*
                                    jazyka romanov Č. Dikkensa i K. Ėmisa) (On the
                                    stylistic effect of multicomponent attributive
                                    nominal collocations. (Using linguistic material
                                    from the novels of Ch. Dickens and K. Amis).

'1603 SENNEWALD), geb. KÖCKERITZ, Ch. : *Die Namengebung bei Dickens, eine Stu-*
                                    die über Lautsymbolik.

1587 WITHINGTON, R.   : *Dickensian and Other Blends.*

DISRAELI, BENJAMIN (1804 - 1881)

' 22 BINDMANN, W.   : *Wortschatz und Syntax bei Benjamin Disraeli (Lord*
                                    Beaconsfield). Unter besonderer Berücksichtigung
                                    der Neologismen und moderner syntaktischer Erschei-
                                    nungen.

DOUGLAS, GAWIN (1474 ? - 1522)

  196 LENZ, K.   : *Zur Lautlehre der französischen Elemente in den*
                                    schottischen Dichtungen von 1500 - 1550 (G. Dou-
                                    glas; W. Dunbar; D. Lyndesay; Clariodus). Mit Be-
                                    merkungen zur Wortbildung und Wortbedeutung.

DUNBAR, WILLIAM (1465 ? - 1530 ?)

196 LENZ, K. : *Zur Lautlehre der französischen Elemente in den schottischen Dichtungen von 1500 - 1550 (G. Douglas; W. Dunbar; D. Lyndesay; Clariodus). Mit Bemerkungen zur Wortbildung und Wortbedeutung.*

FARRELL, JAMES T. (1904 -)

' 50 DIETRICH, H. : *Sprache und Stil James T. Farrells. Möglichkeiten und Grenzen des psychologischen Naturalismus.*

FAULKNER, WILLIAM (1897 - 1962)

876 HAYAKAWA, H. : *Negation in William Faulkner.*

FLETCHER, JOHN (1579 - 1625)

' 91 GIELEN, R. : *Untersuchungen zur Namengebung bei Beaumont, Fletcher und Massinger.*

' 152 KIENDLER, H. : *Wortformen und Wortbildung in den Dramen F. Beaumonts und J. Fletchers. Ein Vergleich mit der Sprache Shakespeares sowie Middletons und Massingers.*

' 186 LANDAU, E. : *Wortspiele bei Beaumont und Fletcher.*

FOSTER, W.

'1802 SOLOV'EVA, T. A. : *O nekotorych neologizmach amerikanskoj političeskoj leksiki XX veka (Po rabotam V. Fostera)*
(On some neologisms of 20th century American political vocabulary. (On the material of the works of W. Foster).

GALSWORTHY, JOHN (1867 - 1933)

' 435 DUBOVAJA, S. I.

: O nekotorych stilisticeskich osobennostjach sloznych slov v proizvedenijach Dz. Golsuorsi " Sasa o Forsajtach" i " Sovremennaja komedija" (On some stylistic features of compounds in John Galsworthy's " The Forsyte Saga" and "A Modern Comedy").

805 JOPP, G.

: Die Modifikation des Verbalbegriffs bei Galsworthy.

' 258 POSSANER-EHRENTHAL, H.: Die Namengebung bei John Galsworthy.

GOWER, JOHN (1325 ? - 1408)

593 EICHHORN, E.

: Das Partizipium bei Gower im Vergleich mit Chaucer's Gebrauch.

GREENE, ROBERT (1560 ? - 1592)

1451 KONKOL, geb. MAYER E. : Die Konversion im Frühneuenglischen in der Zeit von etwa 1580 bis 1600. Ein Beitrag zur Erforschung der sprachlichen Neuprägungen bei Kyd, Marlowe, Peele, Greene, Spenser und Nashe.

373 ZIESENIS, O.

: Der Einfluss des Rhythmus auf Silbenmessung, Wortbildung, Formenlehre und Syntax bei Lyly, Greene und Peele.

HARDY, THOMAS (1840 - 1928)

' 330 STUMMER, P.

: Sprachliche und stoffliche Ausdrucksformen in den Romanen von Thomas Hardy.

HOPKINS, GERARD MANLEY (1844 - 1889)

' 759 BENDER, T. K.   : *Some Derivative Elements in the Poetry of Gerard
                               Manley Hopkins.*

  540 KLÖHN, G.   : *Die nominalen Wortverbindungen in den Dichtungen
                               von Gerard Manley Hopkins.*

  633 LUDWIG, H. W.   : *Die Self-Komposita bei Thomas Carlyle, Matthew
                               Arnold und Gerard Manley Hopkins. Ein Beitrag zum
                               Verhältnis von Sprache und Geist.*

  634   - : *Die Self-Komposita bei Thomas Carlyle, Matthew
                               Arnold und Gerard Manley Hopkins. Untersuchungen
                               zum geistigen Gehalt einer sprachlichen Form.*

JONSON, BEN   (1572/3 - 1637)

' 123 HINZE, O.   : *Studien zu Ben Jonsons Namengebung in seinen Dra-
                               men.*

  250 PENNANEN, E. V.   : *Chapters on the Language in Ben Jonson's Dramatic
                               Works.*

JOYCE, JAMES   (1882 - 1941)

'1695 BORGES, J. L.   : *Joyce y los neologismos.*

' 40 COWDREY, M. B.   : *The Linguistic Experiments of James Joyce.*

' 46 DAVENPORT, B.   : *The Joycean Language.*

' 122 HIGGINSON, F. H.   : *James Joyce, Linguist.*

' 168 KREUTZER, E.   : *Sprache und Spiel im " Ulysses" von James Joyce.*

' 252 PETITJEAN, A.   : *El tratamiento del lenguaje en Joyce.*

268 PRESCOTT, J.   : *James Joyce : A Study in Words.*

'1796 SALEMSON, H. J.   : *James Joyce and the New Word.*

' 287 SCHLAUCH, M.   : *The Language of James Joyce.*

KEATS, JOHN   (1795 - 1821)

602 MASSEY, B. W. A.   : *The Compound Epithets of Shelley and Keats, Consi-*
dered from the Structural, the Historical, and the
Literary Standpoints, with Some Comparisons from
the Greek, the Old English, and the German.

603   - : *The O.E.D. and Some Adjectives of Shelley and Keats.*

' 474 STIASNY, M.   : *Ueber neue Composita bei Keats.*

KIPLING, RUDYARD   (1865 - 1936)

'1591 BERGER, E.   : *Lautnachahmung in den Werken Rudyard Kiplings.*

189 LEEB-LUNDBERG, W.   : *Word-Formation in Kipling. A Stylistic-Philological*
Study.

' 277 RIESS, A.   : *Verbaltechnik bei Rudyard Kipling.*

KYD, THOMAS   (1558 - 1594)

1451 KONKOL, geb. MAYER E. : *Die Konversion im Frühneuenglischen in der Zeit*
von etwa 1580 bis 1600. Ein Beitrag zur Erforschung
der sprachlichen Neuprägungen bei Kyd, Marlowe, Peele,
Greene, Spenser und Nashe.

327 STROHEKER, F.   : *Doppelformen und Rhythmus bei Marlowe und Kyd.*

LAYAMON (FL. 1200)

| 1359 BÖHNKE, M. | : *Die Flexion des Verbums in Laʒamons Brut.* |
| 1371 LANGE, H. | : *Das Zeitwort in den beiden Handschriften von Laʒamons Brut.* |

LANGLAND, WILLIAM (1330 ? - 1400 ?)

' 155 KITTNER, H. : *Studien zum Wortschatz William Langlands.*

LEE, NATHANIEL (1653 - 1692)

'1450 KIENDLER, G. : *Konvertierte Formen in den Dramen Otways und Lees. Ein Vergleich mit der Sprache Shakespeares.*

LOCKE, JOHN (1632 - 1704)

108 HALL, R.	: *John Locke's Unnoticed Vocabulary I.*
109	- : *John Locke's Unnoticed Vocabulary II.*
110	- : *More Words from John Locke.*

LYDGATE, WILLIAM (1622 - 1706)

' 29 BRETZFELDER-THALMESINGER, L. : *Lydgate's Sprache im " Siege of Thebes".*

599 HÜTTMANN, E. : *Das Partizipium Präsentis bei Lydgate im Vergleich mit Chaucer's Gebrauch.*

274 REISMÜLLER, G. : *Romanische Lehnwörter bei Lydgate.*

LYLY, JOHN   (1553 ? - 1606)

373 ZIESENIS, O.   : *Der Einfluss des Rhythmus auf Silbenmessung, Wort-*
                            bildung, Formenlehre und Syntax bei Lyly, Greene
                            und Peele.

LYNDESAY, DAVID   (1490 - 1555)

196 LENZ, K.   : *Zur Lautlehre der französischen Elemente in den*
                            schottischen Dichtungen von 1500 - 1550 (G. Dou-
                            glas; W. Dunbar; D. Lyndesay; Clariodus). Mit Be-
                            merkungen zur Wortbildung und Wortbedeutung.

MALORY, SIR THOMAS   (FL. 1470)

' 81 FROMM, Ch.   : *Über den verbalen Wortschatz in Sir Thomas Ma-*
                            lorys Roman ' Le Morte Darthur'.

MANSFIELD, KATHERINE   (1888 - 1923)

187 LANG, W.   : *Sprache und Stil in Katherine Mansfields Kurzge-*
                            schichten.

MARLOWE, CHRISTOPHER   (1564 - 1593)

'1202 KELLNER, L.   : *Zur Sprache Christopher Marlowes.*

1451 KONKOL, geb. MAYER E.: *Die Konversion im Frühneuenglischen in der Zeit*
                            von etwa 1580 bis 1600. Ein Beitrag zur Erforschung
                            der sprachlichen Neuprägungen bei Kyd, Marlowe, Peele,
                            Greene, Spenser und Nashe.

285 SCHAU, K.   : *Sprache und Grammatik der Dramen Marlowes.*

327 STROHEKER, F.   : *Doppelformen und Rhythmus bei Marlowe und Kyd.*

396 VOGT, R.   : *Das Adjektiv bei Christopher Marlowe.*

MASSINGER, PHILIP   (1583 - 1640)

' 91 GIELEN, R.   : *Untersuchungen zur Namengebung bei Beaumont, Fletcher und Massinger.*

' 118 HASCHKA, G.   : *Studien zur Wortbildung und zu den Wortformen in
Dramen von Philip Massinger und ein Vergleich mit
der Sprache Th. Middletons.*

' 152 KIENDLER, H.   : *Wortformen und Wortbildung in den Dramen F. Beaumon
und J. Fletchers. Ein Vergleich mit der Sprache Sha
kespeares sowie Middletons und Massingers.*

MELVILLE, HERMAN   (1319 - 1891)

' 135 HUMBACH, Ä.   : *Aspekte der Wortbildung bei Herman Melville.*

154 KIRCHNER, G.   : *Amerikanisches in Wortschatz, Wortbildung und Syntax von Herman Melvilles " Moby Dick".*

MIDDLETON, THOMAS   (1570 ? - 1627)

' 118 HASCHKA, G.   : *Studien zur Wortbildung und zu den Wortformen in
Dramen von Philip Massinger und ein Vergleich mit
der Sprache Th. Middletons.*

' 126 HÖLLER, H.   : *Wortbildung und Wortformen in den Dramen Thomas
Middletons. Ein Vergleich mit der Sprache Shakes-
peares.*

' 152 KIENDLER, H.   : *Wortformen und Wortbildung in den Dramen F. Beaumonts und J. Fletchers. Ein Vergleich mit der Spra-
che Shakespeares sowie Middletons und Massingers.*

NASHE, THOMAS   (1567 - 1601)

'1446 FIEBACH, R.-M.   : *Der stilistische Wert der Funktionsverschiebung*
                              bei Thomas Nashe.

' 134 HUFNAGEL, J.   : *Wortschatz von Thomas Nash.*

1451 KONKOL, geb. MAYER, E. : *Die Konversion im Frühneuenglischen in der Zeit*
                              von etwa 1580 - 1600. Ein Beitrag zur Erforschung
                              der sprachlichen Neuprägungen bei Kyd, Marlowe,
                              Peele, Greene, Spenser und Nashe.

' 256 PÖLL, M.   : *Wortformen und Syntax in Thomas Nashs " Unfortunate*
                              Traveller" : ein Vergleich mit der Sprache Shakes-
                              peares.

ORM   (FL. 1200 ?)

1387 THÜNS, B.   : *Das Verbum bei Orm. Ein Beitrag zur ae. Grammatik.*

ORWELL, GEORGE   (1903 - 1950)

  33 CALVET, L.-J.   : *Sur une conception fantaisiste de la langue : la*
                             " newspeak" de George Orwell.

OTWAY, THOMAS   (1652 - 1685)

'1450 KIENDLER, G.   : *Konvertierte Formen in den Dramen Otways und Lees.*
                             Ein Vergleich mit der Sprache Shakespeares.

PEELE, GEORGE   (1556 - 1596)

1451 KONKOL, geb. MAYER, E. : *Die Konversion im Frühneuenglischen in der Zeit*
                              von etwa 1580 bis 1600. Ein Beitrag zur Erforschung
                              der sprachlichen Neuprägungen bei Kyd, Marlowe,

Peele, Greene, Spenser und Nashe.

373 ZIESENIS, O. : *Der Einfluss des Rhythmus auf Silbenmessung, Wortbildung, Formenlehre und Syntax bei Lyly, Greene und Peele.*

POE, EDGAR ALLAN (1809 - 1849)

242 NEUMANN, J. H. : *Poe's Contributions to English.*

PRIESTLEY, JOHN BOYNTON (1894 -   )

369 ZUR MEGEDE, G. : *Wort- und Gestaltungskunst bei J. B. Priestley.*

ROLLE DE HAMPOLE, RICHARD (1290 ? - 1349)

' 198 LINDHEIM, B. v. : *Die Sprache des Ywain und Gawain und des Pricke of Conscience by Richard Rolle de Hampole.*

SHAFTESBURY, ANTHONY (1671 - 1713)

1723 HALL, R. : *Shaftesbury : Some Antedatings and New Words.*

SHAKESPEARE, WILLIAM (1564 - 1616)

3 ABBOTT, E. A. : *A Shakespearean Grammar. (An Attempt to Illustrate Some of the Differences Between Elizabethan and Modern English).*

382 BARTH, H. : *Das Epitheton in den Dramen des jungen Shakespeare und seiner Vorgänger.*

19 BAYLEY, H. : *The Shakespeare Symphony. An Introduction to the Ethics of the Elizabethan Drama.*

868 BECKER, D.   : *Shakespeares Präfixbildungen. Ein Beitrag zur Erforschung der sprachlichen Neuprägungen Shakespeares.*

869   - : *Shakespeares Englisch und seine Erforschbarkeit mit Hilfe des New English Dictionary.*

' 383 BECKERS, G.   : *Die kausative Kraft des Adjektivums in Shakespeares Sprachgebrauch.*

' 1064 DAHL, L.   : *Nominal Style in the Shakespearean Soliloquy, with Reference to the Early English Drama, Shakespeare's Immediate Predecessors and his Contemporaries.*

48 DEUTSCHBEIN, K.   : *Shakespeare-Grammatik für Deutsche oder Übersicht über die grammatischen Abweichungen vom heutigen Sprachgebrauch bei Shakespeare.*

' 384 DIEZ, H.   : *Das Adjektiv in Shakespeares Macbeth.*

' 60 ERLER, E.   : *Die Namengebung bei Shakespeare.*

788 FRANK, A.   : *Das Kausativum bei Shakespeare.*

75 FRANZ, W.   : *Die Wortbildung bei Shakespeare.*

76   - : *Orthographie, Lautgebung und Wortbildung in den Werken Shakespeares mit Ausspracheproben.*

77   - : *Shakespeare-Grammatik.* 2nd ed.

78   - : *Shakespeare-Grammatik.* 3rd ed.

79   - : *Die Sprache Shakespeares in Vers und Prosa unter Berücksichtigung des Amerikanischen entwicklungsgeschichtlich dargestellt.*

80   - : *Shakespeares Blankvers mit Nachträgen zu des Verfassers Shakespeare-Grammatik.*

385 HELMS, G.   : *The English Adjective in the Language of Shakspere.*

' 126 HÖLLER, H.   : *Wortbildung und Wortformen in den Dramen Thomas Middletons. Ein Vergleich mit der Sprache Shakespeares.*

598 HOFFMANN, F.   : *Das Partizipium bei Spenser. Mit Berücksichtigung Chaucers und Shakespeares.*

'1450 KIENDLER, G.   : *Konvertierte Formen in den Dramen Otways und Lees. Ein Vergleich mit der Sprache Shakespeares.*

' 152 KIENDLER, H.   : *Wortformen und Wortbildung in den Dramen F. Beaumonts und J. Fletchers. Ein Vergleich mit der Sprache Shakespeares sowie Middletons und Massingers.*

539 KILIAN, F.   : *Shakespeares Nominalkomposita. Ein Beitrag zur Erforschung seiner Neuprägungen.*

158 KOHL, N.   : *Das Wortspiel in der Shakespearischen Komödie. Studien zur Interdependenz von verbalem und aktionalem Spiel in den frühen Komödien und den späten Stücken.*

448 KOZIOL, H.   : *Shakespeares Komposita in deutschen Übersetzungen*

1455 LINDHEIM, B. v.   : *Syntaktische Funktionsverschiebung als Mittel des barocken Stils bei Shakespeare.*

' 210 MAHOOD, M. M.   : *Shakespeare's Word Play.*

' 389 NOTTROTT, M.   : *Der formale Gebrauch des Epithetons in Shakespeares Dramen ' Othello', ' King Lear', ' Macbeth und 'Coriolanus'.*

' 256 PÖLL, M.   : *Wortformen und Syntax in Thomas Nashs " Unfortunate Traveller" : ein Vergleich mit der Sprache Shakespeares.*

1098 PRIESS, M.   : *Die Bedeutungen des abstrakten substantivierten Adjektivs und des entsprechenden abstrakten Substantivs bei Shakespeare.*

'1105 SCHLOTHAUER, G. : *Der reine Verbalstamm als Substantiv bei Shakespeare.*

' 289 SCHMETZ, L. : *Sprache und Charakter im Drama Shakespeares.*

' 970 STAHL, H. E. : *Studien zum Problem der sprachlichen Neuschöpfungen bei Shakespeare. Die Suffixbildungen.*

321 – : *Schöpferische Wortbildung bei Shakespeare?*

' 519 ŠUBIN, E. P. : *Atributivnye imena v jazyke Šekspira i ich genezis* (Attributive nominal words in the language of Shakespeare and their origin).

337 THEOBALD, R. M. : *Word-Coinage in Shakespeare and Others.*

'1470 VEUHOFF, K. F. : *Shakespeares Funktionsverschiebungen. Ein Beitrag zur Erforschung der sprachlichen Neuprägungen Shakespeares.*

482 VOITL, H. : *Neubildungswert und Stilistik der Komposita bei Shakespeare.*

483 – : *Shakespeares Komposita. Ein Beitrag zur Stilistik seiner Wortneuprägungen.*

' 366 WURTH, L. : *Das Wortspiel bei Shakespeare.*

SHELLEY, PERCY BYSSHE (1792 – 1822)

602 MASSEY, B. W. A. : *The Compound Epithets of Shelley and Keats, Considered from the Structural, the Historical, and the Literary Standpoints, with Some Comparisons, from the Greek, the Old English, and the German.*

603 – : *The O.E.D. and Some Adjectives of Shelley and Keats.*

' 345 VOLKLAND, L. : *Wörterbuch zu den englischen Dichtungen von Percy Bysshe Shelley.*

SIDNEY, SIR PHILIP (1554 - 1586)

' 286 SCHINDL, E.　　　　　: *Studien zum Wortschatz Sir Philip Sidneys.*

SMITH, ADAM (1723 - 1790)

' 119 HASCHKA, H.　　　　　: *Bedeutungswandel und Wortbildung in Adam Smith'*
　　　　　　　　　　　　　　　　　" An Inquiry into the Nature and Causes of the Wealt
　　　　　　　　　　　　　　　　　of Nations".

SPENSER, HERBERT (1552 - 1599)

　598 HOFFMANN, F.　　　　　: *Das Partizipium bei Spenser. Mit Berücksichtigung*
　　　　　　　　　　　　　　　　　Chaucers und Shakespeares.

1451 KONKOL, geb. MAYER E. : *Die Konversion im Frühneuenglischen in der Zeit*
　　　　　　　　　　　　　　　　　von etwa 1580 - 1600. Ein Beitrag zur Erforschung
　　　　　　　　　　　　　　　　　der sprachlichen Neuprägungen bei Kyd, Marlowe, Pee
　　　　　　　　　　　　　　　　　Greene, Spenser und Nashe.

　467 PADELFORD, F. M. - MAXWELL, W. C. : *The Compound Words in Spenser's*
　　　　　　　　　　　　　　　　　Poetry.

SWIFT, JONATHAN (1667 - 1745)

1028 STRANG, B. M. H.　　　　: *Swift's Agent-Noun Formations in -ER.*

SWINBURNE, ALGERNON CHARLES (1837 - 1909)

' 386 KUFFNER, E.　　　　　: *Die Verwendung des Adjektivs bei Swinburne.*

' 392 SCHMITZ, Ch.　　　　　: *Die schmückenden Beiwörter in den poetischen Wer-*
　　　　　　　　　　　　　　　　　ken von Algernon Charles Swinburne.

TAYLOR, JOHN   (1580 - 1653)

' 97 GOTTLIEB, A.   : *Zur Sprache John Taylors.*

TENNYSON, ALFRED LORD   (1809 - 1892)

' 420 BAUMANN, H.   : *Ueber Neubildungen von Wortzusammensetzungen in*
                             Tennysons epischen und lyrischen Gedichten.

  51 DYBOSKI, R.   : *Über Wortbildung und Wortgebrauch bei Tennyson.*

  52   - : *Zur Wortbildung in Tennysons Jugendgedichten.*

  53   - : *Tennysons Sprache und Stil.*

' 388 NEUNER, K.   : *Untersuchungen zur Stilistik des Adjektivs in*
                             Tennysons epischen Dichtungen.

WACE , ROBERT   (1100? - 1175?)

' 140 JENISCH, O.   : *Der Wortschatz des Chronisten Wace. Nach seiner*
                             Chronik.

WEBSTER, JOHN   (1580 ? - 1625 ?)

' 182 KRUSIUS, P.   : *Eine Untersuchung der Sprache John Webster's.*

WHITMAN, WALT   (1819 - 1892)

  607 PELTOLA, N.   : *The Compound Epithet and Its Use in American Poetry*
                             from Bradstreet through Whitman.

 1763 POUND, L.   : *Walt Whitman's Neologisms.*

WOOLF, VIRGINIA (1882 - 1941)

' 12 BADENHAUSEN, I. : *Die Sprache Virginia Woolfs. Ein Beitrag zur Stilistik des modernen englischen Romans.*

1215 RANTAVAARA, I. : *Ing-Forms in the Service of Rhythm and Style in Virginia Woolf's " The Waves" .*

WORDSWORTH, WILLIAM (1770 - 1850)

291 SCHNEIDER, D. B. : *Wordsworth's " Prelude" and the O.E.D. : Word-Combinations.*

ANCRENE RIWLE

'1366 FÜLLER, L. : *Das Verbum in der Ancrene Riwle.*

' 372 ZEISE, A. : *Der Wortschatz der Ancrene Riwle.*

ANDREAS

466 OVERHOLSER, L. Ch. : *A Comparative Study of the Compound Use in Andreas and Beowulf.*

BEOWULF

425 BRYAN, W. F. : *Epithetic Compound Folknames in Beowulf.*

618 - : *Āergōd in Beowulf, and Other English Compounds of aēr.*

' 427 BYERLY, G. : *Compounds and Other Elements of Poetic Diction Derived from an Oral-Formulaic Poetic Tradition, a Comparison of Aeschylus and the Beowulf Poet.*

' 58 ELMAYER v. VESTENBRUGG, R. : *Studien zum Darstellungsbereich und Wortschatz des Beowulf-Epos.*

538 ISSHIKI, M.   : *The Kennings in Beowulf.*

576 KOBAN, Ch.   : *Substantive Compounds in " Beowulf".*

919 LORZ, A.   : *Aktionsarten des Verbums im Beowulf.*

545 MAGOUN, F. P. jr. : *Recurring First Elements in Different Nominal Compounds in Beowulf and the Elder Edda.*

546 MALONE, K.   : *The Kenning in Beowulf 2220.*

' 606 NEELOV, A. A. : *K voprosu o častotnosti nekotorych morfologičeskich struktur v jazyke " Beowul'fa"* (On the Frequency of Compound Two-Stem and Simple One-Stem Adjectives in Beowulf).

466 OVERHOLSER, L. Ch.: *A Comparative Study of the Compound Use in Andreas and Beowulf.*

391 SCHEINERT, M. : *Die Adjectiva im Beowulfepos als Darstellungsmittel.*

317 SONNEFELD, G. : *Stilistisches und Wortschatz im Beowulf, ein Beitrag zur Kritik des Epos.*

' 556 STEPHAN, K.   : *Das Aussterben und Fortleben der Nominalkomposita im altenglischen Beowulfepos und ihr Ersatz im Neuenglischen.*

475 STORMS, G.   : *Compounded Names of Peoples in Beowulf. A Study in the Diction of a Great Poet.*

SIR GAWAIN

1063 CLARK, J. W.   : *The Gawain-Poet and the Substantival Adjective.*

' 198 LINDHEIM, B. v. : *Die Sprache des Ywain und Gawain und des Pricke of*

Conscience by Richard Rolle de Hampole.

183 KULLNICK, M.   : *Studien über den Wortschatz in Sir Gawayne and the Greene Knyʒt.*

368 YAMAGUCHI, H.   : *A Lexical Note on the Language of Sir Gawain and the Green Knight.*

LINDISFARNE GOSPEL

' 914 HOPPER, H. P.   : *A Study of the Function of the Verbal Prefix ge- in the Lindisfarne Gospel of Saint Matthew.*

924 SAMUELS, M. L.   : *The ge-Prefix in the Old English Gloss to the Lindisfarne Gospels.*

WIDSITH

962 MALONE, K.   : *The Suffix of Appurtenance in ' Widsith'.*

XIII. WORD - FORMATION AND APHASIA

'975 WHITAKER, H.   : *Unsolicited Nominalizations by Aphasics : the Plausibility of the Lexicalist Model.*

XIV. WORD - FORMATION AND CHILD LANGUAGE

578 LIVANT, W. P.   : *Productive Grammatical Operations I : The Noun-Compounding of 5-Year-Olds.*

XV. WORD - FORMATION AND THE TEACHING OF ENGLISH

'566 CROFT, K.   : *English Noun Compounds. An Introductory Study for Students of English as a Second Language.*

443 HILL, L. A.   : *'Compounds' and the Practical Teacher.*

715 MECHNER, M.   : *Some Problems of Collocations of Verb and Particle in the Teaching of English as a Foreign Language.*

'972 THORNDIKE, E. L.   : *The Teaching of English Suffixes.*

XVI. WORD - FORMATION AND COMPUTER STUDIES

778 EARL, L. L.   : *Structural Definition of Affixes from Multisylla-*
                               ble Words.

779   - : *Part-of-Speech Implications of Affixes.*

780   - : *Automatic Determination of Parts of Speech of En-*
                               glish Words.

'695 HARRIS, B.   : *Towards Recognizing English Phrasal Verbs for Ma-*
                               chine Translation.

799 HENISZ, B.   : *Derivation, Morphophonemic Alternation Patterns,*
                               Generative Formation Rules and System for Computer
                               Processing.

501 MOESSNER, L.   : *Automatische syntaktische Analyse englischer no-*
                               minaler Gruppen (Automatic Syntactic Analysis of
                               English Nominal Groups).

'502   - : *Automatische syntaktische Analyse englischer no-*
                               minaler Gruppen.

821 MONROE, G. K. jr.   : *Phonemic Transcription of Graphic Post-Base Affixes*
                               in English : a Computer Problem.

837 RESNIKOFF, H. L. - DOLBY, J. L. : *The Nature of Affixing in Written English.*

'551 RÖMER, L.   : *Zur strukturell-syntaktischen Beschreibung und al-*
                               gorithmischen Darstellung produktiver Nominalkom-
                               posita im britischen und amerikanischen Englisch.
                               Versuch einer synchron-linguistischen Untersuchung
                               des englischen Wortbildungsmechanismus beim Vor-
                               gang des Compounding.

'306 SKOROCHOD'KO, E. F.   : *Voprosy teorii anglijskogo slovoobrazovanija i ee*
                               primenenie k mašinnomu perevodu (Theoretical que-
                               stions of English word-formation and their treatment
                               in machine-translation).

XVII. WORD - FORMATION AND SOCIOLINGUISTICS

''224 MEDNIKOVA, E. M. - KARAVKINA, T. Ju.: *Socio-lingvističeskij aspekt pro-
duktivnogo slovoobrazovanija (na materiale anglijs-
kogo jazyka* (The socio-linguistic aspect of productive word-formation in English).

1433 PULGRAM, E.   : *A Socio-Linguistic View of Innovation : -ly and
-wise* .

XVIII. WORD - FORMATION AND STATISTICS

117 HARWOOD, F. W. - WRIGHT, A. M. : *Statistical Study of English Word-Formation.*

XIX. INDEX OF AUTHORS

Tübinger Beiträge zur Linguistik

herausgegeben von Gunter Narr

74 Tübingen 1 · Postfach 25 67

GESAMTVERZEICHNIS

Band 6: **Mario Wandruszka**, Wörter und Wortfelder. Aufsätze, hrsg. v. **Hansbert Bertsch**, Tübingen 1970, ²1973, 154 S., brosch. DM 12.40
ISBN 3−87808−006−9
Mit den Aufsätzen: La Nuance; Angst; Brio und Verve; Das Bild des Menschen in der Sprache der italienischen Renaissance; Echt; Dankbarkeit; Etymologie und Philosophie; Lexikalische Polymorphie.

Band 7: **August Wilhelm Schlegel**, Observations sur la Langue et la Littérature Provençales. Neudruck der 1. Aufl. Paris 1818, hrsg. u. mit einem Vorwort versehen v. **Gunter Narr**, Tübingen 1971, 122 S., Ganzleinen DM 22.−
ISBN 3−87808−007−7

Band 8: **Ernst Gamillscheg**, Studien zur Vorgeschichte einer romanischen Tempuslehre, 2. unveränd. Aufl., Tübingen 1970, 306 S., Ganzleinen DM 29.−
ISBN 3−87808−008−5

Band 9: **Hans-Martin Gauger**, Zum Problem der Synonyme; avec un résumé en français: Apport au problème des synonymes, Tübingen 1972, 149 S., Pbck DM 16.−
ISBN 3−87808−009−3

Band 10: **Jörn Albrecht**, Le français langue abstraite? Ein Beitrag zur Typologie des Französischen und zur Entstehungsgeschichte einer ‚idée reçue' (in deutscher Sprache), Tübingen 1970, 333 S., brosch. DM 24.−
ISBN 3−87808−010−7

Band 11: **Eugenio Coseriu**, Die Geschichte der Sprachphilosophie von der Antike bis zur Gegenwart. Eine Übersicht, Teil I: Von der Antike bis Leibniz. Vorlesung gehalten im Winter-Semester 1968/69 an der Universität Tübingen, autorisierte Nachschrift besorgt v. **Gunter Narr** u. **Rudolf Windisch**, Tübingen 1970, 162 S., Pbck DM 12.−
ISBN 3−87808−011−5

Band 12: **Karl Peter Linder**, Studien zur Verbalsyntax der ältesten provenzalischen Urkunden und einiger anderer Texte mit einem Anhang über das konditionale ‚qui', Tübingen 1970, 109 S., brosch. DM 13.50
ISBN 3−87808−012−3

Band 13: **Jakob Hornemann Bredsdorff**, Über die Ursachen der Sprachveränderungen, aus dem Dänischen übers. u. hrsg. v. **Uwe Petersen**, Tübingen 1971, 56 S., Pbck DM 8.40
ISBN 3−87808−013−1

Band 14: **Eugenio Coseriu**, Einführung in die strukturelle Betrachtung des Wortschatzes. In Zusammenarbeit mit Erich Brauch und Gisela Köhler hrsg. v. Gunter Narr, Tübingen 1970, ²1973, 124 S., brosch. DM 14.80
ISBN 3−87808−014−X

Band 15: **Bengt Sigurd**, Die generative Grammatik, aus dem Schwedischen übers. u. hrsg. v. **Uwe Petersen**, Tübingen 1970, 42 S., Pbck DM 5.50
ISBN 3−87808−015−8

Band 16: **Gunter Narr** (Hrsg.), Griechisch und Romanisch, Tübingen 1971, 185 S., Ganzleinen DM 23.80
ISBN 3−87808−016−6
Mit den Aufsätzen: **Eugenio Coseriu**, Das Problem des griechischen Einflusses auf das Vulgärlatein; **Wilhelm Schulze**, Graeca Latina; **Karl Dietrich**, Neugriechisches

und Romanisches I; **Karl Dietrich,** Neugriechisches und Romanisches II; **Otto Imisch,** Sprach- und stilgeschichtliche Parallelen zwischen Griechisch und Lateinisch; **Friedrich Pfister,** Vulgärlatein und Vulgärgriechisch; **Jacob Wackernagel,** Lateinisch-Griechisches.

Band 17: **Wilhelm Kesselring,** Grundlagen der französischen Sprachgeschichte. Band I: Die französische Sprache im 20. Jahrhundert, Tübingen 1970, 245 S., brosch. DM 12.–
ISBN 3–87808–017–4

Band 18: **Dieter Kastovsky,** Studies in Morphology: Aspects of English and German Verb Inflection, Tübingen 1971, 123 S., DM 12.–
ISBN 3–87808–018–2

Band 19: **Wilhelm Kesselring,** Grundlagen der französischen Sprachgeschichte. Band 4: Die französische Sprache des 17. Jahrhunderts, Tübingen 1973, ca. 200 S.
ISBN 3–87808–019–0

Band 20: **Brigitte Schlieben-Lange,** Okzitanisch und Katalanisch. Ein Beitrag zur Soziolinguistik zweier romanischer Sprachen, Tübingen 1971, ²1973, 65 S., DM 9.80
ISBN 3–87808–020–4

Band 21: **K.-Richard Bausch, Josef Klegraf, Wolfram Wilss,** The Science of Translation: An Analytical Bibliography (1962–1969), Tübingen 1970, 181 S., brosch. DM 12.–
ISBN 3–87808–021–2

Band 22: **Gabriele Stein,** Primäre und sekundäre Adjektive im Französischen und Englischen, Tübingen 1971, 284 S., Pbck DM 22.–
ISBN 3–87808–022–0

Band 23: **Ursula Liehr,** Jour – journée, an – année. Gestalt und Entstehung eines sprachlichen Strukturfeldes, Tübingen 1971, 178 S., Pbck DM 18.–
ISBN 3–87808–023–9

Band 24: **Friedrich Schürr,** Probleme und Prinzipien romanischer Sprachwissenschaft, Tübingen 1971, 351 S., Ganzleinen DM 36.–
ISBN 3–87808–024–7

Band 25: **Göran Hammarström,** Französische Phonetik, aus dem Schwedischen übers. u. hrsg. v. **Uwe Petersen,** Tübingen 1972, 130 S., Pbck DM 12.80
ISBN 3–87808–025–5

Band 26: **Ernst Kemmner,** Sprachspiel und Stiltechnik in Raymond Queneaus Romanen, Tübingen 1972, 252 S., Pbck DM 24.–
ISBN 3–87808–026–3

Band 27: **Lothar H. Mahn,** Zur Morphologie und Semantik englischer Verben auf -ify mit Berücksichtigung französischer und deutscher Entsprechungen, Tübingen 1971, 247 S., Pbck DM 24.–
ISBN 3–87808–027–1

Band 28: **Eugenio Coseriu,** Die Geschichte der Sprachphilosophie von der Antike bis zur Gegenwart. Teil II: Von Leibniz bis Rousseau. Vorlesung gehalten im Winter-Semester 1970/71 an der Universität Tübingen, autorisierte Nachschrift besorgt von **Gunter Narr,** Tübingen 1972, 250 S., Pbck DM 16.80, Ganzleinen DM 22.80
ISBN 3–87808–028–X

Band 29: **Kennosuke Ezawa,** Die Opposition stimmhafter und stimmloser Verschluß-
laute im Deutschen, Tübingen 1972, 145 S., Pbck DM 15.40
ISBN 3–87808–029–8

Band 30: **Wilhelm Kesselring,** Grundlagen der französischen Sprachgeschichte. Band 7:
Die französische Sprache von den Anfängen bis 1300, Tübingen 1973,
400 S., Linson DM 36.– Leinen DM 42.–
ISBN 3–87808–030–1

Band 31: **Rudolf Windisch,** Das Neutrum im Romanischen: Spanisch, Italienisch,
Rumänisch, Tübingen 1973, ca. 250 S., ca. DM 28.–
ISBN 3–87808–031–X

Band 32: **Wolfgang Rettig,** Sprachsystem und Sprachnorm in der deutschen Sub-
stantivflexion, Tübingen 1972, 130 S., DM 14.80
ISBN 3–87808–032–8

Band 33: **K.-Richard Bausch, Josef Klegraf, Wolfram Wilss,** The Science of Translation:
An Analytical Bibliography, vol. II 1970–1971 (and Supplement
1962–1969), Tübingen 1972, 265 S., DM 23.80, Ganzleinen DM 29.80
ISBN 3–87808–033–6

Band 34: **Gabriele Stein,** English Word-Formation in two centuries. In honour of Hans
Marchand on the occasion of his 65th birthday, Tübingen 1973,
ca. 180 S., ca. DM 19.80
ISBN 3–87808–034–4

Band 35: **Barbara von Gemmingen,** Semantische Studien zum Wortfeld ‚Arbeit' im
Französischen. Versuch einer Darstellung unter Berücksichtigung hand-
werklich-fachsprachlicher Texte des 13.–17. Jahrhunderts, Tübingen
1973, ca. 210 S., ca. DM 22.80
ISBN 3–87808–035–2

Band 36: **Albert Mbulamoko,** Verbe et Personne. Les substituts et marques de la
personne verbale en latin, espagnol, français, allemand, lingále et
ngbandi, Tübingen 1973, ca. 300 S., ca. DM 32.–
ISBN 3–87808–036–0

Band 37: **Fritz Abel,** Le Mouvement occitaniste contemporain dans la région de
Toulouse. Festgabe für Gerhard Rohlfs zu seinem 80. Geburtstag,
Tübingen 1973, 106 S., ca. DM 14.80
ISBN 3–87808–037–9

Band 38: **August Sladek,** Wortfelder in Verbänden, Tübingen 1973, ca. 300 S.,
ca. DM 34.–
ISBN 3–87808–038–7

Band 39: **Hans-Martin Gauger,** Die Anfänge der Synonymik: Girard (1718) und
Roubaud (1785). Ein Beitrag zur Geschichte der lexikalischen Semantik,
Tübingen 1973, ca. 220 S., ca. DM 24.–
ISBN 3–87808–039–5

Band 40: **Eugenio Coseriu,** Probleme der strukturellen Semantik. Autorisierte Vor-
lesungsnachschrift von Dieter Kastovsky, Tübingen 1973, ca. 110 S.,
ca. DM 12.–
ISBN 3–87808–040–9

FORSCHUNGSBERICHTE DES INSTITUTS FÜR DEUTSCHE SPRACHE – MANNHEIM,
herausgegeben von Ulrich Engel und Irmgard Vogel

Band 1: I. Arbeitsberichte
Grundsätzliche Bemerkungen zu den Untersuchungen zum Verbalbereich
G. Beugel / U. Suida, Perfekt und Präteritum in der deutschen Sprache der Gegenwart
H. Gelhaus, Das Futur in der deutschen Sprache
S. Jäger, Zum Gebrauch des Konjunktivs in der indirekten Rede
K. Brinker, Das Passiv

II. Diskussionsbeiträge
S. Jäger, Der Modusgebrauch in den sogenannten irrealen Vergleichssätzen
B. Engelen, Zur Semantik des deutschen Verbs
U. Engel, Adjungierte Adverbialia. Zur Gliederung im Innenfeld
Mannheim, Januar 1968, 103 S., DM 8.–. Tübingen ²1972
ISBN 3–87808–601–6

Band 2: U. Engel, Vorbemerkungen
I. Zint, Maschinelle Sprachbearbeitung des Instituts für deutsche Sprache in Mannheim (Teil I)
M. W. Hellmann, Zur Dokumentation und maschinellen Bearbeitung von Zeitungstexten in der Außenstelle Bonn (Teil II)
G. Billmeier, Über die Signifikanz von Auswahltexten (Teil III)
Mannheim, Dezember 1968, 171 S., DM 8.–
ISBN 3–87808–602–4

Band 3: P. Kern, Bemerkungen zum Problem der Textklassifikation
M. W. Hellmann, Über Corpusgewinnung und Dokumentation im Mannheimer Institut für deutsche Sprache
W. Müller, Teilerhebungen und ihre Anwendung auf die Sprachbearbeitung
U. Engel, Das Mannheimer Corpus
Mannheim, April 1969, 84 S., DM 8.–
ISBN 3–87808–603–2

Band 4: B. Engelen, Das Präpositionalobjekt im Deutschen und seine Entsprechungen im Englischen, Französischen und Russischen
M. H. Folsom, Zwei Arten von erweiterbaren Richtungsergänzungen
A. Ströbl, Aus den Überlegungen zur Bearbeitung der Wortstellung für das „Grunddeutsch"
Ch. Winkler, Untersuchungen zur Intonation in der Deutschen Gegenwartssprache
R. M. Frumkina, Über das sogenannte „Zipfsche Gesetz". (Aus dem Russischen übersetzt von A. Schubert)
Mannheim, Mai 1970, 132 S., DM 8.–
ISBN 3–87808–604–0

Band 5: U. Engel, Regeln zur Wortstellung
U. Winkelstern, Corpusanalyse zur Untersuchung der Wortstellung
B. Busch, Erfahrungen bei der Codierung
Mannheim, März 1970, 170 S., DM 8.–
ISBN 3–87808–605–9

Stand 1. 4. 1973